HENRY CLAY AND THE WHIG PARTY

HENRY CLAY

From a portrait painted by G. P. A. Healy in the summer of 1845. This portrait is now in the home of Colonel Charles D. Clay, of Lexington, Kentucky. Photograph by "Cusick," Frankfort, Kentucky.

HENRY CLAY

AND

THE WHIG PARTY

BY

GEORGE RAWLINGS POAGE

GLOUCESTER, MASS.

PETER SMITH

1965

TO

MY WIFE

PREFACE

THE ORIGINAL purpose of this study was to present Henry Clay as a political leader. In particular I sought to examine those aspects of his career which the historians usually pass over with some such phrase as "by methods well known to the politicians," but in which a realistic generation takes well-founded interest. It also seemed desirable to view a great national leader against the background of his state—to approach Clay from Kentucky instead of Washington. As the study progressed, this viewpoint, and also my highly critical attitude toward him, was considerably modified by growing interest and admiration for a great but very human character. It has thus become in effect the last part of a political biography.

To Professors William E. Dodd and Charles E. Merriam, of the University of Chicago, I am indebted for suggesting the original conception of the study and for much kindly criticism and encouragement. The late President C. H. Rammelkamp and Professor John Griffith Ames, of Illinois College, and President L. H. Hubbard, of the Texas State College for Women, gave material assistance of great value. To Mr. George H. Clay, Colonel Charles D. Clay, and Captain Henry Clay, and to their sister, the late Miss Lucretia Hart Clay, I am indebted for access to the Clay Papers while still in their possession, for the memory of a gracious hospitality, and for permission to use the portrait of Henry Clay by Healy. For the photograph of that portrait I am indebted to the Filson Club and its president, Mr. R. C. Ballard Thruston, of Louisville. In common with many other students, I must acknowledge numerous courtesies from the various officials of the Manuscripts Division of the Library of Congress.

My colleague, Professor Max L. Shipley, has read critically the entire manuscript; and Professor Frank H. Holder, of the University of Kansas, has been so kind as to read the chapters dealing with the compromise of 1850. If errors remain, the fault is my own.

G. R. P.

Denton, Texas,
November, 1935

CONTENTS

HENRY CLAY AND THE WHIG PARTY

CHAPTER I

HARRY OF THE WEST

AUTUMN in the Kentucky Bluegrass; bronze upon the beeches, purple on the oaks; long shadows circling over the velvety sward. Nowhere was it lovelier than on the Richmond Pike, some mile and a half southeast of Lexington, where a red brick mansion spread its wide wings in the mellow sunlight. It was autumn too for the master and builder of that gracious house, though his lofty form was still unbowed, his step still light, his magic voice still resonant. Sixty-three years had left a frost upon his head, but the brain within was keen as ever; so too were the exuberant zest for life, that matchless flair for politics; and so too was that overmastering desire for the presidency. For that smiling house was Ashland, and its stately master, Henry Clay.

Autumn it was for Henry Clay; not sere and brown, nor yet a "season of mists and mellow fruitfulness," but rather a season of driving rains and sweeping winds across the gorgeousness of the American forest—the yellow and gold of elm and tulip-tree, the bronze and purple of birch and oak, the flaming crimson of sugar maples, and over all the angry glow of stormy sunsets. Autumn it was; but afterwards the placid days of a long Indian summer, and then a winter of gentle snows and peaceful skies, not over-long, before the eternal spring should break for Henry Clay.

So, in that autumn of 1840, Henry Clay sat in his beautiful home at Ashland, and let the season lay withering fingers on his heart. For with every post came news of the swelling tide of Whig success and Clay, set aside in this year when victory had been all but certain, was too human not to feel the injustice of his lot, not to mingle regret at Harrison's victory with rejoicing at the party's trumph. As he gazed across the wide lawns to the cedars of Lebanon he had planted, their unchanging green sombre against the autumn riot of color, his mind must often have revolved the crowded incidents of his career.

Henry Clay was born in Hanover County, Virginia, April 12, 1777, the son of a poor Baptist minister. Four years later the Rev. John Clay died, "bequeathing to his widow little else than an estate of seven children." After a scanty schooling under a drunken remittance-man, the boy was placed, at the age of fourteen, in a store at Richmond. His step-father, however, had sufficient influence to secure him a place, a year later, as a supernumerary clerk in the office of the clerk of the high court of chancery of Virginia. Here he was so fortunate as to attract the attention of the great Virginia jurist of the time, the venerable Chancellor George Wythe, who borrowed a portion of his services "as amanuensis in recording his decisions, and in other functions of a private secretary."

To a quick-witted youth like young Clay such an association was in itself an education. This arrangement continued for four years, when, at the instance of the chancellor, the young man was transferred to the office of Attorney General Brooke as a regular student of law. A year later, in 1797, young Clay was admitted to legal practice by the Virginia Court of Appeals.

Virginia, even the Virginia of Thomas Jefferson's reforms, offered little opportunity for a young lawyer devoid of powerful connections. Therefore it is not surprising that the fledgling barrister anticipated the famous advice of Horace Greeley by carrying his brand-new license over the mountains to Kentucky. His family had already, five years before, migrated to the new state. In his own words, he established himself

in Lexington, in 1797, without patrons, without the favor or countenance of the great or opulent, without the means of paying my weekly board, and in the midst of a bar uncommonly distinguished by eminent members. I remember how comfortable I thought I should be if I could make one hundred pounds, Virginia money, per year, and with what delight I received the first fifteen shillings fee. My hopes were more than realized. I immediately rushed into a successful and lucrative practice.[1]

Little is known of the details of this rapid rise. Traditions tinged with the roseate glow of myth cluster around Clay's

---

[1] Speech at Lexington, June 6, 1842, quoted by Calvin Colton, *Life and Times of Henry Clay* (hereafter cited as *Life and Times*), I, 29-30.

professional career. At one time he served as state's attorney, but after convicting a slave of murder, he resigned in disgust. Indeed, both Clay's emotional temperament and his peculiar gifts as a lawyer inclined him to prefer the defense. His official biographer says, "It is remarkable, that no person, ever invoked the aid of Mr. Clay, without being saved."

In 1799, Clay married Lucretia, daughter of Colonel Thomas Hart, "a gentleman of high standing in Lexington, and famed for his enterprise, public spirit and hospitality." James Brown, who later played a prominent part in the politics of Louisiana, was another son-in-law of Colonel Hart. The mother of Thomas Hart Benton was his niece and made his home the shelter of her widowhood. Jesse B. Thomas and Felix Grundy are also said to have been youthful protégés of this benevolent gentleman, who seems to have been a sort of impresario for budding politicians. It is therefore only reasonable to surmise, in the absence of positive data, that Clay's notable advancement in the race with so many and such able competitors was a result rather than a cause of his very advantageous marriage.

In 1803, Clay was elected to the legislature, and December 29, 1806, when he still lacked the constitutional age of thirty by three and a half months, he took his seat in the United States Senate for the final session of John Adair's term. The next year saw him returned to the legislature by his neighbors and at the ensuing session he was elected speaker of the Assembly, of which body for the next two years he made himself the active leader. In the winter of 1809-10, he was again sent to the United States Senate for a fractional term of two years. It was in this body that he spoke and voted against the bill for the recharter of the first Bank of the United States.

In November, 1811, he took his place in the federal House of Representatives, and on the first ballot was chosen Speaker by a majority of thirty-one. He made the office of Speaker for the first time one of prime political importance and through his leadership of the House won his earliest national triumphs. As one of the young Western politicians known as "War Hawks" he had much to do with bringing on the second war with Great Britain and was the conspicuous representative of that group among the commissioners who negotiated the Treaty of Ghent. The treaty having been drafted, Clay visited Paris until its ratification, and then proceeded to London. He remained in England from March until September, meeting most of the royal family and making many acquaintances among people of note. This sojourn abroad, from March, 1814, to September, 1815, was Clay's only experience of foreign travel.

In December, 1815, Clay resumed his seat in the House of Representatives and was again chosen Speaker by a large majority. On the election of Monroe, Clay desired the office of Secretary of State, which Monroe gave to John Quincy Adams. Clay and Adams, two intensely antipathetic personalities, had already quarreled violently on the peace commission. Dislike of Adams undoubtedly heightened Clay's chagrin at Monroe's action. He therefore pettishly declined the proffer of the War Department, and from the Speaker's chair began to lead the opposition to the Administration. This factional course was made possible by the absence of a formal opposition party.

Since the particular object of Clay's resentment was the Secretary of State, it might be expected that the foreign policy of the Administration would draw his heaviest fire. Adams's great objective, during Monroe's first term, was a treaty with Spain securing the cession of Florida and delimiting the southwestern boundary between the United States and Mexico. Clay not only violently criticized the treaty as framed, but during its negotiation did much to embarrass the Secretary. At best Spain was a techy party to deal with—proud, suspicious, dilatory. Clay became the mouthpiece of a vociferous agitation for the recognition of the revolted Spanish colonies in South America. None of his resolutions was passed until after the treaty was disposed of, or the negotiations would have come to an abrupt termination. As it was, he strewed many unnecessary thorns in Adams's path.

The "Era of Good Feeling," when no party openly opposed the Republicans and Monroe was reëlected without a competitor, was really one long campaign for the presidential succession. Half-a-dozen aspirants appeared among the younger generation of Republican leaders, each becoming the head of a faction. Andrew Jackson broke into the race as a rank outsider. The outcome was the free-for-all scramble of 1824, with Jackson, Adams, Crawford, and Clay actually on the track and finishing in that order. Clay, who probably would have been the choice of the House, was thus excluded from consideration. Since Crawford had been eliminated by illness, he held the balance between Jackson and Adams. Long and intricate negotiations ensued; and in the end, despite their old antagonism, Clay threw his support to Adams, who was subsequently elected.

Clay was rewarded with the office of Secretary of State in defiance of the charge of "corrupt bargain" which had already been raised. Adams's administration became a four-years' presidential campaign during which party lines came to be fairly well drawn. Adams and Clay got along together surprisingly well, doubtless to some extent because of mutual sympathy as targets for the scurrilous attacks of the opposition. Clay did what could be done to consolidate a National Republican Party, but President Adams gave him no practical help of any kind, even allowing John McLean, the Postmaster General, to use the patronage of his office in the interest of the opposition. The inevitable result was the triumph of Jackson in 1828.

Adams retired to private life and, though elected to Congress in 1830 and kept there until his death in 1848, never thereafter participated in partisan activities. This left Clay at the head of the National Republicans.

No sooner was the Jacksonian coalition in power than internal dissensions appeared. To the original combination of Jackson and Calhoun, Van Buren had added the major portion of the Crawford following, the extreme state rights group accepting Jackson as a lesser evil than Adams. Largely through personal compatibility, Van Buren came to be preferred to Calhoun for the succession by the clique of Jackson's personal advisers known as the "Kitchen Cabinet." These, by raking up Jackson's Florida difficulties, contrived to widen into a chasm the rift between Jackson and Calhoun started by the Eaton affair.

The disruption was advertised by Jackson's anti-nullification toast at the Jefferson's Birthday dinner in April, 1830, by the supersession of Duff Green's *Telegraph* as the administration organ by Blair's *Globe*, and by the remodeling of the Cabinet to eliminate the Calhoun element. Calhoun retaliated by giving his casting vote against Van Buren's appointment as Minister to England. The inevitable result was the nomination of Van Buren for the vice presidency in 1832, plainly as heir apparent to "Old Hickory."

This event, of course, threw the Calhoun group toward the National Republicans. Had the great Carolinian occupied the same ground as in 1824, fusion would have been easy, for Calhoun had come into prominence as an extreme nationalist. The effects of the tariff on the South Carolinian planters, however, had made the nationalist position untenable for any leader of that state, so Calhoun perforce had made a complete about face to extreme particularism. Nevertheless, Calhoun and Clay did effect a rapprochement. McDuffie, Calhoun's chief lieutenant, took the lead in the House in behalf of the Bank of the United States. Clay showed such a weakening in his tariff views as seriously to impair his hold on the New England capitalists.

With the tariff thrown into the background, Clay appeared to have only internal improvements as an available issue. Plans were laid for a challenge to Jackson on this issue, which he was in no wise inclined to reject. The Maysville Road veto brought this issue to a head, and also gave initial impetus to an issue of prime importance in the formation of the Whig Party—the alleged abuse of the veto power by Jackson, one of the chief counts in the charge of "Executive Usurpation."

Little public interest was manifested, however, in these issues, so the opposition politicians seized with avidity the prospect of the injection into the campaign of the question of the recharter of the second Bank of the United States. Jackson had a strong feeling against the Bank, and it may well be doubted whether all the efforts of its suave representatives succeeded in really ameliorating his opposition. But he unquestionably did not desire the issue of a recharter to be injected into the presidential campaign. In proportion as this became apparent, Clay, Webster, and their associates became urgent for an immediate application. Clay even threatened coolness in the future if application were deferred.[2]

Biddle, president of the bank, after a careful canvass of the situation, decided to defy Jackson and apply for a recharter. Then followed a long conflict of six months, characterized by much maneuvering for political advantage and culminating on July 10, 1832, in Jackson's veto of the recharter bill.

In the potentialities of the Bank issue Jackson seems to have been only less mistaken than his opponents. Had he realized the popularity of extinction of the "Monster," it is hard to understand his insistence on postponement of the application. Clay seems never to have sensed the popular antagonism, while Biddle so completely misunderstood the public mind as to circulate Jackson's veto at the expense of the Bank. The result was a crushing defeat of the opposition to Jackson, for "Old Hickory" received 219 of the 288 electoral votes, the remainder being divided among three candidates, with 49 for Clay.

The division of the opposition contributed somewhat to the debacle. Clay went so far toward Calhoun that Webster sought late in the campaign to supersede him as the candidate of the National Republicans. Yet he did not go far enough, for South Carolina threw away her electoral vote by casting it for John Floyd of Virginia. The vote of Vermont was given to Wirt, candidate of the Anti-Masons.

The Anti-Masonic Party had originated in the later twenties in western New York. Beginning as a local movement against the alleged domination of the administration of justice by the Masonic fraternity, it had been seized upon by certain astute politicians who attempted to utilize it as a vehicle for their own advancement. From that strategic central position, the agitation spread westward along the zone of New England migration through Pennsylvania, Ohio, Indiana, and Illinois, and back eastward into New England itself. As an exploitation of the "New England conscience" for political profit, it fore-

---

[2] S. R. Gammon, *Presidential Campaign of 1832,* p. 126, citing S. H. Smith to Biddle, December 17, 1831.

shadowed the later formation of parties on the slavery issue, in which, indeed, many of the same politicians participated.

The appeal of Anti-Masonry especially affected the National Republican element, and this affiliation became more marked as it expanded into a national movement. Jackson was prominent in Masonic circles, as were many of his chief lieutenants and therefore he necessarily antagonized the Anti-Masons. But Clay was also a Mason, though not active in the fraternity, and was therefore unable to coalesce Anti-Masons with National Republicans. In casting about for an available candidate to effect this, the lot seemed to fall by common consent on John McLean.

This statesman for many years played a political part difficult to reconcile with his present obscurity. Monroe's Postmaster General, he had been retained by Adams. He was so close to Calhoun that Clay accused him of using his patronage in Jackson's favor and Adams seems finally to have been convinced of his treachery. Jackson offered to retain him, but he preferred appointment to the Supreme Court. Here he continued to keep his finger on the political pulse.

He seems to have had a considerable popular following, perhaps because of his efficient administration of the Post Office, but more likely on account of the political contacts he had effected at that time. His political correspondents were numerous. Some appeared, at times, to be regular traveling representatives engaged in testing public opinion and directing it toward the Judge. Some were small fry local politicians. Some, in a number of cases to obtain eminence later, were disgruntled politicians of larger caliber who for one reason or another had been excluded by the "organization." Notable among the last was Thaddeus Stevens of Pennsylvania.

For years these correspondents kept the Judge's hopes alive. His affiliation with Calhoun of course inclined him toward the anti-Jackson element, and with every backset encountered by Clay or Webster or Calhoun, he confidently expected the call to emerge from his juridical seclusion to rally and unite the opposition. As the years intervened since his active political service in the Post Office, these hopes of course degenerated into the delusions of vanity, but it is generally conceded that he was the one man who in 1832 might have consolidated the opposition.

McLean was the first choice of the Anti-Masons and encouraged them with the expectation of his leadership. He attached the condition, however, that there should be no other candidate opposing Jackson—in effect, a stipulation that Clay should withdraw or be discarded. On the eve of the Anti-Masonic convention—the first national party convention in American history—having learned that Clay persisted in his candidacy, McLean declined the nomination, which was given to Willam Wirt. Even after this, Wirt himself attempted to concert with Clay a common withdrawal in McLean's favor. While McLean could thus have consolidated the opposition, there appears to be no reason to believe that the outcome of the election would have been changed.[3]

Scarcely was the election of 1832 off the board before public attention became focussed upon South Carolina's attempt to "nullify" the tariff of 1832 and Jackson's militant response which seemed to portend civil war. With Van Buren silent in the vice president's chair, Webster stood forth in the Senate as the administration champion. Clay, on the other hand, saved Calhoun from irremediable catastrophe by securing the passage of a "compromise" tariff providing for gradual reduction of duties. A new alignment of parties on the issue of nationalism seemed imminent, with Jackson and Webster allied against Clay and Calhoun.

This was prevented by Clay's astute leadership. His own compromise tariff was less distasteful to New England than the administration bill fathered in the House by Van Buren's lieutenant, Verplanck. It gave him the prestige of effecting another "compromise" and removing the threat of civil war. Once the nullification threat disappeared, the chief ground of coöperation between Jackson and Webster was gone.

The spring and early summer of 1833, however, were filled with political movements symptomatic of the rapprochement between Jackson and Webster. Biddle was active in the matter,

---

[3] For the latter part of this chapter, I am chiefly indebted to Gammon, *op. cit.;* A. C. Cole, *The Whig Party in the South;* and E. M. Carroll, *The Origins of the Whig Party.*

hoping through Webster to avert further hostile moves by the President. The removal of the deposits, however, led Biddle to change his plans. He now became equally insistent that Webster should join the opposition. This the "god-like" statesman delayed to do until Clay forced his hand. Again effecting a spectacular parliamentary coup, Clay placed Webster at the head of the Senate Finance Committee which shortly was to make a hostile report on the removal of the deposits. As a matter of fact, the negotiations between Webster and the administration had already failed; but the report was a public announcement of Webster's alignment with the opposition.

The high-handed procedure of Jackson in connection with the removal of the deposits, especially his assumption of dictatorial powers over the Cabinet, together with the consequent controversies over censure, protest and "expunging resolution," drove yet another group into opposition and gave the opposition both a ground of combination and a name. Certain leaders, notably Tallmadge of New York, Tyler, Rives, and Archer of Virginia, and Hugh Lawson White of Tennessee, deeply indoctrinated with Jeffersonian constitutionalism, were alarmed at his pretensions and went into opposition, styling themselves "Conservatives."

It was possibly the action of this group that forcibly called attention to the one issue on which all shades of the opposition could unite—"Executive Usurpation." Their real bond of union, of course, was anti-Jacksonism, but in so far as it was based on opposition to his acts instead of mere personal antagonism to the Executive himself, every offensive act could be comprehended under the elastic term of "Executive Usurpation." It covered in a single phrase Jackson's proscription of office-holders, his defiance of the Supreme Court, his repeated vetoes, his assertion of the "unit principle" of the Cabinet, his dismissal of Duane, his removal of the deposits, his protest to Congress, his advancement of Van Buren, his reliance on the Kitchen Cabinet. It centered the attack on Jackson's whole theory and practice of personal leadership and authority. The influence of the Executive in the government having been suddenly and, perhaps, for the period, unduly expanded, the inevitable reaction, the reassertion of influence by the Legislature, was under way. It was therefore for the exploitation of that reaction that the Whig Party drew together.

The name carried stirring patriotic connotations from the revolutionary struggle, and it was especially to the old American stock that the new party appealed. From the first it was imbued with that dislike of naturalized citizens which eventually, on its dissolution, led many of its leaders into the Native American Party of the fifties. But the immediate inspiration of the name seems to have been the contemporary events of British politics.

The English Whigs had always stood for the authority of Parliament as opposed to the prerogative of the Crown. It was they who had worked out the cabinet system of government. More recently, in 1830-31, it was they who had reformed the British parliament, coercing the King into the threat of "swamping" which forced the House of Lords to give its assent. They had then carried through a great variety of reforms. Finally, in November, 1834, it was a Whig cabinet which William IV dismissed, the last time any British sovereign ventured such a step. And by this step he had restored the party's waning popularity, and had been forced to recall it the following April for the rest of his reign. The name of Whig, therefore, in itself designated the new party as a party of reform, as a party dedicated to the maintenance of legislative authority against executive encroachment, as a party ready to vindicate ministerial independence of the chief magistrate. Conversely, it identified Andrew Jackson, "King Andrew the First," with George III and William IV.

Thus, on the issue of "Executive Usurpation" the Whig Party was enabled to comprehend all elements of opposition to Jackson. Followers of Clay, Webster, and Calhoun, Anti-Masons, Conservatives, Bank men, Anti-Bank men, Tariff-men and Nullifiers found it possible to act together in the "Union of the Whigs for the sake of the Union."

Such a combination was truly formidable in its numbers, and even more formidable in its talents. Appealing as it did to the wealthy and conservative, it had ample financial resources for the modest campaign necessities of that day. These appear to have been used in the main by the local managers, and chiefly for subsidizing a numerous and able party press. Even more conspicuous however, were the ability and reputation of its political leaders, as well as their number. In this, indeed, was also a source of weakness, for the new party suffered excessively from personal rivalries and jealousies—a malady which acutely afflicted its Democratic rival only when the Whig Party was passing off the scene.

To this excess of leadership may be ascribed in part the failure of the party to build up an effective organization and to secure good discipline. That defect may also be ascribed, though, to other factors inherent in its membership—wealth, intelligence, independence of thinking, and divergence of aim as soon as the negative program of opposition had to be exchanged for a positive program of administrative and legislative responsibility. Indeed, the party found itself unable to agree upon a candidate to oppose Van Buren in 1836; and after much futile discussion and negotiation fell back on an attempt to reproduce the situation of 1824. Three candidates, Webster, Hugh Lawson White, and William Henry Harrison sought respectively to win the votes of New England, the South, and the West. Although each had some success, and South Carolina again threw her votes away on an individual choice, Van Buren had a safe majority. The most important result of the election, from the Whig standpoint, was the demonstration of Harrison's availability.

Hardly was Van Buren inaugurated when the terrible financial panic of 1837 broke upon the country. The joint result of over-speculation and Jackson's financial policies, the panic and its aftermath practically absorbed governmental energies throughout Van Buren's administration. The President's remedy for the ills which had produced the panic was the creation of an "Independent Treasury" with sub-treasuries in commercial centers. In spite of the emergency and all his urging, he secured its enactment into law only in the closing months of his administration. The Whigs had advocated a new national bank instead; and Calhoun took advantage of the issue to become reconciled to Van Buren and to rejoin the less uncongenial company of the Democrats. The first group to leave the Democratic combination of 1829 was now the first to abandon the Whig combination of 1834.

Clay had recognized his own unavailability for 1836 with anything but resignation, and immediately began a campaign to secure the Whig nomination for 1840. Webster also pressed eagerly toward the goal, and General Winfield Scott was put forward as a military hero. Harrison, however, was the favorite of those who wished to take a leaf from the Democratic book and appeal to popular sentiment. The Webster movement failed to develop, whereupon the Webster managers busied themselves in effecting a combination of all the opponents of Clay to secure the nomination of Harrison. This was accomplished in December, 1839, by a national convention at Harrisburg. As a sop to the Clay men, the vice presidential nomination was given to John Tyler of Virginia, whom they had intended as running mate for the great Kentuckian. In view of the heterogeneous elements composing the party, the leaders wisely abstained from any attempt to frame a platform. Their appeal was to be based on the popularity of their candidate and a general attack on Jacksonism.

Clay was infuriated, declared Harrison utterly unfit for the presidency, and refused to take part in the campaign until it was far advanced. The Democratic press echoed Clay's scorn, and it was one of their sneers that gave the Whigs an effective slogan. Coonskin caps, log cabins, and hard cider became the motifs of a campaign of unmitigated emotional appeal, with the result that Van Buren suffered an overwhelming defeat. Complete control of the House and a narrow majority in the Senate seemed to assure the success of the Whig program— and then, seemingly for the first time, men began to ask what that program was. Could the diverse elements which had not ventured to frame a platform at Harrisburg now hold together to translate their victory into positive legislation?

CHAPTER II

OLD TIPPECANOE

THE WHIG PARTY being essentially a coalition of the most diverse elements of American political life, its sweeping victory in November, 1840, produced what may, without exaggeration, be called a party crisis. A candidate without positive principles or policy, supported by a party which had not ventured to formulate a platform, had, by a campaign of purely emotional appeal, been carried into the presidency. Which of the several factions that made up the party would control the administration? Would the President lean to the planters of the South or to the Abolitionists of the North? Would he follow the ideas of the old National Republican remnant, or those of the State Rights men who had refused to follow Calhoun back into the Democratic fold?

If the National Republicans prevailed, which of their two great leaders would dominate the government? For, whatever might be the belief of the masses who had shouted and voted for "Tip and Ty," the Democratic press and the politicians of all shades were agreed upon one thing, namely, that President Harrison would be kept in tutelage. The Democrats vociferously declared that the power behind the throne would be the United States Bank of Pennsylvania, acting through Clay or Webster. On the other hand, a considerable portion of the Whig press expressed the hope that neither would be taken from the Senate, assuming that the Cabinet must contain neither or both. But that both should be in the Cabinet was impracticable because of their notorious rivalry and their presidential aspirations.[1]

As for Harrison himself, from the undertone of the correspondence which passed between various Whig leaders, the

---

[1] Louisville *Public Advertiser* (hereafter cited as Louisville *Advertiser*), December 1, 1840, also quoting the Cincinnati *Gazette,* Louisville *Journal,* New York *Courier and Enquirer,* and New York *American.* Lexington *Observer and Reporter* (hereafter cited as *Observer and Reporter*), November 11, December 2, 1840. Numerous other citations to the same purport might be given.

abler of them shared to a considerable extent the sentiments confided to his diary by John Quincy Adams: "He is not the choice of three-fourths of those who have elected him. His present popularity is all artificial. There is little confidence in his talents or his firmness. If he is not found time-serving, demagogical, unsteady, and Western-sectional, he will more than satisfy my present expectations."[2]

Even those Whig politicians who had not this disdain of Harrison, felt great anxiety as to the personnel of his Cabinet. They had made campaign pledges, in the observance of which they felt a personal interest. They realized the almost irresistable influence which the experienced statesmen composing the cabinet would wield over the mind of the frontier general. Furthermore, they were determined that this influence should be vested in the President's "constitutional advisers," as they were fond of calling the Cabinet, and not in some unofficial or irresponsible group. This reaction from Jacksonism and the dominance of such leaders as Kendall and Blair was so strong that Tom Corwin wrote to Clay's friend and colleague, John Jordan Crittenden: "I have the utmost confidence in Old Tip, but I also know that his cabinet advisers will and *ought* to have great weight with him."[3]

From Harrison's first movements, it seemed as if Clay were to be the power behind the throne. Hardly had the decisive returns been published before the President-elect turned his steps toward Kentucky. It was announced that he was bound on private business, but no one could doubt that politics would engage much of his attention.

General Harrison was aware of the construction which would be placed upon his journey. Moreover, he was almost morbidly sensitive lest such an opinion gain currency. Accordingly he addressed Clay frankly, suggesting the desirability of their continuing to communicate through Crittenden or other friends

[2] *Memoirs,* X, 366, Washington, December 4, 1840.

[3] Corwin to Crittenden, November 20, 1840; Letcher to Crittenden, January 6, 1841; Zachary Taylor to Crittenden, January 29, 1841; Crittenden Papers. Tyler to Wise, December 20, 1840; L. G. Tyler, *Letters and Times of the Tylers,* III, 86. Washington *National Intelligencer* (hereafter cited as *National Intelligencer*), February 8, 1841, quoting Philadelphia *Inquirer.*

in order to avoid the "speculations and even jealousies" to which their personal meeting might give rise, and intimating that he was about to tender Clay a seat in his Cabinet.[4]

This proposal, however, by no means met Clay's views. He was possibly not unwilling that the very speculations and jealousies deprecated by the President-elect should gain currency. Indeed, a visit of Harrison to Kentucky without a meeting with Clay could not fail to give rise to conjectures, from Clay's standpoint, equally undesirable. To be sure, Harrison was clearly contemplating the offer of a Cabinet position, acceptance of which would serve as a public denial of any coolness between the actual and the titular heads of the party. Clay, however, had already chosen another rôle—one which necessitated at once the rejection of any Cabinet appointment, even the first, and a public manifestation of mutual cordiality.

Aside, moreover, from these larger plans, there were considerations which impelled Clay to go counter to the program laid down by Harrison for their relations during his visit to Kentucky. A long-smouldering enmity between Clay and a group of his personal and political intimates on the one side, and the powerful Wickliffe family on the other, had recently burst into open flame, and all the political elements of the state which were hostile to Clay's extended and dictatorial power were about to draw to a head under a leadership notable both for talent and resources.[5] Since the power of any American statesmen is based primarily upon control of his own state, such a combination was disquieting even to the "Old Chief." Clay, then, had genuine cause for alarm when he was informed by Harrison that the business which was the ostensible reason for his visit to Kentucky would bring him into confidential relations with Charles A. Wickliffe. In fact, the opposition newspapers loudly proclaimed that "Tip's" business was not personal but political, and that it would take him not to

---

[4] Harrison to Clay, November 15, 1840; Calvin Colton, *Private Correspondence of Henry Clay* (hereafter cited as *Private Correspondence*), p. 446.

[5] Letcher to Crittenden, November 30, December 14, 1840, January 6, February 2, February 9, 1841; John White to Crittenden, March 20, 1841; Crittenden Papers. *Observer and Reporter,* December 30, 1840; Louisville *Advertiser,* November 19, 1840. Allusions to this feud run all through the Letcher-Crittenden correspondence.

Clay at Lexington, but to Wickliffe at Bardstown.[6]

In this embarrassing situation, Clay acted with promptness, decision, and characteristic audacity. On the General's
arrival at Frankfort, Clay coolly repaired to the capital and
extended him an urgent invitation to come to Lexington. This
invitation was reinforced by a committee of Lexington citizens,
so that the General had practically no recourse but to accept.[7]

Harrison was splendidly feted at Lexington while the
politicians plied him behind the scenes. On the occasion of his
dining at Ashland, his host engaged him in a long, confidential
conversation, in the course of which Clay declared he desired to
continue in the Senate, and, "to put him at his ease about
Webster," expressed the opinion that that statesman could not
be overlooked. Harrison handled the delicate situation with
great tact, convincing Clay that he was "animated by the best
dispositions," but also managing to avoid mentioning "the
name of one person that he had resolved to invite into his
Cabinet." Just at the point when Clay thought "he was going
to speak freely on that subject," they were interrupted "and
no opportunity afterwards occurred to resume the conversation."[8]

The rival group, meanwhile, was pushing for the appoint-
ment of Charles A. Wickliffe as Postmaster General, and
Robert Wickliffe, Jr., as private secretary. They also managed
to interrupt several attempts to chat with Governor Letcher.[9]
In addition they made the most of a maladroit attempt of the
Clay press to distort a toast to Clay, offered by Harrison at
Versailles, into an endorsement of Clay for the succession, but
this was authoritatively denied before Harrison left
Kentucky.[10]

---

[6] Harrison to Clay, November 15, 1840, loc. cit.; Louisville Advertiser,
November 19, 1840.

[7] Observer and Reporter, November 21, 1849; National Intelligencer,
December 1, 1840; Daniel Webster, Writings and Speeches (National
Edition), XVIII, 90, 91.

[8] Clay to Clayton, December 17, 1840, Clayton Papers.

[9] Letcher to Crittenden, November 30, 1840; Mary Ann (Mrs. Chapman)
Coleman, Life of John J. Crittenden, I, 131.

[10] Observer and Reporter, November 28, December 16, 1840; Louisville Advertiser, December 4, 1840.

The attempt to secure the postmaster generalship for Wickliffe was suggested by the general understanding that Clay would not accept any appointment. With the selection of Crittenden for the post of Attorney General, a fact which was not long in becoming noised abroad, Wickliffe's appointment became impracticable. The attempt, however, to have Robert Wickliffe, Jr., appointed private secretary was more persistent. While General Harrison's son-in-law received the appointment, young Wickliffe travelled to Washington as one of the Presidential entourage.[11]

As a matter of fact, Clay's refusal to enter the Cabinet had been anticipated from the beginning; and as early as November 20, Corwin had written to Crittenden to ascertain what place he would prefer.[12] It is probable that the Ohio anti-slavery men had got wind of the possibility of Wickliffe's appointment and sought to forestall it by pushing Crittenden. That would be good party politics for Harrison anyway, for the appointment of Wickliffe would have been recognized as a direct defiance of Clay, while that of Crittenden minimized the latter's refusal.

Clay evidently felt, whatever the machinations of his Kentucky enemies, that his aims, whether local or national, had been assured; for he left home for the meeting of Congress while the President-elect was still at Lexington.[13] There can be little doubt of his satisfaction at the outcome. A visit which had been viewed in Kentucky as an exaltation of his enemies, had been converted into an advertisement to the whole Union of his apparent dominance over Harrison. The selection of his colleague, Crittenden, proclaimed his triumph over his foes in Kentucky, and in the eyes of national politicians offset the appointment of Webster. It was further conjectured that he had secured pledges for the succession.[14] Withal he had re-

[11] Letcher to Crittenden, December 14, 1840; Coleman, *op. cit.*, I, 132; also January 6, 1841, Crittenden Papers. *National Intelligencer*, February 9, February 11, 1840.

[12] Crittenden Papers.

[13] Clay to Brooke, December 8, 1840, Colton, *Private Correspondence*, p. 446.

[14] Calhoun to J. E. Calhoun, December 26, 1840, J. F. Jameson, ed., *Correspondence of John C. Calhoun (American Historical Association, Annual Report, 1899,* vol. II), p. 470; December 14, 1840, Crittenden Papers.

tained his own independence of action and was proceeding to Washington with the authority of one direct from the side of the President-elect, there to assume in Congress the leadership of the triumphant Whigs.[15]

This leadership of a minority would become, after March 4, the leadership of a majority. The dictator of Congress would be the peer of the holder of the veto-power, against a free use of which the Whigs and their new President were strongly committed. Control of Congress, able and devoted support in the Cabinet, above all the moral superiority already established, left little question as to parity of influence in the councils of the party and the government of the nation. The "Old Chief," set aside by the Harrisburg Convention, would nevertheless determine the policies of the government. Such must have been the ideas with which Clay left Lexington.

Harrison gave Webster his choice between the State Department, originally destined for Clay, and the Treasury, and requested his advice as to the other positions, whether or not he entered the Cabinet himself. Webster accepted the State Department, following up his letter of acceptance with another suggesting his colleagues. Harrison replied thanking him for his suggestions, but stating that he would decide nothing in regard to the Treasury, War, and Navy departments until after his arrival in Washington the latter part of January. The Post Office had already been assigned to Thomas Ewing, of Ohio. The effect of this was that Webster, in consultation with the Whig leaders at Washington, virtually constructed the Cabinet.[16]

Clay's activity in the formation of the Cabinet seems to have been restricted to an attempt to secure the Treasury Department for John M. Clayton of Delaware. He tried various combinations to effect that object, all of which proved abortive. Webster finally blocked the way by shifting Ewing, himself

---

[15] Adams, *op. cit.*, X, 372, December 11, 1840.

[16] Harrison to Webster, December 1, December 27, 1840; Webster to Harrison, December 11, 1840; Webster, *op. cit.*, XVIII, 90-97, *passim*. H. A. Wise, *Seven Decades of the Union*, p. 180. Clay to Clayton, February 12, 1841, Clayton Papers. New York *Express*, February 20, 1841. Louisville *Advertiser*, March 3, 1841. Adams, *op. cit.*, X, 338. Cf. A. K. McClure, *Our Presidents and How We Make Them*, p. 68.

one of the inner circle of Cabinet-makers, from the Post Office to the more important post of Secretary of the Treasury. By the time Harrison reached Washington, the Cabinet was complete with the exception of the Secretary of the Navy, which post had been promised to the South Atlantic States, provided their delegations could decide among the several aspirants.[17]

Harrison reached Washington on February 9, and speedily agreed to the Webster Cabinet slate after conferences with Webster and Ewing. He informed the Southerners that he would give the Navy to whomever they could agree upon. A series of stormy caucuses ensued, until, on the morning of February 12, Stanly of North Carolina finally brought about the selection of his relative, George Badger, who had been mentioned for the place only the day or two preceding. The Cabinet so assembled was announced semi-officially in the *National Intelligencer* of February 13, and was in due time nominated to the Senate and confirmed.[18]

At the end of December, Clay had written to Clayton that he would do for him whatever could be done with propriety; if Harrison consulted him, as Clay presumed he would, he would urge Clayton's appointment in the strongest terms; if Harrison did not consult him, Clay would nevertheless see that his opinions reached the President. Accordingly, on the night of February 11, Clay had an interview with the President to urge Clayton's appointment as Secretary of the Navy. It was probably stormy, culminating in Harrison's exclaiming, "Mr. Clay, you forget that I am the President!"[19] Clay, however, merely reported to Clayton the next day, that "He expressed himself, as he had before done, in the strongest terms of your

---

[17] New York *Express,* December 16, 1840; January 13, January 20, February 12 and 13, 1841; Louisville *Advertiser,* February 5, February 18, March 3, 1841; *National Intelligencer,* February 10, 1841; Harrison to Webster, December 27, 1840, Webster, *op. cit.,* XVIII, 97; Graves to Kennedy, January 20, 1841, Kennedy Papers; Letcher to Crittenden, February 9, 1841, Crittenden Papers.

[18] "The Diary of Thomas Ewing," *American Historical Review,* XVIII, (October, 1912) 98-99; Clay to Clayton, February 12, 1841, Clayton Papers; Wise, *op. cit.; National Intelligencer,* February 10, 1841.

[19] Tyler, *op. cit.,* II, 10, footnote, quoting James Lyons in the New York *World,* August 31, 1880. Since Harrison told Lyons of the incident at his house in Richmond prior to the inauguration, it almost certainly occurred during this interview if at all.

abilities, services, and merits; but he. did not give me much hope of my desire being realized." But he significantly concluded, "We must support his Administration, or rather, I should say, we must not fall out with it."[20]

Clay had staked all on the appointment of Clayton and had lost. Yet his position was little, if any, weaker than Webster's. Crittenden was Attorney General, and to all appearances unswerving in his devotion to the "Old Chief." Ewing's refusal to decline the Treasury at Clay's behest resulted in no personal coolness between them. John Bell of Tennessee, Secretary of War, although far from being a blind partisan, was inclined to follow Clay rather than Webster. Badger was an unknown quantity; but his social affiliations might be expected to swing him into the train of the great Kentuckian. Clay's powerful connections in New York would give him a possible lever even upon Francis Granger, the Postmaster General. The success of the "godlike" statesman, therefore, had by no means eliminated Clay's influence in the innermost circle of the administration.

Clay had arrived in Washington December 1 and established headquarters to which the Whigs hastened as to the court of a sovereign. The next day he made his appearance in the Senate, which nominally consisted of twenty-eight Democrats, two Conservative Democrats (Rives of Virginia and Tallmadge of New York), and twenty-two Whigs.[21] But the Whig minority was so poorly disciplined that it exercised far less influence than its numbers, reinforced by the Conservatives, would lead one to expect. On only one ballot was every Whig in his seat and voting with Clay; on only seven others, out of a total of nineteen, did he have the solid support of those present. Against the two great administration measures of the session, the Prospective Preëmption Bill and the Treasury Note Bill, Clay was able to rally only nineteen and nine votes respectively. In each instance Webster voted with the Democrats.[22] Under these circumstances, it is not surprising that Clay attempted

---

[20] Clay to Clayton, December 29, 1840, February 12, 1841, Clayton Papers.

[21] Cincinatti *Gazette,* December 24, 1840; Adams, *op. cit.,* X, 372, December 11, 1840; *Congressional Globe,* 26th Cong., 2nd Sess., I, 12.

[22] *Congressional Globe,* 26th Cong., 2nd Sess. Only one vote, which had no apparent partisan color, is omitted in this comparison.

nothing constructive at this session and little even of an anticipatory character.

Clay introduced four resolutions only. Two called upon the Secretary of the Treasury for information in regard to the public lands, and were designed to supply ammunition in support of his forthcoming distribution bill. Another called upon the Secretary for his plan for home valuation, and was designed merely to force the Secretary to show his hand. In this action Clay showed his impatience of the more conservative element in the Whig leadership. These three were adopted by the Senate without a vote. The fourth, however, after some debate, was tabled by a vote of twenty-seven to twenty-five.[23]

This resolution declared that the Independent Treasury Act ought forthwith to be repealed, and instructed the Committee on Finance to report a bill to the effect. That Clay expected any action other than that taken may well be doubted. It was probably designed merely as a forecast of future policy, or at most as a test of sentiment both in and out of Congress. It gave opportunity, however, for Clay to deliver himself of an interesting speech characteristic of the tone which pervaded most of his utterances during the session. John Quincy Adams remarked that "Clay crows too much over a fallen foe."[24]

Clay's tendency to taunt the Democrats with their defeat at the polls and to threaten the repeal of their measures came to a climax in a long speech "On the Distribution of the Proceeds of the Public Lands." The original asperity of this speech was probably toned down for publication, but as it stands it approaches the limit of parliamentary decorum.[25] It was marked by a domineering tone and a personal animus

---

[23] *Ibid.*, pp. 14, 16, 105; Clay to Clayton, January 17, 1841, Clayton Papers.

[24] *Ibid.*, pp. 19-20. Another version of this speech, condensed and quite lacking in the vigor and spontaneity of the report, is in Daniel Mallory, ed., *Life and Speeches of Henry Clay*, II, 432-36. Adams, *op. cit.*, X, 387, January 1, 1841.

[25] This speech was not reported, and never appeared in the *Congressional Globe* or its appendix. It was first published in the *National Intelligencer*, May 29, 1841, just four months after its delivery, occupying eleven large columns. It probably is Clay's revised version and considerably different from the speech as actually delivered. This appears to be identical with the speech in Mallory, *op. cit.*, II, 437-81.

unusual in orations of equal political and forensic weight. In particular, the remarks addressed directly to Silas Wright and the allusions to him verge upon insult. In view of the high esteem both as a man and a statesman in which Wright was held by his contemporaries, many of them appear unjustifiable.

Wright replied, but his remarks also are unreported, and Clay explained satisfactorily the personal remarks which had given offense. Tappan of Ohio, however, was reported at length, and his animadversions leave no doubt as to the arrogance of Clay's manner and the bitter feelings he excited among the opposition.[26] These were even more forcibly shown by his collision with William R. King of Alabama.

In spite of Clay's vigorous protests, the expiring Senate had carried out its undertaking to elect Blair and Rives as printers to the Senate for the ensuing Congress. In accordance with Clay's threat, the Whigs lost no time in setting about rescinding the election during the special session of the Senate in March. As soon as the inaugural ceremonies were concluded, delaying only for the adoption of the customary resolution of thanks to the President *pro tempore*, Mangum of North Carolina presented a resolution that Blair and Rives be dismissed. After four days of debate, with intermissions for executive business, the resolution was finally carried by a vote of twenty-six to eighteen. The debate brought out a number of constitutional and legal arguments which are of no special significance in this connection and which were at best mere technical hairsplitting. So far as the equity of the case was concerned, the precedent of the election of Gales and Seaton in 1835, who were allowed to continue for two years, would seem to put the Whigs in the wrong.

Clay spoke every day with great force and some acerbity. Among other things, he touched upon the character of Blair, challenging the opposition to go before the people with the injustice done him. Clay and his friends asked only that they not be associated with him. If there were no other ground for his dismissal, Clay would go "on the ground of infamy of the print and the Printer. They might be indicted on that ground." The

---

[26] *Congressional Globe*, 26th Cong., 2nd Sess., pp. 132 ff.

Democrats owed it to themselves and to the purity of the national character "to disconnect themselves once and forever from these men."

These words provoked a storm on the following day. Smith of Connecticut undertook the defense of Blair without rousing Clay to reply, but King did not escape unanswered. In the course of somewhat lengthy argument on the merits of the case, King referred to Blair as Clay's intimate associate in Kentucky prior to 1825, and declared "that for kindness of heart, humanity, and exemplary deportment as a private citizen, he could proudly compare with the Senator from Kentucky, or any Senator on this floor by whom he had been assailed."

Clay rose to reply and precipitated one of the most sensational incidents in the history of the Senate. He declared that he was perfectly aware of the relation in which he stood to the Senate and to this country—that he was now as heretofore to be the object of concerted attack, but that he stood now, as heretofore, "firm and erect, and ready to repel assaults." In referring to Blair the day before as an infamous man, he had said nothing of the gentlemen who chose to vote for the *Globe*; to say that he had imputed infamy to them was "unlawful inference and illogical deduction." If they had appealed to him he would have denied such views. Yet without such an appeal, Smith of Connecticut, slightingly referred to as "the Senator who sits in the corner yonder, and who must excuse him if he (Mr. Clay) considered him unworthy of his notice," had made remarks evidently intended for him (Mr. Clay). But a Senator who Clay supposed "considered himself responsible," King of Alabama, "had gone a step further, and had chosen to class him with Blair, and to consider Blair equal to him in every point of view—in reputation and in every thing else." Not only was this unparliamentary; "it was false, untrue, and cowardly."

King arose and said, "Mr. President, I have no reply to make—none whatever." Smith however, put no restraint upon himself. He rose, he said, for the purpose of saying but one word in answer to the Senator from Kentucky. He was, it seemed, unworthy of that Senator's notice. "Not at all," interjected Clay, and then Smith not too coherently poured out the vials of his wrath.

Clay did possess a character far more notorious in some respects than his, Smith declared, and one with which he did not wish to be compared. Humble as he might be, "he would not descend to the prominent points" of Clay's character "which gave him so much fame all over the world. He (Mr. Smith) did not belong to those walks." If, however, Clay thought those prominent characteristics of his reputation gave him such elevation as to place Smith beneath his notice, he would not, in return, call him " 'the Senator who sits in the corner,' but would leave him to the people; who, four years hence, will show the Senator [Mr. Clay], as they had shown him heretofore, that they understood his reputation and know how to appreciate it."

William Campbell Preston of South Carolina gained the floor at this juncture, expressed his regret that anything should have occurred to drive honorable Senators "to do anything inconsistent with parliamentary decorum," and proceeded to speak at length on the resolution before the Senate.[27]

The incident, however, did not end here. After the debate, King sat down, evidently much excited. Shortly afterwards, Lewis Linn, one of the Senators from Missouri, bore to Clay either a challenge or an inquiry as to whether he would receive one. There was great alarm among the Whigs at the idea that their leader's life might be so imperilled. That same evening, however, King was arrested but released on bail, Buchanan accompanying him to the magistrate's and becoming his surety.

For nearly a week, nevertheless, the capital was buzzing with the imminence of a duel between two men of such eminence as the Senators from Alabama and Kentucky. The excitement was not the less because the last political duel in the vicinity of Washington, the notorious "Cilley Duel" of 1838, had had a fatal termination. The principals kept their own counsel, which probably only increased the rumors. It was reported that Linn was a "rigid disciplinarian of the duelist school" and "that

---

[27] *Ibid.*, pp. 180, 188-95, 236-56, and *passim.*

there must be a shot, so far as he is concerned, unless Mr. Clay explains or qualifies what he has said." In this, however, it would seem that Linn was done an injustice; for his biographers claim that he was a friend of both parties, and used his best efforts to bring about an honorable and satisfactory understanding between them. Linn's efforts, aided by those of Archer, Preston, and other friends of Clay, brought about mutual explanations and averted a hostile meeting.

Accordingly, on the last day of the special session of the Senate, Preston brought up the matter, evidently by prearrangement, and the episode came to a bloodless conclusion. Preston asserted that the Senators had labored under a mutual misapprehension. Clay then, with a great parade of magnanimity, "under the circumstances as thus explained, and with the understanding which he now had of the real intentions of the Senator," with infinite pleasure now declared every epithet in the least derogatory to him, to his honor, or to his character, to be withdrawn. King thereupon assented to Preston's declaration; and since Clay had explicitly withdrawn his injurious expressions, he felt at liberty to declare that he had not intended to be personally offensive to Clay, or "to derogate from his character as a gentleman or man of honor." When King concluded his explanation, Clay crossed the Senate Chamber and extended his hand, which King grasped amid the applause alike of galleries and Senate. Preston pronounced a benediction upon the reconciliation and ended the scene by moving that the Senate go into executive session.[28]

At the very time, however, when Clay was being reconciled with King, he was coming to a complete rupture with his own party-chief, the President. Harrison appears never to have been endowed with exceptional ability or force. He was now a very old man, and such vigor of intellect and will as he may have possessed in his prime had been greatly impaired. Though honest, conscientious, simple and kindly, he had considerable vanity which made him fear that men would think him subservient to Clay. This vanity was played upon by the personal

---

[28] *Ibid.*, pp. 256-57; New York *Express*, March 13, 19, 1841; Linn and Sargent, *Life and Public Services of Dr. Lewis F. Linn*, pp. 244-45, 249-50; B. H. Wise, *Life of Henry A. Wise*, pp. 80-86.

friends who surrounded him—small men who sought to dis-
place the giants and to control Harrison as Lewis and
Kendall were thought to have controlled Jackson.[29]

The whole past record of the men should have taught Harrison that ordinary recognition was sufficient to retain the
support of Webster, who would follow his party-leader, even
though he grumbled and sulked; while Clay could not and
would not follow, but must have the show as well as the substance of leadership, or fling out into open revolt. In addition,
Webster was the spokesman of no considerable group, while
Clay was the idolized leader of a devoted following which embraced the most considerable and reliable element in the Whig
conglomerate. As between the two, repeated incidents, widely
current in anecdote, had shown that Clay had only to assert
his dominance for "the godlike Webster" to give way. Clay, on
his part, had felt it as an insult that the Harrisburg Convention should prefer such a man to himself.[30]

In this strained situation, definite causes of friction were not
lacking. As one might expect, questions of patronage bulked
large. Clay was violently opposed to the appointment of
Edward Curtis as Collector at New York; Webster was equally
determined on the appointment. Curtis was an intimate personal
and political friend of the latter, had been his spokesman at
Harrisburg, both in the Convention and before its meeting, and
had joined to his exceptional ability the greatest zeal and in-
dustry in defeating Clay's nomination. Thurlow Weed and his
clique were especially anxious for his appointment, and through
the medium of Peter B. Porter, an intimate friend of Clay's,
the wily editor of the Albany *Evening Journal* sought to
placate Clay's resentment and ward off his opposition. This
attempt at conciliation failed, but Curtis was nevertheless appointed.[31]

It has been said that the Curtis appointment was the im-

---

[29] See note 2 above, especially Louisville *Advertiser*, December 1, 1840;
also Adams, *op. cit.*, X, 366.

[30] Louisville *Advertiser*, December 8, 1840; L. P. Little, *Ben Hardin: His
Times and Contemporaries*, p. 180. H. A. Wise, *op. cit.*, pp. 171-72.

[31] Porter to Clay, January 28, 1841; Clay to Harrison, March 15, 1841;
Colton, *Private Correspondence*, pp. 448-49, 452-53. Also *National Intelligencer*, March 20, 1841.

mediate cause of the breach between Clay and Harrison. Clay himself propagated that idea, which cast him in the rôle of aggrieved party and Harrison in that of aggressor. The rupture was precipitated, however, not by patronage but by the question of calling a special session of Congress. Just how early the Whig leaders determined on a special session would be hard to ascertain. Clay asserted that he had "never doubted for a moment about it since November." As early as December 16, he had threatened the Democrats with a special session to repeal the Sub-Treasury. Certainly by the end of January, at the latest, the Whigs were committed to that measure.[32]

As the situation developed Webster cooled toward a special session, or at least sought to delay its meeting. He found himself in confidential relations with Harrison, while Clay was held at arm's length. Already he was largely in control of appointments and was regarded as spokesman for the administration and virtual leader of the party. The adjournment of the special session of the Senate would relegate Clay to temporary obscurity. The Kentucky Senator would find it awkward even to remain on the ground at Washington. He would have no rostrum from which to address the public, while those unfriendly to him controlled the backstairs at the White House. The postponement of the meeting of the special session, therefore, would give Webster that much more time in which to consolidate his own position without effective interference by Clay. Accordingly, he began to suggest delay to the newspaper correspondents and to work toward that end with the President. An argument which appealed to Harrison was found in the existing situation of the Congressional delegation from Tennessee.

The terms of her Representatives had expired March 4, and their successors would be chosen only in August unless Polk, the Democratic Governor, should call a special election. Thus Tennessee, which had given her electoral vote to Harrison in spite of Jackson's strongest efforts on behalf of Van Buren, would be without representation in the House if a

---

[32] *Congressional Globe*, 26th Cong., 2nd Sess., pp. 19-20, 132 ff. Webster to Everett, February 2, 1841; Daniel Webster, *Private Correspondence*, II, 99-101.

special session were convened early in the summer. But the situation in regard to her Senators was even more serious.

At the end of 1839, the Democratic legislatures had "instructed" Senators White and Foster into resigning their seats and chosen Alexander Anderson and the venerable Felix Grundy in their place. A year later Grundy died and Polk appointed A. O. P. Nicholson as his successor, since the regular legislative session met only in October. Thus, whenever the legislature met, two senatorial seats would have to be filled, since Anderson's term was expiring. The present legislative majority was Democratic by a narrow margin, and probably would return two Democrats, whereas the Whigs had high hopes, justified in the result, of carrying the state in the August election. The calling of a special session of Congress during the summer, therefore, would enable the Democrats to discount possible defeat in August by electing two senators at a special session of the legislature, thus blasting the hopes of Whig aspirants to the honor. Jackson and other leaders actually did urge this course on Polk, who for some reason disregarded their wishes, though he issued a public statement pointing out the situation and stigmatizing the calling of the special session by Harrison as "a capital political blunder." The cogency of these considerations was increased by the narrow margin of Whig control in the Senate.[33]

Clay, of course, was fully alive to all these considerations. He undoubtedly chose the rôle of senatorial leader in confident anticipation of a special session. Fully aware as he was of Harrison's suspicious attitude, it is unthinkable that he would tamely submit to leaving Webster in command of the situation for eight critical months while he languished in exile from the seat of government. The suggestions of delay, manifestly emanating from Webster, and the imminent close of the special session of the Senate, determined him to force the issue. Accordingly, on the last Saturday morning before the adjournment, he addressed an imperious "confidential" letter to the President:

[33] E. I. McCormac, *James K. Polk: A Political Biography,* pp. 165-69, 175-83.

Will you excuse me, for suggesting the propriety of a definite decision about an Extra Session, and of announcing the fact? There is much speculation and uncertainty about it, in circles [sic] and among members of Congress. Time is rapidly passing away, and members of your Cabinet have, it is alleged, added to the uncertainty.

After all that has occurred; after what you have said at Richmond and elsewhere, if the purpose of calling one should be abandoned, there is danger of the implication of vacillating counsels.

I have never doubted for a moment about it since Novr. In my deliberate opinion, the good of the Country and the honor and interest of the party demand it.

By way of stating the grounds for the convocation, I have sketched the rough draft of a proclamation which I respectfully submit for your perusal, as best indicating what strikes me as expedient.

I think your election should occupy the front and most prominent ground. The financial difficulties of the Gov't. alone form too narrow a basis to put the call upon; but the draft now enclosed covers that and all other grounds.

Altho' not well, I shall have the honor of dining with you today, when I should be most happy to learn your final decision.[84]

The enclosed draft proclamation recited as reasons for the summons "the just expectations of the people of the United States, in regard to measures adapted to their prosperity, as evidenced by a recent political event; the great and general embarrassments in the Commerce, Currency, and Business of the Country; and the financial condition of the Government of the United States."

Harrison, construing this letter as a renewed attempt at dictation made immediate and emphatic response. With his own hand that same afternoon he wrote:

My dear friend, You use the privilege of a friend to lecture me and I take the same liberty with you.

You are too impetuous. Much as I rely upon your judgment there are others whom I must consult and in many cases to determine [sic] adversely to your suggestion. In the matter to which your communication of this morning refers there is no difference of opinion as to the manner and there would be none as to the time

---

[84] Clay to Harrison, March 13, 1841, Clay Papers.

but for the situation of Tennessee to whom we owe so much. Her feelings and interest must not be sacrificed if it can be avoided. The question will be finally settled on Monday having been adjourned over from a discussion which took place this morning.

I prefer for many reasons this mode of answering your note to a conversation in the presence of others.[35]

This note, carrying its sting in its tail like a scorpion, threw Clay into transports of rage. A newspaper correspondent found him alone that evening, pacing his room in great perturbation and crumpling the note in his hand with an energy which showed the state of his feelings:

"And it has come to this!" he exclaimed.

I am civilly but virtually requested not to visit the White House —not to see the President personally, but hereafter only to communicate with him in writing. The prediction I made to him at Ashland last fall has been verified. Here is my table loaded with letters from my friends in every part of the Union, applying to me to obtain offices for them, when I have not one to give, nor influence enough to secure the appointment of a friend to the most humble position![36]

That evening Clay was present at a state dinner at the White House with a large company of Whig leaders, but he never had another private interview with Harrison.[37] On Monday the Senate adjourned, and Clay dispatched a final letter to the President.[38]

It was skillfully written to becloud the issue. Ascribing the letter to the difficulty of finding opportunity for a private conversation with the busy Executive, Clay brought up the charge of "dictation" in such terms as to imply that Harrison had suggested it in an interview on Saturday, thus making possible the later suppression of the two notes written that

---

[35] Harrison to Clay, March 13, 1841, Clay Papers. At some time this letter was prepared for publication, even to the page it was to occupy, but, so far as I can discover, it is hitherto unpublished, as is the note to which it is a reply.

[36] N. Sargent, *Public Men and Events,* II, 115-16.

[37] *Ibid.,* p. 116; Adams, *op. cit.,* X, 444, March 13, 1841.

[38] Clay to Harrison, March 15, 1841, Clay Papers. According to endorsements in Clay's handwriting, he recovered this letter and that of March 13 through Harrison's grand-nephew in June, 1841.

day. This charge Clay categorically denied and countered by accusing his enemies of poisoning Harrison's mind against him.

> In what, in truth can they allege a dictation, or even interference, on my part? In the formation of your Cabinet? You can contradict them. In the administration of the public patronage? The whole Cabinet as well as yourself can say that I have recommended nobody for any office. I have sought none for myself, or my friends. I desire none. A thousand times have my feelings been wounded, by communicating to those who have applied to me, that I am obliged to abstain inflexibly from all interference in official appointments.

Clay next took up the Curtis appointment. While admitting, and repeating, the harshest denunciation of Webster's friend, he stigmatized as "utterly unfounded" the charge that he had said that "Curtis should not be appointed"; nor had he used such language in regard to any other appointment. He asserted that he had not dictated unless "to express freely my opinion, as a citizen and as a Senator" was dictation. The only alternative to such expression would be retirement, and so he concluded on a plaintive note of injured innocence.

In spite of his breach with the President, the Cabinet decision was substantially a victory for Clay. The special session was summoned to meet May 31. The proclamation, issued on Wednesday, March 17, did not, however, follow Clay's draft either in phrasing or in ideas.[39]

Clay left Washington immediately, to return to his home in Kentucky. Before he again set foot in the capital, Harrison was no more, John Tyler was in the White House, and all political calculations had to be recast.

---

[39] J. D. Richardson, ed., *A Compilation of the Messages and Papers of the Presidents*, IV, 21.

CHAPTER III

TYLER TOO

JOHN TYLER was one of the most distinguished sons of the Old Dominion. At the age of fifty-one he had been honored with practically every office in the gift of the commonwealth and had become the youngest man up to that time to occupy the presidency. He was notable for suavity, geniality and tact, and was said to possess the rare gift of retaining the personal friendship of his opponents through heated contests. He was fond of social intercourse and was a model of the domestic virtues. His conscientiousness amounted to punctilio. These estimable and amiable qualities, which are universally conceded to him, readily explain his indisputable popularity in his own state. On the other hand, the vanity, stubbornness, opinionated self-sufficiency, and priggishness sometimes attributed to him seem equally out of keeping with that popularity.[1]

As the respectable figurehead of a powerful machine, Tyler's qualities might well have carried him into high office. The politicians with whom he was affiliated, however, were conspicuous for their failure to grasp the principles or the necessity of party organization, and indeed for their futile and querulous opposition to all that tended toward it. In such a situation as existed in the Virgiina of that day, the possession of considerable talents is the only possible explanation of Tyler's advancement, yet there is nothing to indicate that he was endowed with intelligence of the highest order. His nature seems to have been rather simple and confiding, with great capacity for friendship and a disposition to rely strongly on the personal relation.[2] At the same time, where his conscience was involved, his courage was inflexible. The man who could vote at a great national crisis in a minority of one was hardly a weakling. It was, however, equally incontestable that he was an "Impracticable."

Historians have been inclined to criticize or ridicule Tyler

---

[1] Tyler, *op. cit.,* II, 13, 21.
[2] Tyler to Tucker, April 25, 1841, Tyler, *op. cit.,* p. 32.

for his devotion to consistency. Yet he had been highly praised for that very quality by men who later as strongly condemned him for it. Such a man was Philip Hone, the very *beau ideal* of a high-minded Whig—a representative of the old Federalist leaven. Hone had met Tyler at the table of Webster in 1830 and on the occasion of his resignation from the Senate expressed in his dairy the general sentiments of his class.[3] "Thus it ever is," he wrote. "The honorable, high-minded men viewing personal consistency as of greater importance than party fidelity do not hesitate to maintain the one at the expense of the other, and persons less scrupulous usurp their stations in the government."

It has been claimed with considerable plausibility that Clay was responsible for Tyler's nomination as vice-president. Tyler and William Cabell Rives, a "Conservative," were rival opponents of the Democrats for the Virginia senatorship. Their rivalry seemed not only to endanger an anti-Van Buren seat in the Senate, but even the Whig chances of success in carrying Virginia for the presidency in 1840. Clay, who expected to be the presidential candidate, attached a sentimental importance to securing the vote of his native state. He accordingly accepted Tyler as his prospective running-mate with the understanding that Tyler's friends would support Rives for the Senate.[4] If this be true, it is one of the ironical turns of American politics that Rives became Tyler's spokesman in the Senate and a chief factor in thwarting Clay's designs.

There can be no doubt, however, that, up to the demise of Harrison, Clay's relations with Tyler were friendly. It was believed, indeed, that by Tyler's succession the position of the great Kentuckian had favorably changed from what it had been under Harrison. Tyler concluded a long letter to Clay with the assurance that "My attention is turned to the removals from office after the manner you suggest, and I hope that to recent appointments, you have nothing to object. The P. office at Lexington shall be attended to." It seemed feasible for

---

[3] Bayard Tuckerman, ed., *The Diary of Philip Hone,* I, 201-2, March 2, 1836.

[4] H. A. Wise, *op. cit.,* pp. 156-61; Tyler, *op. cit.,* I, 556-65 and III, 204. Cf. New York *Express,* September 1, 1841.

Crittenden to seize the capacity of the administration from Webster.[5] Yet even before the opening of the session Clay and Tyler had come to a political rupture on the subject of the Bank.[6]

On no subject was Tyler's record longer or more consistent. The very first act of his public career was to introduce a resolution in the Virginia legislature condemning Senators Giles and Brent for their suport of a Bank bill. In 1819, he voted, along with General Harrison, for the issuing of a *scire facias* to rescind and annul the charter of the second Bank of the United States, declaring in a speech his belief in its unconstitutionality. In 1832, he voted both against renewing the charter and in support of Jackson's veto. In 1833, while holding the withdrawal of the deposits improper, he reiterated in a speech, and again in a report, his position on the constitutional question. He had never deviated from this opinion, and during the campaign repeatedly expressed it in letters and speeches. Yet the accession of Tyler brought surprisingly little apprehension to the northern Whigs.[7]

On April 6, Tyler took oath of office as ninth President of the United States. The extra session of Congress had been called to convene on May 31. The new President had not quite eight weeks in which to bring his invalid wife and large family from their plantation home and settle them in the White House, to adjust himself to his new duties, and to prepare his recommendations to Congress. Meanwhile the flood of office seekers which had overwhelmed Harrison continued to beat about the White House. Tyler was "surrounded by Clay-men, Webstermen, anti-Masons, original Harrisonians, old Whigs and new Whigs—each jealous of the others, and all struggling for the offices."[8]

---

[5] David Lambert to Mangum, May 7, 1841, Mangum Papers; Tyler to Clay, April 30, 1841, Tyler, *op. cit.*, III, 94; John White to Crittenden, April 15, 1841, Crittenden Papers.

[6] Tyler, *op. cit.*, II, 33-34.

[7] Tyler's "Statement," written "at the time of the tariff bills in 1842," Tyler, *op. cit.*, II, 66 ff. See also Webster to Hiram Ketcham, July 16, 1841, Webster, *Writings and Speeches*, XVI, 345; Tuckerman, *op. cit.*, I, 393, 394, December 9, 1839 and II, 73, April 7, 1841.

[8] Tyler to Tucker, July 28, 1841, Tyler, *op. cit.*, II, 53-54.

Tyler was peculiarly handicapped by the circumstances of his becoming president. He was the first vice-president to succeed to the presidency and there was a quite reasonable uncertainty as to his status. This was somewhat mortifying to Tyler, but his prompt and decisive claim to the full presidential title met with little serious opposition and established an interpretation of the constitution which has never since been disputed. His assumption of full presidential prerogatives, however, met with more determined resistance, and that from his own party.

Unfortunately, but, under the circumstances, quite naturally, he retained the newly installed Harrison cabinet. When it became apparent that there was a serious difference of opinion between the President and the party leaders in Congress on some of the cardinal measures of the Whig program, there was a tendency on the part of the latter to exalt the Cabinet appointed by Harrison as holding by a better popular title than did the new President, and to seek to use the "ministers" to coerce him into compliance with their wishes. When, feeling that the Cabinet sympathized with his opponents, Tyler took counsel with personal friends, and even dispatched veto messages which he knew the Cabinet would disapprove, without consulting his "constitutional advisers," the congressional Whigs raised the old cry of "Executive Usurpation."

In the measures which had most incensed the Whigs, which had indeed sent into their ranks the very contingent that included John Tyler, Jackson had acted either without consulting his Cabinet, or in opposition to its advice. The issue which had united former Federalists like Webster and Adams, former Jeffersonians like Clay, radical State rights men like Calhoun and Tyler, Tariff men, Bank men, Nationalists, Nullifiers, and Abolitionists, was "Executive Usurpation," as exemplified by one measure or another which ran counter to the interests or sensibilities of the respective groups.

The Whigs, therefore, laid great stress upon the Cabinet, even regarding it as in some manner a check upon the President. The Whig newspapers of 1841 quite consistently referred to the secretaries as "Ministers" or "constitutional advisers"—and if they were "constitutional advisers," was not their advice a constitutional necessity? The character of Harrison, the manner in which his Cabinet was constructed, the circumstances of Tyler's succession—all these factors combined to further this attitude. Archer had the strange idea that Tyler might follow his opinion in vetoing the Bank Bill, but must then resign—[9] an awkward approximation to the status of the British Prime Minister. This shows the trend of Whig thinking, and apparently differed from the ideas of Clay mainly in that it identified the presidency with the premiership instead of with the Crown.

Of course, all these hazy ideas were grist to Clay's mill. Passed over for the presidency, he saw in them his opportunity still to wield, as leader of the party in Congress, the reality of power. With characteristic opportunism, he sought to create an approximation to the British system. Realizing that the power of the Prime Minister rested not upon his ministerial position but upon his parliamentary leadership, he essayed the rôle of Prime Minister in the Senate. Experience had taught him that to this program Webster could make no effective resistance. As Judge Rowan, of Kentucky, no great admirer of Clay's, once said, "If the two should go duck hunting together, Mr. Clay would expect Mr. Webster to assume the office of spaniel, to bring out the birds, and the latter would not perceive that there was any degradation in his assumption of such an office!"[10] Hence the Clay press insisted that the President was practically obligated to accept whatever legislation the congressional majority might frame in alleged fulfillment of campaign pledges. The weakness of this position was, of course, the fact that the Whigs had adopted no platform at Harrisburg.

It was generally thought that Clay dominated the Cabinet, and while his control was not so absolute as commonly assumed, the sequel proved that it was sufficient to effect his purpose. Tyler thus had at one and the same time to combat the subordination of the Executive department to the Legislative, and the exaltation of the Cabinet at the expense of the President. That he succeeded was probably due to the constitutional power

---

[9] Wise to Tucker, June 27, 1841, Tyler, *op. cit.*, II, 53-54.
[10] Little, *op. cit.*, p. 180.

inherent in the presidential office rather than to any wisdom or skill on his part.

With the approach of the special session, various plans for a Bank began to appear in the Whig newspapers, in spite of the fact that a great deal of uncertainty had all along been felt as to Tyler's position.[11] One of the Whig publicists whose mind was engaged in this work was Judge N. Beverly Tucker of Virginia, half-brother to John Randolph. As early as April 3, Judge Tucker had sent his plan to Clay, who definitely rejected it in a letter dated April 15. In this letter Clay presented an elaborate argument for a national bank of the old type and enclosed the resolutions which outlined his legislative program.

Tucker had written to Clay before learning of Harrison's death. On the eleventh, therefore, he sent his plan to Tyler, who replied under date of the twenty-fifth. The President expressed his anxiety at the uncompromising spirit of the Whig "Ultras" and his fear that nothing but "an old-fashioned bank" would satisfy the leaders. He indicated his own views and expressed interest in Tucker's plan, promising to ponder it. He discussed it freely and fully with Wise, and, as a result of his discussions and cogitations, became much pleased with the plan, Wise left Washington on May 8. On the following day the President wrote Tucker requesting him to work out details of the plan with Wise, Preston, and Upshur, and this was duly done. The detailed plan was brought to Washington by Wise, who arrived on May 25, but found no opportunity for private or extended conference with the President until the twenty-eighth. He then delivered the plan to Tyler, but it proved to be too late to serve as a basis for the administration plan presented to Congress by Ewing.[12]

In the meantime, there had been important developments. On April 14, the day before he rejected the Tucker plan, Clay wrote to Tyler and probably sent him a copy of his program resolutions. Tyler replied with great frankness under date of

[11] *National Intelligencer*, April 7, 1841, and others; Waddy Thompson to Tyler, January 30, 1843, Tyler, *op. cit.*, II, 16-17, and *ibid.*, II, 44, quoting *National Intelligencer*, June 15, 1841.

[12] Tyler to Tucker, May 9, 1841; Wise to Tucker, May 29, June 5, 1841; Tyler, *op. cit.*, II, 30-37, *passim*.

April 30, informing Clay of his insuperable objections to an "old-fashioned United States Bank."[13] Clay reached Washington May 26. He gave Wise an "audience" the next day, at which the two leaders broke. Clay's breach with Wise was speedily followed by a breach with the President himself.[14]

Tyler would have preferred Tucker's plan, but there was not time for the Cabinet to be brought to accept it. He therefore took up Judge White's suggestion, for which he had voted in 1832 along with all the other State rights senators. This he recommended to Ewing, who, with the coöperation of the other members of the Cabinet, framed the bill in accordance. The details were almost entirely worked out by the members of the Cabinet, and the completed bill received the acquiescence of all of them.[15]

The new President flattered himself that the most formidable difficulty in the way of a peaceful administration had been overcome. He himself had little confidence in the efficacy of any bank to correct the disorders of the country, but he strongly desired to meet the wishes of the Whig party in so far as he could. He therefore sought a common ground upon which all could meet without any sacrifice of principles.[16] His plan was for Congress, as the local legislature of the District of Columbia, to establish a bank there, empowering it to establish offices in any State with the assent of the State.

Congress met, and his flattering delusion vanished. The urgent solicitations of the Cabinet availed nothing. The President had the fullest conversation with Clay,[17] and in the strongest manner urged upon him the adoption of the bill. He made his appeal in the strongest terms. He asked if he could be required to surrender the consistency of his whole life

---

[13] Tyler to Clay, April 30, 1841, Tyler, *op. cit.*, III, 92-94.

[14] Wise to Tucker, May 29, 1841; Tyler to Tucker, July 28, 1841; Tyler's "Statement," Tyler, *op. cit.*, II, 33-34, 67-70.

[15] This account is compiled from Tyler's "Statement," and Tyler to Tucker, July 28, 1841, *loc. cit.*

[16] Wise's evidence is to the contrary. "Ewing's report is not to be regarded as Tyler's measure. Tyler would hardly sanction all of the features, but even that Clay will oppose; and he is determined to oppose everything coming from Tyler," Wise to Tucker, June 18, 1841, Tyler, *op. cit.*, II, 46.

[17] Tyler places this interview "upon the opening of the extra session," Tyler to Tazewell, October 11, 1841, Tyler, *op. cit.*, II, 46.

upon a great question of policy, and whether the President, no
matter how he became so, could be asked to commit a wanton
and deliberate act of perjury. Clay remained stubborn, and
then Tyler became incensed and exclaimed:

Then, sir, I wish you to understand this—that you and I were
born in the same district; that we have fed upon the same
food, and breathed the same natal air. Go you now, then, Mr. Clay,
to your end of the avenue, where stands the Capitol and there perform your duty to the country as you shall think proper. So help
me God, I shall do mine at this end of it as I shall think proper.[18]

Up to this time, three forces had been working upon Tyler.
First, there were his old Virginia associates, who were urging
him to a course in accord with their extreme State rights
views. They disliked Webster as heartily as they did Clay,
and seem to have feared him more. Therefore, one of their
primary objects was to destroy the influence he had established
over the President. Yet they were willing to avail themselves
of his aid to defeat Clay. Wise was the most active of this
group. Later they may have been in coöperation with Calhoun,
but at this early stage there is no evidence that they were in
communication with the Carolinian, but rather to the
contrary.[19]

In the second place, there were the ultra-Whigs of the Clay
school, who were represented in the Cabinet by Crittenden, Bell
and Ewing. So far as the evidence goes, Crittenden made no
attempt whatever to realize Reverdy Johnson's anticipation
that he could make himself the "captain" of the administration.
Except Ewing, none of these seems to have had any influence
with Tyler.

In the third place, there were the moderates. The chief of
these was Webster, who early began to exercise, within certain
limits, a preponderating influence over the President. His
deferential attitude and the consideration he showed for Tyler's
cherished principles established his position, based as it was
upon a mutual antagonism to Clay. Furthermore, his constituents were interested in a Bank for strictly commercial

---

[18] This version of Tyler's final words is given by Lyon G. Tyler, apparently from family tradition, *op. cit.,* II, 34.

[19] Wise to Tucker, June 18, 1841, *loc. cit.;* Jameson, *op. cit., passim.*

reasons, and therefore it was with him rather a question of constructive legislation than of political strategy. He was much
more disposed to assure some kind of a Bank than to haggle
over the kind, and therefore influenced Tyler for moderation
and compromise, which happened to be the wisest political
strategy for the President.

This was perceived by Tyler, as we have seen, as well as by
the opposition (considerably to the disappointment of
Calhoun), and no less by Clay.[20] The latter therefore resolved
to force upon Tyler either complete submission or open rebel-
lion, and insisted upon an ultra-national measure. Webster, perceiving this, was impelled by self-interest, if by no higher
motives, to redouble his efforts at compromise, which the opposition at the last joined with Clay to prevent. For six weeks
Webster succeeded in foiling Clay's designs, and for a month
longer still held Wise and the Virginians at bay. In all this,
whatever personal interests may have been advocated, Webster
was essentially carrying on, through the maintenance of the
Whig party, the great work of his life—the maintenance of the
Union. The victory of Clay and Wise over Webster was a long
step toward the sectionalization of parties which precipitated
the Civil War.

The Extraordinary Session of Congress convened on May
31. The Senate had a membership of fifty-one, there being one
vacancy from Tennessee. The Democrats numbered twenty-two,
leaving a nominal Whig majority of seven.[21] Clay's control
was revealed by the election of the standing committees. He
himself headed that on Finance, which would manage all the
great Whig measures except the Land Bill. That would go
to the Committee on Public Lands, the chairman of which was
Clay's devoted follower, Oliver H. Smith of Indiana.

Yet on the most important measure of the session, the Bank
Bill, Clay was unable to count upon a full partisan majority.
No less than five Whig Senators, Archer and Rives of Virginia,
Merrick of Maryland, Preston of South Carolina, and Barrow
of Louisiana, had constitutional scruples which seriously em-

---

[20] Calhoun to Gleason, June 13, 1841, Jameson, *op. cit.*, p. 478; Wise to
Tucker, June 27, 1841, *loc. cit.*
[21] *Niles' Register*, LX, 195.

barrassed their leader.[22] In addition, he had to cope with the disposition of certain New England senators to look to Webster rather than to himself for leadership.

On Friday, June 4, several Senators presented petitions in favor of a general bankrupt law. Whereupon Linn of Missouri suggested to Clay "the necessity of introducing some such resolution as he had introduced in the called session of 1837, for the purpose of confining the business within proper limits." Clay said he would willingly adopt Linn's suggestion, if such was the sense of the Senate. He would reflect upon the suggestion "with a view of making up a sort of protocol of the subjects which in his opinion, it would be necessary to take up during the session." After some further remarks, on Clay's motion the Senate adjourned until Monday.

Accordingly, on Monday, Clay introduced the series of resolutions which he had prepared at Lexington six weeks before. The first declared that the business of Congress should be restricted to measures of an urgent nature. The second declared that the deliberations of Congress ought, "first, if not exclusively," to be devoted to

The repeal of the sub-Treasury; the incorporation of a bank adapted to the wants of the people, and of the government; the provision of an adequate revenue for the Government by the imposition of duties, and including an authority to contract a temporary loan to cover the public debt created by the last Administration; the prospective distribution of the proceeds of the public lands; the passage of necessary appropriation bills, and some modification of the banking system of the District of Columbia, for the benefit of the people of the District.

The third resolution suggested the distribution of these measures between the two Houses in order to prevent loss of time through simultaneous consideration of the same measure. Clay asked that these resolutions be printed and laid upon the table, where they reposed throughout the session.[23]

In the House, Clay's ascendancy was shown by the election of John White of Kentucky as Speaker. Fillmore of New York headed the powerful Ways and Means Committee and Cost

---

[22] Wise to Tucker, June 27, 1841, *loc. cit.*

[23] *Congressional Globe,* 27th Cong., 1st Sess., p. 22.

Johnson of Maryland, that on Public Lands. Both were strong Clay men. A specially created Committee on the Currency was headed by Clay's old running mate of 1832, John Sergeant of Pennsylvania. The Whigs appeared to have a majority of forty-eight, with twelve vacancies. This was sufficient to disregard two insurgent movements which appeared in the early days of the session. Wise had assumed the functions of leader in the routine of organization, but had speedily given way to Sergeant, his father-in-law, and had received only eight votes for the Speakership. Five members, radical anti-slavery men, including John Quincy Adams and Giddings, had voted for Lawrence of Pennsylvania. From the nature of things, a union of these two groups was impossible. The Whig majority in the House was as determined as it was numerous, and assured its control of legislation by a more drastic rule for limiting debate.

Meanwhile, on June 1, the President's message was received. Its longest and most significant section dealt with the subject of a financial agency for the government. On this point the message was noncommittal, but gave fair warning that the Executive was not to be ignored by the leaders of the Legislature.[24]

Clay immediately announced his intention of moving on the morrow for a select committee on so much of the President's message as related to the currency and the finances, with a view to suggesting a remedy. Upon being questioned as to the nature of the remedy he proposed, he replied that it was a National Bank. This committee, of nine members, was duly authorized, and Clay, who was already chairman of the Committee on Finance, became chairman also of the select committee. The other members were Choate, Berrien, Tallmadge, Bayard, Graham and Huntington, Whigs; and Wright and King, Democrats.[25]

Clay's first move, however, was for the repeal of the Sub-Treasury Law. On June 3, he introduced and carried the resolution which had been defeated at the preceding session. The next day, Friday, he reported a Repeal Bill from the Finance Committee. It was read, ordered printed, and made the

[24] *Ibid.*, pp. 6-8, 11, 12.
[25] *Ibid.*, pp. 8, 11, 12.

order of the day for Monday, June 7. After some attempts to amend and a good deal of wrangling, the bill was passed on the ninth by a vote of 29 to 18. Clay's haste was not, however, reflected by the House for the bill was not even committed until June 21, and it was exactly a month later that Sergeant reported it with amendments, simultaneously with the Fiscal Bank Bill.[26]

On the seventh, Clay, after referring to Ewing's Treasury Report, introduced a resolution "That the Secretary of the Treasury be directed to communicate to the Senate, with as little delay as practicable, a plan of such a bank to be incorporated by Congress, as, in his opinion, is best adapted to the public service." He briefly stated that his purpose "was to obtain for the consideration of Congress the Secretary of the Treasury's plan of a United States Bank." King, Woodbury, Wright, and Calhoun criticized Clay's deviation from Ewing's own phrasing in the Report, claiming that the resolution unduly limited the Secretary. Rives joined in suggesting a modification; whereupon Clay rather pettishly expressed the hope that he would write the modification himself. Upon hearing that modification, Clay at once declared that he could not vote for it, but would accept it if changed to the alternative "bank or fiscal agent." This was done and the resolution agreed to, as follows.[27]

Resolved, That the Secretary of the Treasury be directed to communicate to the Senate, with as little delay as possible, the plan of such a Bank or fiscal agent, as being free from constitutional objections, will, in his opinion, produce the happiest results, and confer lasting and important benefits on the country.

In accordance with Clay's resolution, on June 12, Ewing reported a plan of a "Bank and Fiscal Agent," incorporated as a bank located in the District of Columbia. The details of this plan, except in one particular, are of no importance for this study. The Bank should have "Power to establish branches or offices of discount and deposit in the several States with the assent of the States," and Congress might order the location of offices of discount where the same were needed for fiscal

---

[26] *Ibid.*, pp. 13, 21-36, 83-84, 238.
[27] *Ibid.*, pp. 22-23.

operations. This plan came to be referred to as the Ewing Bill, and, on Clay's motion, was referred to the Select Committee.[28]

Even before Ewing's plan came before Congress, it had been known, at least in its main features, and discussed. As early as June 5, Wise informed Tucker that it was "Judge White's old notion of a District Bank here, the branches to depend on State incorporation and State compact with the Federal government." At the same time he outlined the political situation at the Capital. Clay was "beyond all advice." Well knowing that Tyler would veto "his full-grown central monster," in his mad jealousy of Tyler's candidacy for a second term, he sought to drive him to a veto. That would compel Webster to take shelter under Tyler. Clay had "consummate nerve and ability to stand alone." Webster had not and fled before him. Clay was "the opposition ultimately to the Tyler Administration." Nor was Clay less suspicious of Tyler and his personal friends. He thought him likely to abandon the great body of the Whig party to coalesce with Calhoun, Duff Green, and their associates. If he did this, it would be upon the Bank.[29]

The Whig press, however, took a more moderate stand than the politicians. It was understood pretty generally that Ewing's plan had been framed by the Cabinet and represented a compromise between their views and those of the President. The powerful *National Intelligencer*, long regarded as the organ of the Whigs, took strong ground for the bill. It was "obviously a well-considered project," it declared,

which if cast into the form of law in the precise shape into which it had been molded by the Secretary of the Treasury, could not fail, in our opinion, to be fruitful of benefits to the country and facilities to the Government. . . . We would ourselves willingly see one or two of its features changed. But . . . for the mere gratification of a personal wish, we should never dream of hazarding the success of a great measure.

The *Intelligencer's* New York correspondent also reported that the plan "meets the public expectations and is far more

[28] *Ibid.*, pp. 48-49.
[29] Tyler, *op. cit.*, II, 37-38; Clay to E. M. Letcher, June 11, 1841, Coleman, *op. cit.*, I, 156-57.

satisfactory than any other that has been proposed."[30]

In spite of the attempts of the moderates, followers of Webster, to bring about concession from the "Ultras" to the views of the "Impracticables," the former proceeded with their program, but not without friction which could not altogether be veiled from the opposition.[31] Repeated caucuses of the Whig Senators were trying to frame a bill which could pass. There was sufficient disagreement over the branching power to render highly dangerous Clay's insistence upon the inclusion of that power without limitations. The moderates felt that this was an unimportant point inasmuch as "wherever the Bank wishes for a branch, a State Legislature will allow one," and that the majority of the Whigs if necessary, must give way to the scruples of the "Impracticables."

The day after Clay reported his Fiscal Bank Bill, an unusually well-informed correspondent reported that while the bill could pass the Senate it was uncertain if the President would approve a bill granting unrestricted branching power, and that a compromise would be necessary.[32] About the same time, however, Silas Wright wrote Van Buren that "It will pass both Houses substantially as it is to be reported I do not doubt, as I think everything has been settled in general caucus."[33] That able politician, veteran of the well-disciplined Democracy, could not credit the reckless politics of the Whig leaders.

Thus the Ewing bill was quite acceptable to the moderate Whigs and business men of the East. It also seems probable that Tyler would have signed that bill if it had been presented to him without undue delay or controversy.[34] Furthermore, it was generally known in Washington that the Ewing Bill was practically an administration measure, while there was a strong probability that Tyler would veto any bill that

[30] Clay to E. M. Letcher, June 14, 1841, *loc. cit.;* New York *Express,* June 14, June 26, 1841; *National Intelligencer,* June 15, June 17, June 18, 1841.

[31] Calhoun to Clemson, June 15, 1841, Jameson, *op. cit.,* p. 478; Louisville *Advertiser,* June 15, 1841.

[32] New York *Express,* June 18, June 28, 1841.

[33] Wright to Van Buren, June 21, 1841, Van Buren Papers.

[34] New York *Express,* September 18, 1841.

conferred unrestricted branching power. Clay knew this at least a day before Ewing's report was sent to the Senate, and according to Tyler he had known it for a month. In addition, as early as June 11, Clay knew that the controversy was likely to lead to a breach between the Whigs and their own President, and a "distinguished and experienced" correspondent of the Louisville *Public Advertiser* informed that newspaper that Clay knew that Tyler would veto such a bank bill as the "Ultras" desired, and that Clay "might find it necessary to alienate" the Whigs from the administration.[35] And finally, it was known to the correspondents, and must have been known to Clay, that if he got his bill through the Senate at all, it would be by a bare majority and consequently there would be no chance whatever of overriding a veto.

In the light of all these considerations, one thing appears certain: Clay was far more concerned with the political implications of the Bank bill than he was with the actual setting of the Bank in operation. Wright had no doubts at all in regard to his motives. Writing to Van Buren in full confidence, he said:

I have little doubt that Clay will succeed with all the measures he proposed for the extra session. . . . I have less that if he does that he will immediately give Tyler his choice to surrender or fight & that poor Daniel will have to fight or run, as I do not think surrender will be received from him. . . .[36]

This situation was understood by a considerable circle in Washington and the general public could have been apprised of it had the press so desired. A correspondent wrote on June 25, that it was "not at all certain either that Tyler would approve the bill, or that twenty-six senators could be found to vote for it." This correspondent went on to urge concession and to suggest a "back fire" to force it upon the Congressional leaders. Most ominous of all, he was at pains to state that the President "is of the best accord with all the members of his Cabinet, while at the same time he has an enlightened and liberal courtesy for the opposition." The only conceivable

---

[35] Clay to E. M. Letcher, June 11, 1841, Coleman, *op. cit.,* I, 156-57; Louisville *Advertiser,* June 15, 1841.

[36] Wright to Van Buren, June 21, 1841, Van Buren Papers.

purpose of these statements would be to allay incipient rumors of discord between the President and his "constitutional advisers," and of undue intimacy with the opposition. Three days later there was a suggestion of the inauspicious presence and unfortunate influence of Duff Green.[37]

This Extraordinary Session from which so much was expected had been in session barely four weeks. Already, however, Clay had defeated the plan of the moderates, sown the seeds of distrust between President and Cabinet, laid the basis for a revival of the "Executive Usurpation" issue, and goaded Tyler into compromising counsels. Webster was about to be placed in an untenable middle position, exposed to the attacks of the Democrats and the two extreme wings of his own party. Everything had gone well, though not perfectly smoothly, with Clay's plans for eliminating all rivals and securing an uncontested nomination in 1844 to "Harry of the West."

[37] New York *Express*, June 26, 1841, Washington correspondence dated June 25. This dispatch contains the first suggestion I have found of the "Clay compromise amendment." Cincinnati *Gazette*, July 5, 1841.

CHAPTER IV

THE DICTATOR

It was on June 21 that Clay made his report from the select committee, but only on the twenty-fourth that he was able to deliver his speech on the Fiscal Bank Bill. The speech, which was not reported in full, consumed about an hour. It was devoted to an exposition and defense of details; the crucial question of the constitutionality of the "branching power" was ignored. The opposition then sought a postponement, to which Clay emphatically objected and even demanded the yeas and nays. This impatience of delay characterized his whole management of the bill. It appeared repeatedly, in various connections, and usually resulted in a discussion which still further blocked proceedings and goaded Clay to fury. Yet he seemed unable either to profit by experience or to control his temper.[1]

On the twenty-fifth, at Buchanan's suggestion, it was agreed that the bill should be read by sections, the Whigs presenting their amendments. When they had made the bill that they wished, the Democrats should have their turn. This procedure was the more necessary since the Whigs themselves were not fully agreed on details, especially in the matter of branches. It was rumored, however, that such a compromise was in process of negotiation as "will not weaken the usefulness of the Bank if the States were disposed to obstruct the establishment of Branches, and such as will not, at the same time, commit the Executive to principles he cannot constitutionally approve."[2]

Tyler's course was already uncertain. It was reported that the branching feature of the bill ran counter to his constitutional opinions and that "if the bill should pass with that feature in it, he will veto it." Uneasiness was felt as to his intentions in regard to the election of 1844, which was not allayed by the friendliness of the Nullifiers and certain Loco Foco

---

[1] *Congressional Globe,* 27th Cong., 1st Sess., pp. 79-81, 97, 108-16, 121; New York *Express,* June 26, June 30, 1841.

[2] *Congressional Globe,* 27th Cong., 1st Sess., p. 121; New York *Express,* June 30, 1841.

elements, to say nothing of intimacies at the White House which boded no good to orthodox Whigs. There was also complaint of the slowness of removals, and not entire satisfaction with such new appointments as were made.[3] Meanwhile, the New York *Evening Post* exultantly declared "There is certainly a Senatorial conspiracy on foot to counteract Mr. Clay's scheme of forcing Mr. Tyler to veto this bill. . . . The votes will be, it is supposed, for the bill 24, against it 27 in full Senate."[4]

While the Whigs were thus descending into the depths of discouragement and Clay's control appeared to be threatened, the conditions of the session were telling upon the temper of the Senators. The Senate was sitting nearly seven hours a day, beginning at ten o'clock and continuing until nearly five. There is little wonder that such a program, together with the necessary preparation and correspondence, amid the summer humidity of Washington, caused the members to feel debilitated and to display a good deal of irritability.[5] Nor was Clay's manner in debate calculated to encourage a spirit of sweet reasonableness. Although Buchanan and Wright were said to be treated with great courtesy and consideration by the Whigs, the latter wrote Van Buren that he never saw Clay "more apparently irritable, and yet he looks across the Chamber to King and controls his tongue unusually when used towards our side of the house."[6]

The climax of the debate came with the consideration of the amendment which Rives presented on July 1. This represented the extreme concession of the "Impracticables," and as such was supported by Webster in order to prevent a veto, the complete failure of bank legislation, and the probable disruption of the party. The discussion, lasting three days, marked

---

[3] Cincinnati *Gazette,* July 5, 1841, Washington correspondence dated June 28. The concluding sentence contains the first hint to the public of Duff Green's influence with Tyler.

[4] Louisville *Advertiser,* July 5, 1841, quoting New York *Evening Post.*

[5] Calhoun to Mrs. Clemson, June 28, 1841, Jameson, *op. cit.,* p. 479. Two weeks later, he says that the Senate was sitting thirty-six hours a week. Calhoun to Clemson, July 11, 1841, *ibid.,* p. 481.

[6] Cincinnati *Gazette,* July 5, 1841, Wright to Van Buren, June 21, 1841, Van Buren Papers.

the lowest ebb of Clay's leadership.[7] For a time, it seemed as if Webster would be victorious, which probably explains the brutality of Clay's treatment of Choate, Webster's spokesman in the Senate.

The Rives amendment referred to the "branching power." In the precise words of Ewing's project, it required the assent of the state legislatures for the establishment of any "office of discount and deposite in any State," but once established, such a branch could not be withdrawn without the assent of Congress. Rives declared that the restoration of the principle of the Ewing Bill was the purpose of his amendment, in support of which he spoke at great length.[8]

Omitting the general constitutional arguments, which were those customary to the State rights school, Rives's argument declared for a bank located in the District of Columbia, which might send its paper all over the Union, but which otherwise was as unlike the old Bank of the United States as possible. He based this contention upon the decision of the Supreme Court in *Bank of Augusta vs. Earle.* Taking up the question of State assent, he declared that it represented not an extension of Congressional power by assent of individual States, but a mere exercise of State sovereignty. Reviewing the history of the Bank question, he declared that its constitutionality was not settled, nor did the election of 1840 prove the popular judgment in its favor. Other issues were involved, notably "the odious sub-treasury." Harrison's early record was against the Bank, and at least in Virginia he had been regarded as personally opposed to it still. Tyler's opinions must have been considered in view of the potentialities of the vice presidency, and his unvarying opposition to a National Bank on constitutional grounds for nearly a quarter of a century was a matter of public record.

At this point, Clay called Rives to order for referring "to the opinions of the President on a pending subject of deliberation." Rives protested that he was merely giving an historical survey of the election of 1840, making no reference to what

---

[7] New York *Express,* July 3, 1841.
[8] *Congressional Globe,* 27th Cong., 1st Sess., App., pp. 354-55.

might or might not be Tyler's opinion at that moment, nor
had he any view to influencing the independent action of the
Senate. After some further conversation, Rives was declared
in order. Asserting that the question was in a state of balance,
he appealed for consideration for the scruples of the strict
constructionists, declaring that policy called for the adoption
of the Ewing compromise, which practical business men as well
as the Secretary of the Treasury assured him would work
well.

Clay replied, also at great length. He assailed Rives's plan
of a district bank as an attempt to do by indirection something
which Rives believed Congress had no power to do. Assuming
that Congress had such power, the asking of State assent
would create a bad precedent. As to forbearance in its exercise,
this was a case of such marked and peculiar character that forbearance in exercise was tantamount to surrender. Rives's project proceeded from the supposition that Congress lacked the
power to create a national bank. A branch admitted thus would
be subject to State jurisdiction, in effect a local institution.
The States would impose conditions for its admission, including
the taxing power, and its location would become a bone of contention. Again, such a great district bank, stript of all essential power of banking within the District and transacting
all its important business beyond the boundaries of the District,
would indeed be a monster. This was no occasion for compromise. "The question is a National Bank or no National Bank,
constitutionality or unconstitutionality, power or no power.
There is no mean or middle term."

He did not think it "compatible with respect due to the
Chief Magistrate, or to the dignity and independence of the
Senate" to allude to the possibility of a veto. He was confident
the President had authorized no such intimation. His "confidence in the patriotism and honor of the President, and in his
devotion to the cause which brought him into power" was so
great that he felt "perfectly persuaded" that he would have
"an anxious desire . . . to conform his judgment to that of the
Legislative department." It would be improper for him to
"advert to the facts and circumstances" from which he drew
"inferences variant from those which have been expressed."

What was their duty? Their conviction, he continued, coincided with the wishes of the people. The theory of our government inculcated the independence of the Legislative and the Executive. Could they give up their judgments to mere presumption as to the judgments of others? Their duty was to perfect the measure, then to present it to the coördinate branch of the government, whose duty and rights would then accrue. They should hope for concurrence—he would not anticipate disagreement—but that, if it came, would not be so great a public calamity as a voluntary surrender of the conscientious judgment and constitutional independence of the one to the other.

Preston closed the debate of that day, supporting the amendment on the ground that it was their imperative duty to create some kind of Bank, that it was inexpedient on slight grounds to risk the unity of the Executive and the Legislature, and that he concurred with Ewing and Rives as to the practicability of the plan. He pointed out the possibly disastrous political results of continued disagreement, and concluded with another plea for conciliation and forbearance as the only means of achieving practical results.[9]

On Friday, Choate, Webster's successor, spoke in favor of the amendment, which, after a good deal of hesitation, he had resolved to support, although he had no doubts as to "the constitutional power of Congress to establish branches all over the States, possessing the discounting function, directly and adversely against their united dissent."[10] But it is not always expedient to exercise a power. He felt that his urgent duty was to give the people a national bank as speedily as possible, and he believed he could affect that sooner and more surely by "voting for the bill as it came from the Secretary, the bill of the Administration, than for the bill as it came from the committee."

There was no doubt that the united Whigs could enact such a bank at that session, and it might begin operations by January 1. He did not believe that the capitalists would refuse to subscribe because the establishment of branches was contingent on

[9] *Loc. cit.*
[10] *Ibid.*, App., pp. 355-58.

State consent, even without which it could "perform all of the offices, earn all the profits, and do all the good a Bank can do, except that it may not make a local loan." If the capitalists did refuse, they could remedy the defect at the next session, and the independent discounting power would have been proved an indispensable necessity before which all constitutional theories must give way.

If the State adhered to the bill reported by the committee, he "fully believed" they would pass no bank charter. He doubted whether they could carry it through Congress; he had no doubt they would fail to make it a law. "The rules of orderly proceeding here, decorum, pride, regret," would prevent his stating the reasons of his belief. He had "no personal or private grounds for the conviction," but judged on "notorious and . . . decisive indications."

Here Clay interrupted to demand that Choate "give the grounds" on which he made "this broad assertion" that he *knew* that no Bank could be chartered at that session unless the amendment were adopted. Choate replied that he was sure Clay would allow him without interruption, "the right of expressing manfully" his "firm conviction" without giving reasons which he could give only by a breach of privilege or a violation of a parliamentary rule. But he repeated that there would be no bank at that session without the amendment.

Choate then resumed his argument. The same situation would prevail at the next session—they would have to wait two years, or four, or even longer, for a National Bank. The people should not be kept waiting so long, but should be relieved at once. Another reason for his vote was that the adoption of the amendment would preserve the harmony and unity of the party.

This was the crisis of the debate. Preston's calm reasoning had revealed the impolicy of following Clay in his uncompromising course. But Preston was a South Carolinian with self-confessed preference for the employment of the State banks, were that course a possibility. Choate, however, stood in no such invidious position. Senator from Massachusetts in succession to Webster, his constitutional principles were beyond criticism except by those who, in his assertion of them, scented

Federalism. By every social, professional, and political association, he was the representative of the financial power of State Street, then relatively far greater than today. He was recognized as one of the foremost lawyers of the nation, one whose opinion, on a question of pure law, carried far more weight than that of Clay. Such was the man who insisted that the proposal of Ewing and Rives involved no surrender of the constitutional power of Congress to establish branches all over the Union; that a vote for it required no abandonment of principles; that the plan was practical, alike in its legal, its political and its financial aspects; who, from the seat of Webster, seemed, with the very voice of the Secretary of State, to declare that without this amendment no Bank Bill could be enacted; who presumed to argue that the proposal was deserving of consideration because it originated with the administration—with John Tyler and Daniel Webster! This able advocate's logic and luminous phrase cleared up the obfuscations of Rives, paled the persuasive eloquence of Preston, and pitilessly revealed the superficiality, the disingenuousness, the peevish impracticableness of "the Dictator." That plea for conciliation placed squarely upon the Senator from Kentucky the responsibility for compromise or party disruption.

All these considerations must have seethed through the mind of Clay as he saw the effect of his own speech overcome, and all the uglier passion which lurked in the depths of his ardent nature mounted to the surface. Simmons of Rhode Island followed Choate, speaking against the amendment. But the interval thus afforded was insufficient for the return of Clay's calmer judgment, and Archer, either by accident or design, afforded him an opening. Forgetting alike the respect due to Choate's personal and professional standing, the courtesy which the oldest member of the Senate owed to the youngest, the consideration of a party-leader for his party-associates, even the amenities of debate, Clay attempted to use in the Senate the brow-beating methods of a cross-examination. Unfortunately also, in seeking a cooler part of the torrid chamber, Clay had accepted the seat of Young of Illinois, which brought him within one seat of Choate. The heated colloquy which ensued thus occurred with the participants in close proximity.

In this colloquy, Clay endeavored to extort from Choate the source of his statement that he knew that there would be no bank at that session unless the Rives Amendment were adopted, finally attempting to pin him down to a categorical answer to his question. Choate denied that he had implied Executive authority for his statement of his convictions, and asserted his right to explain what he said in his own words. The scene ended only when Preston called the Senators to order. The next day the incident was closed by a statement from Clay which was tantamount to an apology.[11]

That day, Bayard introduced an amendment to the Rives Amendment which later was to have great significance. When it came to a vote, however, it was supported by only nine senators.[12]

Huntington of Connecticut spoke next, maintaining the orthodox Whig position on the question of expediency and emphasizing the dilemma upon which Clay had impaled Choate. Who could speak with authority as to the President's intentions, or, if he could, ought to do so? But it made no difference—the Senate was "an independent branch of the Congress" and they should not inquire in advance what were the opinions either of the House or the President—"to others must be left their share of responsibility." The Senate was not yet "called upon to bow to any such implied dictations." They did not know their opinions. He would vote "uninfluenced by any supposed embarrassments" which might arise elsewhere. But

---

[11] *Ibid.*, p. 145: "Clay pounced upon him with the utmost ferocity. The Massachusetts gentleman cowered and quailed before the violence of Mr. Clay, when he should have repelled his insolence with equal violence, even at the risk of his life. The people of Massachusetts are a pacific, and order-loving, and a law-abiding people, but they will not sustain a representative who permits their rights to be outraged, their dignity to be insulted, in his person. Mr. Choate must be utterly deficient in energy and spirit, or he would never have submitted to the tyrannical insolence of Mr. Clay. The Dictator is a man of unquestioned courage but since the lesson taught him by Col. King last March, he manifests great discrimination in the selection of subjects for the exercise of his bullying disposition. His overshadowing preponderance in the Senate causes him to forget himself sometimes, but it will be seen that he will not tyrannize over or insult any Senator who recognizes the 'point of Honor,' " Louisville *Advertiser,* July 16, 1841, quoting New York *Herald.*

[12] *Congressional Globe,* 27th Cong., 1st Sess., p. 152.

the topic was "irrelevant"; they should forget that it had been mentioned.[13] Such talk was the very abdication of political commonsense, but it brightly illuminated Clay's tactics. Tyler must either submit or again raise the issue of "Executive Usurpation."

Clay had intended to carry the bill that day, but despairing of success, had consented to go into executive session. The opposition were delighted at the quandary of the Whigs, and, as was manifestly their policy, resolved to vote *en masse* against the Rives Amendment in order to increase the confusion of the Whigs. Choate's stand was attributed by many to Webster's prompting—"Massachusetts leads off against Clay." Others said, "Here's a coalition of Tyler and Webster against Clay." Still others, "Now the Whig Party is broken up. Clay has got the Senate turned against the Administration." A well-informed correspondent wrote: "It is rather a fight among great men than any other kind of a fight at all. It is a trial of power ahead." The Fourth of July recess did little to help the situation. On July 6, a correspondent wrote that the Virginia Whig press generally demanded that Clay accept the Rives Amendment. This may have had some influence on Rives's colleague, Archer, who was wavering in his support of Tyler.[14]

When the Senate resumed consideration of the measure, after the national holiday, Bates, in a brief speech, stated the grounds of his vote, and these proved to be practically identical with those of Choate. He cut clearly through the tissue of sophistry and parliamentary fiction woven by Huntington, and threw out a challenge to Clay which the latter did not think fit to take up. "Without doubt, the honorable chairman (Mr. Clay) indulges the belief that the bill will become a law, for nothing short of the barest dementation could originate a bill with us, . . . the friends of the Administration, that could not."

The Bayard Amendment having been defeated, the Rives Amendment also was defeated by a vote of ten to thirty-eight. Eight Whigs and two Democrats voted in the affirmative. The

[13] *Ibid.,* App., pp. 358-61.
[14] New York *Express,* July 7, 1841. Wise to Tucker, June 27, 1841, Tyler, *op. cit.,* II, 47-48.

majority consisted of eighteen Democrats and twenty Whigs. Of the eight Whig senators from New England, four voted for and four against the amendment; of five from the Middle States, all voted against it; of eight from the South Atlantic States, two voted for and six against it; of two from the Gulf States, one voted for and one against it. One Whig and two Democrats were absent or abstained from voting.[15] Webster had been able to detach only four senators from Clay's leadership, and Tyler as many more, but those eight votes would be enough to defeat the bill. To be sure, the four New England Senators had voted for the amendment only to obviate Tyler's veto, and would vote for the unamended bill if necessary. The opposition of the four Southern Senators, however, was more deeply seated and unless at least one of them could be brought over, the bill was doomed to defeat by a vote of twenty-six to twenty-five. It was for Clay the crisis of the conflict.

Clay's anxiety was shared by others. The galleries were daily crowded by a different class of men from those usually seen in Washington. Of this unusual group were merchants and manufacturers whose grave, reflective countenances indicated the concern of their personal interests in the manoeuvres of the politicians. While the Webster press denounced the "petty conflict for the mere triumph of individual opinion—or what is worse, for the purpose of testing personal influence in the Senate," a panic fell upon the hitherto confident Whig members. It was reported that five or six Whig Senators who had voted for Rives's amendment would not vote for the bill as it stood, and this would insure its defeat. Should it pass, said the Webster papers, it would be vetoed. Then the only hope would be a new bill, and the session must be prolonged to the end of August. On July 7, Clay admitted to John Quincy Adams that passage by the Senate was doubtful.[16] Tyler's friends had brought forward the Rives Amendment as a peace-offering, hoping to unite the Whig party upon it. "But through the uncontrollable desire of Mr. Clay to exercise the entire dictatorial power, and control the action of his party," said a contem-

---

[15] *Congressional Globe,* 27th Cong., 1st Sess., App., pp. 361-62.

[16] New York *Express,* July 10, 1841; Adams, *op. cit.,* X, 498, July 7, 1841.

porary press analysis, the breach in the Whig ranks was made wider than before.[17]

On July 6, the action of the Democrats in voting against the Rives Amendment seemed to have produced an irrevocable breach in the Whig majority, to have made Bank legislation all but impossible, and even to have broken Clay's leadership.[18] Webster had emerged as the great conciliating force, the one leader who might unify the party after the elimination of the irreconcilable leadership of Clay and Tyler. A week later, Clay had succeeded in altering the whole situation. Tyler had been led into an attitude so extreme that he would not accept even the Ewing Bill, Webster had been weakened by Tyler's having thus been thrown into the arms of the Virginian clique, and Clay's own ascendancy among the Whig Senators had been restored.

Clay's manoeuvres appear to have been along two lines, one public, through the press, the other secret through the party caucus. The New York *Courier and Enquirer* took the lead in the former, which was well under way by mid-July. Any desire on Clay's part to dictate was disavowed and his imperiousness was ascribed to excessive zeal, "surrounded as he is by instances of *treachery*." Then followed an exposé of the Virginian intrigue representing the extreme conjectures of the Clay men. It correctly explained the later objective of Wise and his intimates in the formation of a new party composed of the moderates from both the old parties, but was mistaken, apparently, as to the means they planned to use, and also as to the attitude at the time of Webster, Granger, Rives, and Tyler. The nub of the alleged plan was that if Clay "should lose his *Bank Bill and Land Bill, and the Whig party break up before it has redeemed its solemn pledge to the people, his political ruin is deemed certain.*" Other newspapers followed this lead, and the Democratic press was not slow to reveal its purpose.[19]

Meanwhile, the Whig Senators were holding repeated

[17] New York *Express*, July 13, 1841, quoting Louisville *Advertiser*.
[18] Calhoun to Hammond, August 1, 1841, Jameson, *op. cit.*, pp. 484-85.
[19] New York *Courier and Enquirer*, July 10, 1841; Cincinnati *Gazette*, July 22, 1841; Louisville *Advertiser*, July 21, 1841; New York *Express*, July 14, 1841.

caucuses in a vain attempt to agree upon their course of action. The names of the recalcitrants were now made public by the press. Merrick appeared to be the only one whom there was any chance of moving, although through two caucuses he "mulishly" stuck to the Ewing-Rives compromise. The Whig press therefore mingled denunciations of the four Whig insurgents with predictions of defeat. Under pressure of these conditions, even the New York *Express*, which had heretofore supported Webster and the Ewing plan, was forced into line and began to belabor the State rights Senators and to praise Clay.[20]

In addition, however, to the cry of treachery, the attempt at back-fire, and the pressure of party regularity, Clay appears to have held out another inducement to those Senators who were more interested in creating a bank than in making a president. This was nothing less than the promise of the Ewing bill as a compromise in case Tyler really did veto Clay's bill. In other words, if they would allow Clay to use the Bank bill to ruin Tyler's chance for the succession, he would then allow them to pass such a bill as Tyler could accept. This actually was tried after the veto. Where these calculations failed, however, was in the fact that Tyler had already thrown over the Ewing bill.[21]

The Rives Amendment had been disposed of July 6, and on the following day, in pursuance of the agreed procedure, the Democrats began to present their amendments. During the whole period of the party manoeuvres detailed above, these amendments were under consideration, and, although Clay stubbornly opposed every change proposed, a number were adopted. The debate was occasionally enlivened by some witty rejoinder, but was for the most part a dreary wrangle.[22]

On the eighth it was calculated that the bill would be disposed of in the Senate by the seventeenth, and it was anticipated, thanks to the newly evolved gag-rule of the House, that not more than a fortnight would be required to carry it through

---

[20] Cincinnati *Gazette,* July 22, 1841; Louisville *Advertiser,* July 21, 1841; New York *Express,* July 14, 1841.

[21] New York *Express,* July 14, 1841; Cincinnati *Gazette,* July 22, 1841; Wise to Tucker, July 11, 1841, Tyler, *op. cit.,* II, 52.

[22] *Congressional Globe,* 27th Cong., 1st Sess., pp. 157-59, 162-64, 172-73.

that body. The Senate would employ that time in passing the Land Bill, which had already passed the House and been referred by the Senate, and the Loan Bill, with which the House was then engaged. This program would enable the session to end in the first or second week of August. Meanwhile public interest had largely subsided, for the galleries were comparatively empty. The absence of ladies was especially noticeable, with a consequent falling off in the eloquence of the Senators.[23]

By the end of the week, in order to hasten proceedings, the Whigs were beginning to adopt the tactics of silence. Clay also had tightened the reins of discipline and between July 10 and July 14 he succeeded in rallying practically the whole party strength of the Whigs for the defeat of opposition amendments.[24]

However, Clay began to show impatience at the delay and on the twelfth allowed Calhoun to provoke him into the threat of a gag-rule, or, as he put it, "a measure to place the business of the Senate under the control of a majority of the Senate." This set Calhoun off on a tirade which was even exceeded by Linn who followed him. Indeed Linn became so bitter that Benton, after encouraging his colleague as loudly as he could from his seat, crossed the Senate chamber and took his station close by him to support him. Linn's bitterness gave rise to fears, at one time, that some "personal ill consequences" might ensue, but "the Whigs had the sound discretion to remain silent." Linn's reputation as a duelist may have contributed to this discretion.[25]

The very night following this stormy scene, the Whig caucus agreed upon a compromise procedure. Therefore the correspondent of the New York *Express* exultantly wrote on Tuesday:

A Bank Bill will be passed, and it will be Clay's Bill with an immaterial amendment, so far as any principle is involved. The States asking for Branches of the mother Bank, will have them of course, and in addition to this, I predict that power will be given

[23] New York *Express,* July 10, 1841.
[24] *Congressional Globe,* 27th Cong., 1st Sess., pp. 167-200, *passim.*
[25] *Ibid.,* pp. 183-88; New York *Express,* July 17, 1841.

to Congress to establish a Bank where Congress may determine to establish it. . . .[26]

The launching of Clay's "compromise" amendment thus coincides with the restoration of Whig discipline, a week after the defeat of the Rives Amendment. Obviously the amendment was not shown at this time to the State rights Senators, for its promise far outran performance. When it was submitted to Tyler by John Minor Botts, Tyler rejected it "emphatically, unhesitatingly and unequivocally," with the positive declaration that its incorporation into the bill would ensure his negative. This, combined with the absence of Graham and Rives, led to further postponement and for the first time it was suggested that a new compromise bill should be initiated in the House.[27]

Clay's movements, however, were reducing Tyler to such a state that he was inclined to regard any Bank legislation whatever with extreme suspicion. Under these circumstances, he naturally fell more and more under the influence of the Virginian clique and became distrustful even of Webster. That statesman, at this juncture, initiated a new drive for the Ewing bill through his two letters to Hiram Ketchum written on July 15 and July 17 respectively. These reiterated the arguments already voiced in the Senate by Choate.[28]

Hitherto Clay had been all for action; now, on Thursday, July 15, he suddenly proposed to lay aside the Bank Bill in order to consider the Loan Bill passed by the House, which he had the day before reported from the Finance Committee. The Democrats made a counter-proposal to finish up their amendments and let the Bank Bill come to a vote on Saturday or Monday at latest. Clay rejected this, frankly avowing as his reason the absence of two of his supporters. But it was only on Friday, by a formal motion to postpone the order of the day, that Clay succeeded in giving the Loan Bill precedence over the Bank Bill. On Tuesday, the twentieth, the Bank Bill was again before the Senate, with no significant action,

---

[26] New York *Express*, July 17, 1841.
[27] Tyler's "Statement," Tyler, *op. cit.*, II, 70; New York *Express*, July 17, 1841.
[28] Webster, *Writings and Speeches*, XVI, 844-52.

and Sergeant reported a similar bill from his committee in the House. Wise declared that Clay's purpose was to have the House pass the measure by a large majority so as to bring pressure upon the Senate and the President.[29]

Wise wrote thus on the twenty-fourth. That day the New York *Express* published an undated dispatch saying that appearances pointed to the Democrats helping the passage of the Bank Bill in the Senate, if necessary, by absenting themselves in numbers sufficient to offset the Whig defections. Their purpose was, of course, to precipitate a veto and consequent disruption of the Whig party. The day before, Calhoun had written, "The only thing that seems settled is that Clay's project of a bank will either not pass or be vetoed."[30]

The night of Friday, July 23, was marked by a caucus of Whig senators at which they finally agreed upon a formula which was acceptable to all except, at most, one or two of their number. Botts appears to have misrepresented Tyler's attitude toward Clay's "compromise," for it was confidently asserted that he "would approve such a Bill as was there proposed."[31]

With the customary wrangling, on Wednesday, July 21, the last of the opposition amendments were defeated by straight party votes. Then Berrien offered an amendment designed to forward by a month the commencement of operations by the Bank. This was adopted by a party vote of twenty-seven to twenty-two. Clay then moved to lay the bill on the table and print. Calhoun opposed tabling, wishing it to remain the unfinished business. Clay did not consent to this and his motion prevailed. Berrien gave notice that he would call up the Bankrupt Bill on the next day, which was done. The purpose of this manoeuvre, was, of course, to afford an opportunity for the final formulation of Clay's "compromise" and the consolidation of the party in its support. This was thought to be accomplished Friday night, yet Saturday night saw some still

---

[29] *Congressional Globe*, 27th Cong., 1st Sess., pp. 203, 205, 207-9, 230-31, 238; New York *Express,* July 21, July 24, Wise to Tucker, July 24, 1841, Tyler, *op. cit.,* II, 53.

[30] New York *Express,* July 24, 1841; Jameson, *op. cit.,* p. 482.

[31] New York *Express,* July 28, 1841, Cf. Tyler's "Statement," Tyler, *op. cit.,* II, 80.

holding out and further delay became almost equivalent to postponement. On Saturday, the twenty-fourth, the Bankrupt Bill having been disposed of, on Clay's motion the Bank Bill was taken up and the amendments made in the committee of the whole were considered separately. This continued throughout Saturday and Monday.[32] In the end, Clay succeeded in defeating all but one of the opposition amendments.

King then proposed that both sides drop all further amendments and allow the bill to go to engrossment. This proposal of King's was of course a mere *ruse de guerre*, for the opposition understood that the Whigs had a "compromise" amendment behind all the other amendments, and that yet another caucus was needed to unite their forces. Preston and Merrick of Maryland were still doubtful and had the question been put on the twenty-sixth, the bill would have been defeated. That night, however, they were brought to the support of the "compromise" amendment.[33]

The Senate met Friday morning in "a state of sombre dubiosity." The hope for unanimity was not very apparent. The Senate had already been four hours in session when Clay introduced the "compromise" amendment. Clay said that it was generally known, both to the Senate and to the country, that the bill in its present shape could not pass the Senate, but would probably be rejected by a vote of twenty-five to twenty-six. To reconcile these differences, a conference has been held, which had agreed to a "compromise" amendment, which he then moved. It provided for the establishment of branches in the States with their consent, but unless, at the first session of the Legislature held after the passage of the act the Legislature should "unconditionally assent or dissent to the establishment" of the same, "such assent of the said State shall be thereafter presumed; and provided, nevertheless, that whenever it shall become necessary and proper for carrying into execution any of the powers granted by the Constitution to establish as office or offices in any of the States whatever, and the establishment thereof shall be directed by law," it should be done.

---

[32] *Congressional Globe*, 27th Cong., 1st Sess., pp. 203-36, 240, 245, 248-52; New York *Express*, July 28, 1841.

[33] New York *Express*, July 28, 1841; Jameson, *op. cit.*, pp. 482-84.

Offices once established were to be withdrawn only with the assent of Congress.[34]

Rives denounced the amendment because "it paltered with them in double sense; while it kept the promise to the ear, it broke it to the sense." Calhoun had heard of Clay's forthcoming "compromise" and had been curious in regard to it. His curiosity was now satisfied. One said that it asserted power, the other that it condemned power. "How can you compromise between assent and dissent?" But he would leave that to be settled among the Whigs. He rose to present a solemn protest against the amendment. What was it? "That the sovereign power of any State shall be presumed to be surrendered because it does not answer a demand which it does not recognize the right of being asked. It is a proposition to authorize the Congress to say to any State, 'You have declined giving your assent and therefore we take it'." How would such a proposition work in case Congress undertook to interfere with the interstate slave-trade?—or to emancipate the slaves? How could the representatives of the slaveholding states vote for such an amendment?

It would be unprofitable to pursue further the details of the debate which lasted four weary hours. When Clay expressed surprise at Rives's declaration of an intention to vote against the amendment, Rives retorted that Clay believed Congress had power to establish branches within the States without their consent, which he denied. "And those who believed as he did, could not, either by a vote in that body, or the exercise of powers elsewhere, sanction the principle contained in the Senator's amendment without violating the oath they had taken to support the Constitution of the United States."

Nevertheless, the amendment was then adopted by a vote of twenty-five to twenty-four, Archer and Rives voting in the minority. Even this majority of one was secured only by the fact that Henderson of Mississippi, who was "irreconcilably opposed" to the amendment, left the chamber to avoid voting. The Clay "compromise" amendment was thus adopted, although it was unacceptable to a majority of the Senate. By

---

[34] New York *Express*, July 31; *Congressional Globe*, 27th Cong., 1st Sess., p. 254; Adams, *op. cit.*, X, 351-52, August 14, 1841.

the same vote, the bill was ordered to engrossment. On Wednesday, July 28, the bill came up for final passage. Henderson, after explaining his action, voted for the bill, which was thus passed, twenty-six, to twenty-three, the Virginia Senators voting with the Democrats, and Thomas Clayton of Delaware and Cuthbert of Georgia being absent.[35]

Clay had passed his measure by the barest margin. Had Tennessee been fully represented, or had either Clayton or Henderson voted on the "compromise" amendment, or had Cuthbert and Clayton been present, according to Calhoun, the final vote would have been twenty-six to twenty-five. The latter wrote:[36]

It seems to be conceded that should it pass the House, in its present shape, it will fall under the veto. To avoid that, the only alternative seems to be, to adopt Ewing's project. Whether the House can be brought to adopt it, or if it should, the Senate would concur, is doubtful. Nor is it at all certain, if it should whether it would receive the executive sanction. . . . The loss of the Bank Bill would probably break up the Whig party, and lead to a remodelling of the Cabinet. Whatever may be the result of the session, I cannot doubt the overthrow of the Whigs, at the next session. Discord and division have entered their ranks. The split between Clay and Tyler cannot be healed. They are both aspirants for the next term, and it is now or never for both. Neither will yield.

The historian can add nothing to this contemporary summary, the forecast of which was borne out to the letter.

---

[35] New York *Express*, July 31; *Congressional Globe*, 27th Cong., 1st Sess., pp. 254-60.

[36] Calhoun to Hammond, August 1, 1841, Jameson, *op. cit.*, p. 484.

CHAPTER V

EXECUTIVE USURPATION

THE VERY DAY on which Clay's bill was passed by the Senate, Tyler wrote to his friend Tucker that his back was to the wall and he would, if practicable, beat back the assailants. He had not authorized the newspaper assertion that he would veto the bill, but his conversation with Congressional leaders had been "free from concealment." However, "that which was devised for harmony" was "declared to have arisen from a spirit of executive dictation." Yet, three days later, a letter, clearly emanating from Clay's headquarters, was sent to his Lexington organ, declaring that rumors of a veto should not be credited, and asserting "that the slightest doubts are not entertained by those who have opportunities of information."[1]

Thus was initiated the campaign which had been foreshadowed by Clay's altercation with Choate. Every intimation of Tyler's opposition was excluded from the debate. Now the same policy was to be pursued by the press, the great *National Intelligencer* doing its part by maintaining a discreet silence. The object of these tactics, of course, was to let the veto fall upon the unwarned Whigs as an absolute surprise. The consequent dismay of the rank and file was then to be whipped up by cries of "Treason" until the unhappy President was irremediably alienated from his party.

On August 2, Monday, the bill was taken up by the House in Committee of the Whole. Morgan of New York gave notice of a motion to end the committee consideration at noon on Friday. Morgan called up his motion on Wednesday, and moved the previous question. Adams and others protested, and at their request he modified his motion, substituting Tuesday for Friday. Sergeant of Pennsylvania and Rhett of South Carolina tried to have the modification ruled out of order, but failed and the motion was defeated 55 to 136. Sergeant then

---

[1] Tyler to Tucker, July 28, 1841, Tyler, *op. cit.,* II, 53-54; Lexington *Intelligencer,* August 10, 1841.

renewed the original motion, moved the previous question, and carried the motion 104 to 97.[2]

The debate of Thursday was enlivened by an attack on the bill from Thomas F. Marshall, the member from Clay's home district. He proposed to strike out the Clay "compromise" provision, and to give the Bank unconditional power to establish branches. Without that change he could not vote for the bill. Wise followed, denouncing the manner in which the bill was jockeyed through the Senate. Adams also assailed the "compromise" provision as unconstitutional, since, he said, it "contained the whole poison of nullification."[3]

Promptly at noon on Friday, the committee began to vote down amendments. Finally the committee was able to rise for Sergeant to report the bill unamended to the House. It was then ordered to its third reading under the previous question, and passed by a vote of 128 to 97. John Quincy Adams and Irwin of Pennsylvania voted in the negative, along with Marshall of Kentucky, Foster of Georgia and the Virginians Wise, Gilmer and Hunter.[4]

At twenty minutes past one on Saturday, August 7, the enrolled bill was placed in the hands of the President, who perplexed and somewhat disturbed the committee by remarking that it was important that the hour should be noted. It was also considered inauspicious that a number of Virginians visited him at the White House that night.[5]

From the time the bill was presented to him, despite all assertions to the contrary, there was great uncertainty as to Tyler's course. So closely had he kept his own counsel, that, on the preceding night, even the members of the Cabinet did not know his intentions. By agreement, Webster had said nothing to him on the subject. Although he had no better means of judging than others, the Secretary of State nevertheless inclined to the opinion that Tyler would sign the bill. His judgment was doubtless influenced by his own dread of the

---

[2] *Congressional Globe,* 27th Cong., 1st Sess., pp. 282-83, 294.

[3] *Ibid.,* pp. 299-300.

[4] *Ibid.,* pp. 312-14.

[5] New York *Express,* August 11, 1841; Cincinnati *Gazette,* August 16, 1841; Webster to Mrs. Webster, August 8, 1841, *Writings and Speeches,* XVIII, 107-8.

commotion which would follow a veto. Calhoun, on the other hand, who foresaw profit in turmoil, had little doubt of a veto. He only feared that, instead of being placed on high ground, it would leave the way open for a compromise bank. Monday night, Tyler's intentions were still unknown, wild rumors were afloat, and there was betting on both sides. Democratic reports declared emphatically that there would be a veto, followed by a dissolution of the Cabinet.[6]

On Tuesday and Wednesday, of course, the rumors became wilder, the wagers grew larger. Every day of delay increased the probability of a veto, while conjecture as to its results grew like a snowball. It was rumored that Rives was to become Secretary of State and Balie Peyton, Secretary of War. In this uncertain situation, the nominees before the Senate felt very uneasy. Up to Wednesday morning, if Tyler had made up his mind, he had informed no one of his conclusions. That day a Cabinet meeting was held, from which rumor said the members emerged without being able to form an opinion of the result. "The President's most intimate friends profess not to know, and do not know his intentions. His political enemies, however, are yet sure of a veto. . . . They are ready, too, to back their opinions with any amount of money." The moderate Whigs kept up their courage by the thought that Tyler was following the example of Washington, "who noted the exact time when the first United States Bank Bill was presented to him, and who retained it for eleven days, when he signed it." The real sentiment of the "Ultras," however, was revealed by the caricature, published by the reporter of the *National Intelligencer*, representing Tyler "seated before a table, with a most lugubrious and careworn visage, and a pen in his hand, looking over the bill, with the words 'To sign or not to sign— that is the question,' above him."[7]

By Thursday, the prevailing opinion was that there would be a veto, although optimistic Whigs declared they would not believe it until they saw the veto or heard it read. That opinion

[6] Cincinnati *Gazette*, August 12, 1841; Calhoun to Clemson, Jameson, *op. cit.*, p. 486; New York *Express*, August 11, 1841; Louisville *Advertiser*, August 19, 1841, quoting New York *American*, August 11, 1841.

[7] Cincinnati *Gazette*, August 16, 1841; New York *Express*, August 14, August 18, 1841.

was based upon inference from "the character of some of the President's associates, such articles as appear in the *Madisonian* newspaper, and from the avowed opinions of some of the President's more intimate friends." Meanwhile, there was complaint of the "most unaccountable mystery and secrecy existing as to the President's intentions," which was declared to be unprecedented. Bets continued to run high and good Whigs held that, since Tyler had long before made up his mind, this secrecy about his intentions was "injudicious and impolitic."[8]

Nevertheless, that very day evidence which could not be ignored was given of Tyler's intentions. In the lobby of the House, where all bystanders could hear, Robert Tyler, the President's son and private secretary, entered into a discussion with one of the New York representatives. After denouncing the bill as unconstitutional, "he concluded by declaring that 'to suppose that his father could be gulled by such a humbug compromise as the bill contained, was to suppose that he was an ass'." The effect was "electrical." The declaration was communicated to the members and spread like wildfire. The Whig members became indignant, and all was gloom and uncertainty.[9]

It is inconceivable that any considerable number of men in Washington, either members of Congress, correspondents of the press, or politicians holding or seeking office, could have been so ignorant of the opinions which the President apparently expressed with the greatest freedom while the bill was pending before Congress, as really to have been overwhelmed by surprise when the veto became certain. Such a situation is explicable only on the assumption that the public men to whom the President expressed himself deliberately suppressed his sentiments. Choate, Bates, and Rives had gone to the very bounds of propriety in warning the Senate, the Democratic reporters announced it as a certainty from the moment the bill was passed, the public uncertainty was such that wagers were laid, and yet the Whig press failed to warn the party. In proportion as

---

[8] New York *Express*, August 14, 1841; Cincinnati *Gazette*, August 18, 1841.

[9] Cincinnati *Gazette*, August 18, 1841.

that press was cool toward Clay, it reported uncertainty. As it was committed to Clay, it was silent, or expressed confidence in the signature of the bill. Although its editors were informed of all the abortive negotiations with Tyler, the *National Intelligencer*, from which a large proportion of the Whig country papers derived their Washington items, gave not the slightest warning, but allowed it to fall like a thunderbolt.[10] All this bears the earmarks of deliberate contrivance for political effect. Whether planned or not, to it was due in great part the impression that Tyler betrayed the Whigs by an unanticipated veto.

A committee of Ohio representatives, with one or two Senators, waited upon the President on Friday, to ascertain his intention, and to prevail upon him, if possible, to sign the bill. Tyler frankly avowed his perplexity, but admitted that he felt he should be obliged to veto the bill. He would recommend in his message on Monday such a bank as he could approve. His mind was, however, still open to conviction and he would, on Sunday, "go to church and pray earnestly and devoutly to be enlightened as to his duty."[11]

That day the President signed the bill for the repeal of the Independent Treasury. He thus forced upon the Whigs the alternative of framing such a bank bill as he would sign, or of incurring in their turn all those denunciations they had heaped upon the Democrats in Jackson's time anent "the union of the purse and the sword." This action, in view of the growing belief in a veto of the bank bill, filled the Whigs with wrath and dismay.[12]

By Saturday, however, even the most optimistic of the reporters despaired of the approval of the bill. Those who were not informed of the game in progress thereupon despaired of Bank legislation, believing that the "Ultras" had meant what they said when they rejected the Ewing plan and declared that the Clay "compromise" was their extreme concession. Even to the uninitiated, however, the next move in the war on

---

[10] Adams, *op. cit.*, X, 531-32, August 14, 1841.

[11] Cincinnati *Gazette*, August 26, 1841.

[12] *Congressional Globe*, 27th Cong., 1st Sess., p. 336. As Calhoun supported the Independent Treasury, this tends to confirm the judgment that he was not at this time coöperating with Tyler. Cincinnati *Gazette*, August 26, 1841; New York *Express*, August 18, 1841.

Tyler was evident, namely, agitation against "Executive Usurpation."

"Mr. Ewing's plan from appearances, by no possibility could receive the sanction of the two Houses of Congress," wrote a well-informed correspondent. However, on Sunday night, the Whigs held a caucus, at which they tentatively determined to take up and pass the Ewing Bill, and on Monday negotiations for an entirely new measure were begun.[13]

By Sunday it was definitely known to the Washington public that a veto would be sent in on Monday. The delay had at least brought about some decrease in the irritation felt a week before, although it was still feared that Clay's friends, who were particularly angry, might prevent anything further in the way of bank legislation. In order to keep the Whigs in as good temper as possible, Webster invited them to a "man party" for Monday night. The party was duly held, and according to Adams was a jovial affair, so Webster's purpose would appear to have been accomplished. Even more than to Webster's good cheer, however, the joviality of the Whigs was due to the prospects of Bank legislation by means of the new bill already in process of negotiation.[14]

That day, Monday, August 16, President Tyler had, as foretold, returned the Bank Bill to the Senate with his objections. He touched upon the disputed nature of the constitutional question, and upon his own record of consistent opposition. In view of these opinions, to sanction the bill would be to violate his oath of office. As to his reasons for his convictions, they had been repeated over and over. He could not see the necessity or propriety of a bank of discount. "What can the local discounts of the bank have to do with the collecting, safe-keeping, and disbursing of the revenue? . . . what influence . . . in the regulating of the currency and the exchanges?" In the history of the late Bank of the United States, this power was almost exclusively exercised in its early years, and during that period it failed to realize anticipations. Later ex-

---

[13] Adams, *op. cit.*, X, 531-32, August 14, 1841; Cincinnati *Gazette*, August 26, 1841.

[14] Cincinnati *Gazette*, August 26, 1841; Webster to Mrs. Webster, August 16, 1841, *Writings and Speeches*, XVI, 353; Adams, *op. cit.*, X, 534, August 17, 1841.

pansion of its exchange business had produced those results. Few losses were incurred thus, but enormous ones through discounts, which had been a source of favoritism and corruption. If local discounts could relieve the currency, the great capital of the state banks was sufficient to produce that result. As for the Clay "compromise," which he quoted in full, he denounced it in the most scathing terms as "irrational," unconstitutional, and contrary to "all that is established in judicial proceeding."[15]

During the reading of the veto message, the excitement in the galleries was intense, its conclusion being greeted with mingled applause and hisses. The presiding officer speedily checked the disturbance, but Benton demanded with great indignation the punishment of the offenders. Rives, probably considering that publicity would be of no advantage to the President, denied hearing the hisses, thus throwing the Senator from Missouri into a state of great excitement. Preston, Buchanan, Merrick, and Linn united in various and characteristic ways to soothe the choleric Missourian, who appeared likely to provoke a personal issue with Rives. While this scene was enacting, Walker, with his usual commonsense, directed the sergeant-at-arms in the arrest of the offender, who, in excuse, professed ignorance and avowed contrition. Benton was finally calmed and the incident closed.[16]

In order to gain time for negotiations for a second, or rather third, bank project, consideration of the veto was postponed on Monday and Tuesday, and only on Wednesday did Clay take the floor against the President. Considering the speaker and the occasion, Clay's speech was as temperate as could well have been expected.[17] He began by reciting the history of the Bank Bill from the accession of President Tyler. After a moving reference to the circumstances of that accession, he spoke of Tyler's address of April 10, which was, he said, "in the nature of a coronation oath, which the chief of the state in other countries, and under other forms, takes,

---

[15] *Congressional Globe*, 27th Cong., 1st Sess., pp. 337-38.

[16] *Ibid.*, pp. 338-39.

[17] *Niles' Register*, LX, 403-6, August 28, 1841. The *Congressional Globe* gives only a summary, and Colton, *Life and Times*, II, 358-69, a summary with extracts.

upon ascending the throne." He referred particularly to the
final sentences of the paragraph dealing with the currency,
which, he insisted, had been given but one interpretation by
friend and foe—"that the President intended to occupy the
Madison ground, and to regard the question of the power to
establish a national bank as immovably settled." He therefore
came to Washington confident that the Whigs would have the
President's cordial coöperation in passing a bank bill.

With the opening of the session, they found reason to apprehend that the address had been misunderstood; but it was
hoped that mutual concessions might solve the difficulty. Under
the influence of this spirit, concession was made to the President's scruples in regard to the name and the location of the
institution, and finally, in regard to the branching power. The
last compromise was so repugnant to some friends of the bank,
that they finally voted against the bill. Clay had stated that
he did not know whether it would be acceptable to the President, but he "did entertain the most confident hopes and expectations" that the bill would receive his sanction—Clay had
"presumed he would not fail to feel and appreciate their
sacrifices." In this case they were mistaken.

Clay then turned to a consideration of the President's objections. In reply to the claim that opinions were essentially
even for and against the constitutionality of the bank, he endeavored to show an overwhelming preponderance in its favor
through the action of all three branches of the government,
while President Tyler had wholly omitted to notice the decisions of the Supreme Court. As to consistency, could he
have been disgraced and dishonored in yielding "his private
opinion to the judgment of the nation?" Why could not Tyler
"have suffered the bill to become law without his signature?"
As candidate for vice president his opinions had not been
scrutinized as carefully as they should have been. Had the
present situation been anticipated, Clay hazarded nothing in
expressing the opinion "that he would not have received a
solitary vote in the nominating convention." Clay contended
that such passivity would not have drawn in question Tyler's
honor, firmness or independence. Besides, the presidential office is "a sacred trust, created and conferred for the benefit

of the nation, and not for the private advantage of the person who fills it." He then pointed out a third alternative, that of resignation, citing Tyler's own action in refusing compliance with instructions to vote for the expunging resolution, given by the Virginia Legislature.

Clay next passed to the sixteenth fundamental condition, in regard to which he endeavored to controvert the President's arguments in detail and rested the weight of Tyler's objections upon the establishment of branches without the assent of the States. Thus he ignored the fact, of which he was well aware, that the real objection was against those branches having the power of discount.[18]

Clay then took up the future program of the party, laying a public foundation for the forthcoming Fiscal Corporation Bill and indicating his own attitude. While he regretted that the message was not more explicit, he thought it might "be collected from the message, with the aid of information derived from other sources, that the president would concur in the establishment of a bank whose operations should be limited to dealing in bills of exchange, to deposit and to the supply of a circulation, excluding the power of discounting promissory notes." He understood that some of his friends were trying to frame such a bill. While he could take no active part, and must reserve his support until he saw the bill in mature form, he would in no way impede their efforts. Meanwhile, let them at the east end of Pennsylvania Avenue do their whole duty by passing the other measures of the Whig program.

If nothing can be done at this extra session to put upon a more stable and satisfactory basis the currency and exchanges of the country, let us hope that hereafter some way will be found to accomplish that most desirable object, either by an amendment of the constitution limiting and qualifying the enormous executive power, and especially the veto, or by increased majorities in the two houses of congress competent to the passage of wise and salutary laws, the president's objections notwithstanding.

Clay thus once more forecast the ground of the fight to drive Tyler from the party—the old issue of "Executive Usurpation."

---

[18] This passage is omitted by Colton, *Life and Times*, II, 367.

To those who shared Clay's views as to the constitutionality of first and second Banks of the United States his arraignment of the President was highly satisfactory.[19] Those who shared Tyler's views, however, appear to have been equally delighted by Rives's reply.[20]

He declared that two-thirds of Clay's speech, instead of dealing with the question at issue, was devoted to an arraignment of the President, most of the allegations ranging themselves under a general charge of faithlessness to his party and to the people. He took up Clay's treatment of the inaugural address, and answered it by emphasizing Tyler's specification of a constitutional measure. After an elaborate array of Republican precedents, in which he quoted Clay's own speech of 1811 in answer to his arguments of 1841, Rives held Tyler justified in questioning the constitutionality of the bill. He further upheld his right to act upon his own judgment and conscientious convictions.

Turning to Clay's references to the Harrisburg Convention, he impaled the Kentuckian on the dilemma of admitting that the Bank was not the major issue at Harrisburg, or asserting that the convention nominated a vice presidential candidate whose adverse opinions on the major issue were well known. Rives further endeavored to prove that Harrison was not a Bank man; that the Bank was not the great issue in the campaign, being rejected with the rejection of Clay; that indeed, the Democrats tried to fasten the Bank issue on the Whigs, who avoided it, restricting themselves to attacks on the Sub-Treasury.

Speaking not by authority, but from the language of the message, Rives concluded that Tyler would hold the assent of the States to be necessary for any bank beyond "a mere fiscal agency," dealing in exchanges generally. As to the unanimity of the Cabinet, the President could acknowledge no control in his official conduct save that of his own conscience. As to resignation, his previous action was no precedent, for while the Legislature of Virginia were the constituents of the

---

[19] "The Diary of Thomas Ewing," *American Historical Review*, XVIII (October, 1912), 97-112.

[20] *Congressional Globe*, 27th Cong., 1st Sess., App., pp. 366-68.

Senator, the President derived his authority from the sovereign people of the States, the same as the members of both houses of Congress. Much had been said about Executive dictation, but Clay's doctrine would set up "a standing legislative dictation and supremacy."

Clay interrupted to explain that he regarded the people as having given instructions for the Bank. Rives denied the competence of Congress to voice that instruction, and contended further that the particular clause to which Tyler took exception, the Clay "compromise," had not received the approval of a majority of the whole membership of either House. Rives concluded by advising against further attempts at this time to legislate on the currency.

In reply, Clay made up for his restraint toward Tyler by pouring the vials of his wrath upon the President's defender.[21] Though Rives professed not to know the President's opinions, the sequel proved that they coincided remarkably with his own. He defended the President as solicitously as if he were a member of the rumored Kitchen Cabinet which aimed at the dissolution of the regular Cabinet and the Whig party and the defeat of the objects of the special session. He himself had no conceivable motive for quarrelling with the President or breaking up the Whig party, but certain individuals apparently designed to place him in opposition to the President. They were "beating up for recruits, and endeavoring to form a third party, with materials so scanty as to be wholly insufficient to compose a decent corporal's guard." He did not charge Rives with being one of these individuals, but they, who boasted and claimed to be Tyler's "exclusive and genuine friends" were the "bitter, systematic, determined, uncompromising opponents of every leading measure of John Tyler's administration."

Clay repelled Rives's charge that he would have vetoed the bill in Tyler's place. He hoped he might without disparagement compare with other men in all that related to personal firmness, but he neither possessed nor coveted the kind of courage to use official power to obstruct the welfare and happiness of his country. Men sometimes were rash and inconsiderate for fear of the imputation of want of courage. "But pride, vanity,

[21] *Ibid.*, pp. 368-69.

egotism, so unamiable in private life," become crime in public life. Their unfortunate victim can see only his own personal interests—"All his thoughts are withdrawn from his country, and concentrated on his consistency, his firmness, himself"; he is incapable of the unselfish patriotism which is "the noblest and the sublimest of all public virtues."

Rives retorted in kind to Clay's personalities, saying in conclusion:

Rumor is busy alleging that there is an organized dictatorship, in permanent session in this Capitol, seeking to control the whole action of the Government, in both the Legislative and Executive branches, and sending deputation after deputation to the President of the United States to teach him his duty, and bring him to terms. I humbly hope it may not be true; but if it should unfortunately be so, I will say that it is fraught with far more danger to the regular and salutary action of our balanced Constitution, and to the liberties of the people, than any secret cabal that ever existed or ever will exist.[22]

After further remarks by Archer and Berrien, at half past five the vote was taken. The count stood twenty-five to twenty-four and the veto was sustained.[23]

---

[22] *Ibid.*, pp. 369-70.

[23] *Ibid.*, p. 352. Clayton of Delaware and Phelps of Vermont are not recorded.

CHAPTER VI

THE FISCALITY

THE WHIGS met in caucus Sunday night, August 15, to determine what to do about the veto, which was to be delivered the next day. There was much difference of opinion, but the President was denounced in unmeasured terms. It was finally decided to receive the veto without a word, lay it on the table and order it to be printed, while as quietly as possible a sort of steering committee should settle on their course Monday night. The caucus tentatively decided to take up and pass the Ewing bill, to which the President and his Cabinet were thought to be fully committed, though it was believed he would take ground in the veto which would make his assent to it impossible. In that case the Cabinet would resign. If he did accept it, they expected it to prove unworkable through failure of the stock subscription, which would force Tyler to agree to such modifications as they might dictate. In either event, he could be charged with inconsistency. Two representatives informed "a gentleman of the strictest veracity" of these proceedings, who sent Tyler a full account the next day, adding that it was confidently asserted that Crittenden would resign.[1]

The Cabinet, however, were reluctant to assume the rôle assigned to them, for it meant a disarrangement of their personal plans, a surrender of honors and influence, and even considerable direct financial loss.[2] They were therefore delighted to perceive the next morning an apparent way out of the predicament. Ewing called at the White House and found Tyler at work on the veto message. A conversation ensued, in the course of which Tyler read parts of the message, especially

---

[1] Tyler, *op. cit.,* II, 81, footnote. A. H. H. Stuart's "Statement" in T. H. Benton, *Thirty Years View,* II, 344-47.

[2] The statement is justified by their manifest reluctance to resign a fortnight later (*vide infra*) and by contemporary press comment. For their financial involvement, cf. New York *Express,* September 15, 1841. The Letcher-Crittenden correspondence indicates that Crittenden's dependence on his official salaries made it all but necessary that he remain in office.

that dealing with the sixteenth fundamental article. Bell joined
them during the conversation, which ended with Tyler's assertion that the message sufficiently indicated the kind of bank
he could approve.[3] These ministers thus learned the real onus
of Tyler's objections, of which the Cabinet had hitherto been
ignorant. They apparently carried their information straight
to Crittenden, for before the reading of the message in the
Senate had made its contents public he wrote to Clay suggesting a new scheme which would meet the President's views.
Various circumstances connected with the disruption of the
Cabinet tend to confirm this view, but also to indicate Bell
rather than Ewing as the news-bearer.

The plan thus suggested was to confer upon the proposed
bank and its branches "*all* the usual banking powers," but to
restrict it from discounting promissory notes, the exercise of
the latter power without state consent, not the mere creation
of branches, being the center of Tyler's objections. In that
case, observed the Attorney-General, "the moneyed transactions
of men" would be "put into the shape of bills of exchange."[4]
Since the Cabinet wished to retain office, it is impossible to
doubt that they believed such a bill would meet Tyler's chief
objection, though by evasion. They clearly did not understand
the "impracticable" type of politician, represented by Tyler,
who could not be satisfied by a mere concession in form. Their
mistake arose, of course, from Tyler's persistent use of the
term "local discounts" in the general sense of "local loans."
This may have been mere looseness of expression, or it may
have arisen from actual ignorance. The use of bills of exchange
is from its nature peculiar to the mercantile community, and
may well have been unknown to a planter like Tyler. Certain
remarks of Rives in debate give weight to that view.[5]

The objectives of Clay, however, were quite different from
those of Crittenden and Bell. Perhaps he now knew Tyler well
enough to know that he would not accept such a way out. At
any rate, he clearly grasped all its potentialities as a device

---

[3] "The Diary of Thomas Ewing," *American Historical Review*, XVIII, 99.

[4] Crittenden to Clay, August 16, 1841, Crittenden Papers; also in Coleman,
op. cit., I, 159-60.

[5] *Congressional Globe*, 27th Cong., 1st Sess., App., p. 348.

to "head" the President. Crittenden had urged Clay himself to assume the authorship of the new bill, and on Tuesday a report was sent out that he was to do so.[6] But to propose it himself would at once excite Tyler's suspicion. Besides, the charge of inconsistency would be the more surely fixed on Tyler if the new project could be made to appear to have originated with the President himself. This was clearly the purpose of the ensuing negotiation.

One of Clay's chief lieutenants in the House was Millard Fillmore, chairman of the Ways and Means Committee, who was one of the closest Congressional intimates of James A. Pearce of Maryland. That gentleman has a place in history because nine years later he was to upset Clay's "omnibus bill" at the behest of this same friend, Fillmore.[7] This intermediary rôle of Fillmore's rests on mere surmise, for the part may have fallen to Corwin, also an intimate of Pearce, and always a rival of Ewing. At any rate, it is inconceivable that Pearce, being the man he was, acted on his own initiative that Monday afternoon when he called on Alexander H. H. Stuart and urged him to approach the President in regard to a new bill. It was to be based on the rejected Bayard amendment, omitting the last clause, which authorized, under certain contingencies, the conversion of the agencies into offices of discount and deposit. Stuart at first declined, but at length yielded to Pearce's insistence, and late that afternoon secured an interview with the President.[8]

Tyler, informed of the action of the caucus and aware of his danger, eagerly seized upon Stuart's proposition as a way out. After some discussion they agreed upon a modification of the Bayard amendment, which Tyler pencilled upon a copy torn from the Senate journal that Pearce had given to Stuart. He then sent Stuart to Webster to have the bill prepared at once, but with a caution not to expose him to the charge of dictating to Congress. As Stuart departed, Tyler grasped his hand with the declaration that if he could be instrumental in passing the bill, he would esteem him the

[6] Cincinnati *Gazette*, August 23, 1841.
[7] *Vide infra.*
[8] Stuart's "Statement," Benton, *op. cit.*, II, 344

best friend he had on earth. Stuart drove at once to Webster's lodgings but failed to find him, a mischance which may account for the subsequent omission of Tyler's own modification of Bayard's amendment from the bill as framed.[9]

Stuart informed his messmates of what had occurred and went early to the meeting of the committee to confer with Sergeant. After discussion of various plans, Sergeant called on Stuart to inform the committee of what had passed between the President and himself. After much deliberation the committee decided to recommend accession to the President's views. Sergeant and Berrien were intrusted with the management of the affair and were to confer with Tyler for assurance against misunderstanding. Mangum pledged himself that Clay, who was not present, would offer no obstacle, and promised to obtain his consent to a postponement of the veto until the full caucus could act on the recommendation of the committee. Accordingly, Clay concurred in postponement on both Tuesday and Wednesday.[10]

A night's reflection, however, had cooled Tyler's ardor; so in a conference with Berrien and Sergeant on Tuesday, in which Ewing participated, he merely referred them to his message and professed to think it unbecoming in him to draw up a specific plan. He made no objection, however, to Ewing's summary of his views as embracing a bank located in the District of Columbia, employing agents in the States to perform its fiscal duties and incidentally to deal in exchange and to do all other acts allowed by the vetoed bill, except the making of local discounts.[11] The same morning, he desired Bell to furnish certain data calculated to support such a bank, together with a statement of his views on the subject. Bell acted with such promptitude that he presented the desired information that evening, only to have the President receive it with manifest

---

[9] Tyler's "Statement," Tyler, *op. cit.,* II, 99; Stuart's "Statement," Benton, *op. cit.,* II, 344; Badgar to Gales & Seaton, September 18, 1841, *Niles' Register,* LXI, 53.

[10] Stuart's "Statement," Benton, *op. cit.,* II, 344-47; Tyler's "Statement," Tyler, *op. cit.,* II, 66-70, 77-79, 98-102.

[11] "The Diary of Thomas Ewing," *American Historical Review,* XVIII, 99-100.

indifference. He also alarmed Bell by remarking that he began to doubt whether he would give his assent to any bank.[12]

By Tuesday night, Tyler was clearly desirous of having the whole matter postponed, but Wednesday morning Berrien and Sergeant forced his hand by informing him that the Whig caucus had acceded to his terms. Together with Dawson of Georgia, they engaged him in a long conference which delayed the regular Cabinet meeting over an hour. In the two hour discussion by the Cabinet which ensued, the President showed great uneasiness, but was apparently satisfied by the assurances given by his ministers. He was especially cheered by the powerful legal support which Webster gave to his constitutional views. A reference to the Ewing Bill drew from him an impatient repudiation of it as containing "that odious feature of local discounts" which he had repudiated in his message. He also declared that "he would not sanction a bank in the form just agreed upon, if he supposed that it would be made the groundwork or basis of a bank with the power of the late bank of the United States." Tyler appealed to the Cabinet to secure the passage of such a bill, the features of which Ewing again recapitulated. No State assent was to be required for the establishment of agencies within the States, but Congress might not confer the power of local discount, even with the assent of the States. The President desired Webster and Ewing to see that the bill took that form. On his urging that it be entrusted to one of his friends, they suggested Sergeant, to which he agreed. He cautioned them not to commit him personally to any desire to dictate to Congress, but to express their confidence of his approval as a matter of inference from the veto message and his general views. He also expressed a wish to see the bill before it was presented to the House, if it could be managed.[13]

As to the ensuing negotiations, we have few details. Webster and Ewing conferred with the Congressional leaders separately,

---

[12] Bell's "Statement," *Niles' Register*, LXI, 54.

[13] "The Diary of Thomas Ewing," *American Historical Review*, XVIII, 97-112; Bell's "Statement" and Berrien's "Memorandum," *Niles' Register*, June 7, 1842.

thus opening the way for any number of misunderstandings. Also, in his very first interview with Berrien, Webster sanctioned the omission of Tyler's proviso to Bayard's amendment, an omission to which Tyler took instant exception. He then made an appointment for Ewing to confer with them that evening. They informed him that Webster had suggested the particular frame and had referred them to Ewing for his concurrence. The result was, they agreed to present the project to the caucus, and if approved by the Whigs of both branches, to introduce it into the House.[14] Thus the negotiations between the Cabinet and the Congressional leaders were virtually completed by Wednesday evening, August 18. Up to this point the testimony of the various participants is in complete agreement on all essential points, differing only as to minor details. But now, Tyler claims that the bill was not submitted to him before introduction as promised, and in this he is supported by Webster. Sergeant, however, claims to have sent a copy to Webster for submission to the President, and Ewing declares that Webster told him, on September 5, that he had done so. The fact seems to be that Sergeant did send Webster a copy, but too late for submission to the President before its introduction in the House.[15]

The proposed bill could not be brought in, however, until the veto was disposed of, which was done on the nineteenth. Clay's speech, considering the speaker and the occasion, was as temperate as could well have been expected, yet it could hardly fail to exacerbate the sensitive feelings of the President, heighten his suspicions, and in general increase the tension between the White House and the Capitol. The veto disposed of, Sergeant called up House Bill Number 14 (Ewing's project), and moved to amend it by striking out all after the enacting clause and inserting the new bill. This was in committee of the whole.[16]

That very day, however, John Miner Botts's "coffee-house letter" was received by the editor of *The Madisonian*, Tyler's

[14] "The Diary of Thomas Ewing," *American Historical Review*, XVIII, 97-112.
[15] "Statements" of Berrien, Sergeant, and Ewing; cf. Tyler, *op. cit.*, II, 85-86, 99. Ewing's "Statement" is in *Niles' Register*, LXI, 55.
[16] *Congressional Globe*, 27th Cong., 1st Sess., p. 364.

Washington organ, and at once communicated to the President. It accused Tyler of trying "to set himself up with the *locofocos*," declared that he would "be headed yet," and that a bank bill would be passed which would "serve only to fasten him."[17] This letter, together with the omission of his proviso from the sixteenth provision, could only redouble Tyler's suspicion of the Whig leaders and confirm him in repudiation of the bill. That night, therefore, he took pains to apprise all members of the House whom he saw of his inability to sanction the bill as it stood, probably forty or fifty members thus being informed of his objections. He gave some an amendment which would remove the constitutional difficulty. He sought to inform Sergeant of his view through Williams of Connecticut and Greig of New York, expressed an earnest desire to see him. This message was either not delivered or ignored.[18]

Indeed, no further attempt was made to conceal the "joker" in the bill, the possibilities of which were immediately explained in the press.[19] Tyler was so deeply committed to the bill that it was immaterial whether it received his signature or his veto. Either way, his chances for 1844 were ruined.

Saturday morning, Sergeant moved to end debate in the committee at four o'clock that afternoon, at once invoking the previous question. The Democrats used dilatory tactics until Sergeant, on private remonstrance, consented to extend the debate until the same hour on Monday. The opposition amendments were then voted down, the new bill adopted, 113 to 55, and the bill reported to the House. Stanly immediately moved the previous question, which was carried, the bill rushed through all its stages, and, still under the previous question, passed by 125 to 94. After reconsideration had been moved and denied, Sergeant moved to amend the title, the name "Fiscal Corporation of the United States" being greeted with roars of laughter. This was also carried under the previous question. Wise then moved a reconsideration, by which means he at last secured the floor to deliver himself of his indignation. This he

---

[17] Tyler, *op. cit.*, II, 112, footnote, Botts's letter was dated and postmarked, Washington, August 16, 1841.

[18] Tyler's "Statement," Tyler, *op. cit.*, II, 99.

[19] New York *Express*, August 25, 1841, Washington correspondence, August 2.

did for half an hour amid constant interruptions on points of order, ending by withdrawing his motion. Finally, at seven o'clock, the House adjourned.[20]

Tyler continued to make no secret of his dissatisfaction. Both on Saturday and on Monday, while it was passing through the House, he plainly intimated to various members of the Cabinet that he would probably veto the bill. At a Cabinet meeting on Wednesday, he was gloomy and depressed and intimated in strong terms that he would not sign the bill. He was earnest and exigent that his ministers should get the bill postponed, which he thought they could do as easily as they had got it up. The next day Tyler again urged this course on Ewing in the presence of Granger, and in order to consider the matter the ministers gathered at Webster's on the evening of August 27. "After much discussion and a full interchange of opinions," Ewing wrote in his diary, "it was agreed to endeavor to postpone, if we found it could be done by general assent of the Whigs." They evidently realized that the "bills of exchange" scheme had failed, so far as getting a bank bill passed, and that its recoil might destroy its initiators. It was only five days later, however, that Ewing confided to his diary the full bearing of Clay's course and its implication for him personally.[21]

The Fiscal Corporation Bill was received by the Senate August 24, read twice, and referred to a select committee headed by Berrien. There it reposed while Smith of Indiana pushed through a land bill, embodying Clay's familiar program, which had occupied the Senate since August 6. Clay seconded Berrien's motion to refer, requesting the Chair not to place him on the committee, in order that he might preserve his independence of action on the bill. That same day, Bates and Choate consulted Webster as to the general policy the Whigs should follow in respect to the bill. Webster replied the next day, advising postponement in deference to the President's

---

[20] *Congressional Globe,* 27th Cong., 1st Sess., pp. 364, 366-68, 370-72; Adams, *op. cit.,* X, 528.

[21] "The Diary of Thomas Ewing," *American Historical Review,* XVIII, 103-4.

manifest desire. The Botts letter made this imperative, he thought, if only to disprove its imputations.[22]

While the political barometer was thus rapidly falling, that stormy petrel, General Duff Green, put in his appearance. He had been in Washington, on confidential terms with the President, before the passage of the first Bank Bill, and had gone thence to Kentucky.[23] There he negotiated an alliance between Tyler and the Wickliffes. Those leaders were at once enemies of Clay and friends of Calhoun, whose oldest son had married Green's daughter, and whose correspondence with Green was intimate.[24] Now, at the end of August, Green was a frequent visitor, if not a constant inmate, of the White House. He was often seen stretched at full length on one of the sofas in the President's audience chamber, and would not retire even when he knew men desired to speak with Tyler on personal and secret matters.[25] Green now undertook to negotiate another alliance between Tyler and Judge McLean, but without success.[26]

There can be no question that this situation was well understood in Washington. "There are ten thousand rumors here at least," wrote a well-informed correspondent on the night of August 25, "and more mischief-makers than would fill any locality in Bedlam if the mischief designed and executed were all accomplished." It being the evening of the Marine Band concert, most of the distinguished men of the city, including Clay, were in the walks. The President and his particular friends were watched with lynx-eyed vigilance. It was noted that the Cabinet were mostly with him and upon the most

---

[22] *Congressional Globe*, 27th Cong., 1st Sess., pp. 372 ff.; Webster to Bates and Choate, August 25, 1841, *Niles' Register*, LXI, 54-55.

[23] Letcher to Crittenden, September 3, 1841, Crittenden Papers. Also in Coleman, *op. cit.*, I, 161, with the significant sentence omitted. Cf. Clay to E. M. Letcher, June 11, 1841, Coleman, *op. cit.*, I, 156-57.

[24] Letcher to Crittenden, September 8, 1841, Crittenden Papers; Jameson, *op. cit., passim.*

[25] Cincinnati *Gazette*, September 9, 1841.

[26] "The Diary of Thomas Ewing," *American Historical Review*, XVIII, 107-9; Green to McLean, August 26, 1841, McLean Papers. Cf. Letcher to Crittenden, September 3, 1841, Crittenden Papers; Cincinnati *Gazette*, September 8, 1841.

social terms, but it was said that Clay had not seen him for four or five weeks.[27]

The country at large should have been aware of what was so well known at the capital, for the correspondents of such Whig newspapers as the New York *Express* and the Philadelphia *Enquirer* were sending forth frank and voluminous dispatches of the most ominous import, forecasting not only the veto of the Fiscal Corporation Bill, but the dissolution of the Cabinet. The *National Intelligencer*, to be sure, was still playing Clay's game of silence, yet finally these reports could no longer be ignored. On August 31, it reprinted a graphic letter to the Philadelphia *Enquirer* only to denounce the writer as a traitor to the Whig cause. "This correspondence," declared the great party organ, "grossly and most unjustly misrepresents the state of public opinion, and the motives of public action here. . . . Of this letter it would take more time than we have to expose the fallacies. . . . The prediction of the dissolution of the Cabinet is one which no friend of the President or any Whig would either make or willingly publish." Thus were the rank and file of the party deliberately deceived, first by intentional silence and finally by overt falsification.[28]

Saturday night, August 28, there was a promiscuous party of Whigs of all shades at Crittenden's. Mrs. Crittenden was the only lady present and doubtless retired early. There was a sideboard supper with madeira and champagne. The President had been invited but had sent an excuse. At a late hour, however, a regular delegation, headed by Dawson of Georgia and Triplett of Kentucky, went over to the White House, which was closed for the night, roused the President, "took him by storm after the Kentucky fashion," and led him back to Crittenden's in triumph. At the door, Clay greeted him with, "Well, Mr. President, what are you for, Kentucky whiskey or champagne?" "Champagne," responded Tyler, with evident meaning, and entered into the jollification as well as he could. "But all this was false and hollow as it was blustering and

---

[27] New York *Express*, August 28, 1841.

[28] New York *Express*, August 27, 1841; *National Intelligencer*, August 31, 1841, quoting Philadelphia *Enquirer* correspondence dated August 28, 1841.

rowdyish," commented Adams, who had left early, before the arrival of the President.[29]

The political significance of this party was well understood. It was the final effort of the Cabinet, under the mellowing effects of a social gathering, to bring about a reconciliation between Tyler and the orthodox Whigs in Congress, and to draw him from under the influence of the Virginian clique. One rumor said that the reconciliation had been effected by an agreement to postpone the bank bill until the next session. As to the actual events of the party, there is no evidence save a brief entry in the diary of John Quincy Adams, which, as published, ends with the arrival of the President. Whatever occurred thereafter, the object of the entertainment was not attained. The very correspondent who on Saturday had written complacently of reconciliation, on Monday was forced to admit that he had been mistaken and that since then the signs of the times were more disastrous than before.[30]

On the following Monday, August 30, Berrien reported the Fiscal Corporation Bill without amendment, giving notice that he would call it up on Wednesday. The Senate then receded from its amendments to the Land Bill, which was thus passed and sent to the President, either in anticipation of a breach over the Bank Bill or as an additional embarrassment to him. Tyler meanwhile continued negotiations for a new Cabinet.[31]

The events of Monday and Tuesday thoroughly alarmed Ewing, who attempted, through Evans of Maine, to persuade Berrien to postpone the Bank Bill until after the passage of the Revenue Bill. Evans used every effort to postpone the bill, but Clay insisted on taking it up, appealing to the Democrats and receiving their support for proceeding. Many of the Whigs were much incensed at Clay's course but were powerless to control him. At the Cabinet meeting that day, Tyler's manner was "courteous and kind—not perfectly frank though evidently striving to appear so." He read the Land Bill to the Cabinet, objected to one clause and "talked jocosely about a Veto."

---

[29] Adams, *op. cit.*, X, 544-45.

[30] New York *Express,* September 1, 1841; Cincinnati *Gazette,* September 6, 1841. Cf. Wise to Tucker, August 29, 1841, Tyler, *op cit.*, II, 90-91.

[31] *Congressional Globe,* 27th Cong., 1st Sess., pp. 404-6; Reverdy Johnson to Crittenden, August 30, 1841, Crittenden Papers.

"The events of the day caused me much reflection," wrote Ewing that night. "On the one hand Mr. Clay was evidently hurrying matters to a catastrophe, intending to hasten the new Bank Bill upon Mr. Tyler; force him to approve or Veto— in the latter event compel the Cabinet to resign—denounce the Administration and make himself as the head of the Whig party an opposition candidate for the Presidency."[32]

This situation set the ministers to conferring with one another. Should they cling to office or follow Clay? They realized that in either case their motives would be impugned and charges of disloyalty preferred, but that adherence to Tyler would probably result in political ruin. Ewing, Bell and Granger concurred in the opinion that they should not resign unless Tyler vetoed the Land Bill as well as the Bank Bill, because that would be conclusive evidence that he had betrayed the party. Under no circumstances would they agree to the nomination of Clay at that time. Granger thought that Clay had "lost many friends by the hot haste with which he pressed the Bank Bill forward," and thought him imprudent in putting it before the Revenue Bill "if he really desired that the Land Bill should be approved."[33]

Evans's private expostulations having failed, Rives nevertheless objected to consideration of the Bank Bill before the Revenue Bill was finally disposed of. Clay, however, declared himself unprepared to go on with the Revenue Bill and announced his intention of voting for the Fiscal Corporation Bill, which it was generally understood should be taken up that day. Calhoun and Woodbury, of all men, supported him. Nineteen Whigs and fifteen Democrats voted for immediate consideration and eight Whigs and six Democrats against it. Berrien then opened the debate with a speech of two hours which is quite as significant for what it did not say as for what it did. There was no mention of the proposed use of bills of exchange in lieu of promissory notes for local loans, but he did claim that the bill conformed to the President's opinions, knowledge of which, however, he declared that he derived only from the

---

[32] "The Diary of Thomas Ewing," *American Historical Review*, XVIII, 106.

[33] *Ibid.*

official messages. Berrien certainly knew too much to make such a speech unless he were a party to the intrigue against the President.[34]

Rives replied to Berrien, pointing out the evasion in the matter of discounts, and Benton, by no means a friend of Tyler, joined in the attack on the subterfuge. During the day, Rives submitted to Tyler an amendment which would enable him to support the bill, but the President refused to have anything to do with it. He preferred that the bill should be sent to him in the form it then had. Tyler thus definitely committed himself to a breach with the Whig party. The next day, after a brief debate, the Senate passed the Fiscal Corporation Bill by twenty-seven to twenty-two—except for Rives in the negative, a strict party vote. As John Quincy Adams recorded, it passed "with the certainty that it would be vetoed by President Tyler."[35]

---

[34] *Congressional Globe*, 27th Cong., 1st Sess., pp. 417-18.

[35] *Ibid.*, App., p. 348; "The Diary of Thomas Ewing," *American Historical Review*, XVIII, 107-8; Adams, *op. cit.*, XI, 4.

CHAPTER VII

DISRUPTION

THE CONNECTION between a Bank veto and a dissolution of the Cabinet, which by September 1 was engaging the minds of correspondents, politicians, members of Congress, Cabinet ministers and the President himself, was no new or sudden development. A hint that all was not well with the administration appeared as early as June 25, and only three days later there came an intimation of the presence and sinister influence of General Duff Green at the White House. By July 7, rumors of discord between Tyler and his Cabinet were current in New Orleans and about the same time in Kentucky. On July 28, in a private letter, Tyler referred to a veto of the Fiscal Bank Bill as a "contingency which might lead to a rupture." Calhoun also, on August 1, expressed the opinion that "The loss of the Bank Bill would probably break up the Whig party, and lead to a remodeling of the Cabinet." A week later the probable resignation of a part or all of the Cabinet was referred to as a common rumor at Washington, doubted by Whig reporters, accepted by the President's intimates.[1]

This was the posture of affairs when the Tyler faction dropped a bomb in the ranks of the enemy by the famous "Truisms" editorial in *The Madisonian* of August 12. This editorial asserted the independence of the Executive against the Legislative and the Judiciary, and denied the subordination of the President to the Cabinet, who "are chosen by him and are removable at his will."[2]

Under these circumstances, rumor ran riot, and even the

---

[1] New York *Express*, June 26, August 14, 1841; Cincinnati *Gazette*, July 7, August 12, August 16, 1841; Louisville *Advertiser*, August 19, 1841; Jos. Eve to Crittenden, July 7, 1841; Nicholas to Crittenden, July 9, 1841; Crittenden Papers. Tyler to Tucker, July 28, 1841, Tyler, *op. cit.*, II, 54; Gilmer to Minor, August 7, 1841, *ibid.*, II, 706-7; Calhoun to Hammond, August 1, 1841, Jameson, *op. cit.*, p. 484.

[2] *National Intelligencer*, August 14, 1841, quoting *Madisonian*, August 12, 1841.

Whig correspondents who deprecated the action had to report
the prevalence of a belief that Cabinet changes were impending.
The *National Intelligencer* immediately took up the gauntlet of
The Madisonian. "The doctrine of Executive supremacy and
infallibility which it includes," declared the great Whig organ,
"is of the growth of other climes, and can never flourish in the
atmosphere of this free Republic. It is one of the most odious
of those Jacksonian pretensions upon which the people set the
seal of condemnation at the Presidential election in November
last." About this date "a distinguished gentleman, now in
Washington" wrote to the editor of the Cincinnati *Gazette* that
"Should the Cabinet *throw up,* another Whig Cabinet cannot
be formed. *But will they throw up?* That is another question."
Whereupon the editor comments: "Why should they *throw up?*
Do the hopes of the country . . . rest solely upon the charter
of a Bank? For ourselves, whatever others may think, we are
ready to answer—No !"[3]

Already, however, negotiations destined to lead to the Fiscal
Corporation Bill, were in progress. Accordingly, talk of a
break-up of the Cabinet subsided. On August 21 it was reported that the difference of opinion in regard to a bank
would not lead to a dissolution, but that the Cabinet would
cling together to carry out the Whig measures, to which there
seemed to be no real obstacle "if Tyler would assent to a fiscal
agent of any sort." This was written two days after the Fiscal
Corporation Bill was reported, and of course after Tyler had
already informed the Whigs in Congress of his insuperable
objections.[4]

By the end of August, the correspondents were spreading
abroad reports of the impending veto of the Fiscal Corporation Bill, and once more the dissolution of the Cabinet became
the subject of speculation in political circles. It was stated,
moreover, that a dissolution would come regardless of the
President's action on the Fiscal Corporation Bill, although
no one understood why. The only reason given was lack of con-

---

[3] Louisville *Advertiser,* August 19, 1841; New York *Express,* August,
1841; Cincinnati *Gazette,* August 16, 1841; *National Intelligencer,* August
14, 1841.   [4] Cincinnati *Gazette,* August 8, 1841.

fidence, both by Tyler in some of the ministers, and by some of the ministers in Tyler. Also, Crittenden was named as most determined to resign, instead of Webster as previously believed, who was declared to be on good terms with the President. The Webster newspapers went on to warn the Whigs that vetoes were not so unpopular as people took them to be, and that a rupture with Tyler and his friends and their reinforcement of the Democracy would not further the cause of a Bank. Several functions which the Cabinet ladies gave this week were interpreted as farewell parties.[5]

The situation had become so tense by this time, that Ewing took counsel with the Ohio delegation in Congress. In the event of a veto of the Bank Bill, or even of the Land Bill, they felt that the Cabinet should hold on until actually dismissed, for the country regarded them as holding by a higher tenure than merely Tyler's appointment, and a resignation would be regarded as a desertion of the post to which General Harrison and the nation had assigned them. If Tyler chose "to add this last crowning sin to his already great transgressions," let his and not theirs be the act and the responsibility. This policy was speedily communicated to the Ohio press, together with a forecast that Congress would hold together just long enough to prevent a pocket veto.[6]

Meanwhile, September 3, the Fiscal Corporation Bill passed the Senate.[7] The next morning Ewing called on the President, finding Bell and Granger already with him; Webster soon joined the group. The Land Bill was under consideration, Tyler being disposed to approve it, but objecting to one clause. A declaration on the subject was drawn up, apparently for later discussion by the Cabinet. The President then asked their opinion as to the time of sending up the Land Bill, immediately, or together with the Bank Bill, which probably would be vetoed. He accepted their advice to act at once "as the more frank

---

[5] New York *Express*, September 4, 1841.

[6] "The Diary of Thomas Ewing," *American Historical Review*, XVIII, 107; Cincinnati *Gazette*, September 8, 1841, Washington correspondence dated September 2, 1841. *Ibid.*, September 13, 1841, Washington correspondence dated September 6, 1841.

[7] *Congressional Globe*, 27th Cong., 1st Sess., p. 428; Adams, *op. cit.*

and generous—he having known of the passage of the Bank Bill—before he approved the other."[8]

At this juncture, the Committee on Enrolled Bills delivered the Bank Bill and withdrew. Tyler then expressed a wish to converse with the ministers on the subject. He said he would probably be compelled to veto the bill, and "he thought of accompanying the veto with a solemn declaration that he would not be a candidate for the Presidency another term." The Cabinet members did not concur in these views, and he readily surrendered them, though generally "tenacious of his opinions." Tyler was evidently anxious and unhappy. He unburdened himself of his sense of isolation and the ruin of all who ventured to support him. He spoke of his veto message, which should criticize the bill with much severity. Webster counselled against this course as both imprudent and undignified, and some of the others expressed the hope that he might yet approve the bill.[9]

Ewing walked to the department with Webster, who said they must prepare the public through the press, and desired Ewing to call upon him the next morning. It was probably due to this idea of Webster's that the New York *Express* received a letter from an "occasional correspondent" denying the certainty of a dissolution, or that Webster would "throw up his place in a huff," provided his friends would allow him to stay. In the event of a change, it averred, only Whigs would be admitted to the Cabinet. Much would depend on the reception which the veto met from Congress. Meanwhile, the President was on the most pleasant social terms with the Cabinet, even to the novel extent of going to the parties of their wives.[10]

On reflecting, however, upon Webster's remarks, Ewing made up his mind that they "ought not yet to give up the question or attempt to bring the public mind into accquiescence in it." In accordance with Webster's request, he called upon him and gave

---

[8] "The Diary of Thomas Ewing," *American Historical Review*, XVIII, 109.

[9] *Ibid.;* Tyler, *op. cit.*, II, 25, 27-28.

[10] "The Diary of Thomas Ewing," *American Historical Review*, XVIII, 109; New York *Express*, September 8, 1841.

him a full exposition of his views. Ewing thought that Tyler had given Webster a fine opening for a free and confidential discussion of the political situation and the certain effects of a veto. He could point out the relations of the various ministers to Clay, who "exacted great sacrifices of his friends and was willing to sacrifice nothing to them," only Crittenden being his personal intimate. He should point out the embarrassment produced by his repudiation of the Fiscal Corporation Bill to both himself and the Cabinet, and their inability to postpone or defeat it after initiating it.[11] Webster concurred in all of this, and wrote a note to the President, asking an interview the next morning. Unfortunately, no evidence is available as to what occurred at that meeting between the President and the Secretary of State.

It is significant that Ewing's argument was directed quite as much toward prevailing upon Tyler to retain the Cabinet as toward securing his acceptance of the Fiscal Corporation Bill. This is the more striking since Ewing goes on to note in his diary certain moves of Tyler probably designed to meet the contingency of a disruption of the Cabinet, but which might as well refer to an intention on his part to change his "constitutional advisers."

As early as mid-July Duff Green was in Kentucky effecting an alliance between Tyler and the Wickliffes. In August, he sounded Judge McLean as to accepting either the State or the Treasury department as he might choose. A few days later, General Alexander Hamilton went to Baltimore, approached J. V. L. McMahon, counsel of the Baltimore and Ohio Railroad, and held a private conference of several hours with Upshur. A few Whigs learned of these activities and connected them with cabinet making. Reverdy Johnson immediately informed Crittenden, for whose post they believed McMahon had been considered.[12]

As the tension increased, the three factions, through their presses, put before the public their explanations of the im-

---

[11] "The Diary of Thomas Ewing," *American Historical Review*, XVIII, 110-11.

[12] *Ibid.*, pp. 107-9, 111; Reverdy Johnson to Crittenden, August 30, 1841, Coleman, *op. cit.*, I, 160; *Congressional Globe*, 27th Cong., 1st Sess., pp. 404-6. See also authorities cited in note 26, chap. VI.

pending disruption. The Clay papers held that the Cabinet had "performed their own duties with unexceptionable fidelity, and abstained from interference either with the President's duties (except in cases where their advice was officially required) or those of Congress." It was asserted that between President and Cabinet there had never been "the slightest discord, no passage of warm debate, no discourtesy," nor anything giving ground for suspicion that "the President either meditated or desired a change." Yet a change was impending. "But it ought to be understood," wrote Horace Greeley, "that this Cabinet change was *meditated, planned, and advised*—I do not say by Mr. Tyler, *but by those who now possess his confidence—months ago, and entirely independent of the Bank collision.* No effort has been spared to draw invidious distinctions between a Cabinet formed by General Harrison and one selected by Mr. Tyler for himself."[13]

These persons were referred to as a "cabal," a "corporal's guard," a "Kitchen Cabinet."

Such are the terms now in vogue here to designate those—a very few persons—who are supposed to have busied themselves in undermining this Cabinet by secret, stealthy and back-door intercourse with the President. They are supposed to have whispered ambition in his ears; to have suggested the necessity of a new and third party for the next Presidential campaign, and of finding occasion, in some one or more of the measures brought forward by a Whig Congress, to break with the party, dissolve the Cabinet, and ride into importance on a new tide of their own creation. . . . Tyler was not warm in his seat as successor, if report speaks the truth—before the magnificent scheme of a reorganization of parties broke its shell and began to peep. Soon it strutted forth with pride, and since, as you know, it has crowed with much boldness.[14]

On the other hand, the Tyler press claimed that the Clay men were trying to alienate the party from Tyler, aided by the treacherous coöperation of the Cabinet. All the restraint shown in their reception of the vetoes was the result of un-

---

[13] Letter of September 8, 1841, quoted in *National Intelligencer,* September 16, 1841.

[14] *National Intelligencer,* September 11, 1841, quoting Philadelphia *North American.*

willingness to precipitate an immediate break-up of the Cabinet, which would follow open denunciation of the President. The work of the moderates in the Cabinet was stigmatized as actuated by the same motives. While the secretaries thus directed their efforts "to undermine and circumvent the President" in Washington, during the calm interval of a few weeks, their friends in Congress in accord with their counsel, were "to go home, and raise the standard of revolt there," "in the shape of indignation meetings, newspaper denunciation and other affiliated hostile movements, extending all over the country." Meanwhile, the Government had come almost to a standstill, for Tyler knew full well "the secret objects the leading members of his Cabinet" had in view, and was constrained to do almost everything himself, working early and late on matters many of which would have been handed over for the action of the secretaries, had they been men who were really his friends. They were invited to act like men and hand in their resignations so that the President might bring to his aid men in whom he had confidence. Tyler, they claimed, had neither a clear field nor a fair fight, but was forced to play into the hands of either Clay or Webster.[15]

The best exposition of the moderate position is to be found in the letters of the "occasional correspondent" of the New York *Express*, who, if not Webster himself, was certainly inspired by him. They of course urged acceptance of a veto and postponement of bank legislation, and deprecated a disruption of the Cabinet.[16]

And so the issue was joined, even before the resignations were sent in. That neither the public facts nor the personal relations of the President and the ministers justified a disruption, and that, from the standpoint of the party, it was suicidal,

---

[15] The substance of this paragraph is taken mainly from a letter to the New York *Herald*, from its Washington correspondent, John Howard Payne, the poet and playwright, quoted in the *National Intelligencer*, September 11, 1841. Payne was said to derive his information from Tyler's sons, one of whom, Robert, had similar literary and dramatic tastes. The contemporary sources are replete with allusions, frequently scurrilous, to these associations. Cf. Tuckerman, *op. cit.*, II, 89, where Payne's name, probably through an easily conceived error in transcription, appears as "Parmely."

[16] New York *Express*, September 11, 1841.

all sides were agreed. So too, that this unnecessary and disastrous action was precipitated by intrigues—but whose intrigues? Those of Wise and the "Kitchen Cabinet," or those of Clay and the "Caucus?" The Clay version was openly paraded by the Whig press at the time, and has since been accepted by most historians.[17] That Wise, Gilmer and their associates actively desired a change and even disruption of the Whig party cannot be doubted, but it appears highly improbable that, at the time of the resignations, they had brought the President into accord with their views.

Throughout all this excitement, the *National Intelligencer*, the great organ of the Whigs, had given not a hint of the movements behind the scenes. Now, on September 9, it published a conservative warning:

To prepare our readers for the possible event, however, we now state that the prevalent impression here is that the president will not approve the bill, but will return it with his objections today, or shortly. We do not vouch for the truth of this report . . . but give it our readers as the rumor of the day.[18]

That very day, indeed, the veto message was sent to the House. After a defense of the veto power as "a great conservative principle" designed by the framers to safeguard the Constitution and necessarily to be exercised against the will of a legislative majority, mere regard for which might in no way control the Executive in the exercise of this function, Tyler proceeded to examine the proposed Fiscal Corporation Bill and concluded that "it cannot be regarded as other than a bank of the United States, with powers seemingly more limited than have heretofore been granted to such an institution. It operates *per se* over the Union by virtue of the unaided and,

---

[17] James Schouler, *History of the United States,* IV, 380-83, 387-88, 390-94; H. E. Von Holst, *Constitutional and Political History of the United States,* II, 414-16, 421-38; Carl Schurz, *Life of Henry Clay,* II, 212-15. E. Channing, *History of the United States,* V, 464-65, is laconically noncommittal; and only G. P. Garrison, *Westward Expansion,* pp. 55-64, discredits the charge. Von Holst places some blame on the Clay men, but seems to lay more on the "Kitchen Cabinet." Schouler takes the extreme Clay view, probably following Benton, *op. cit.,* II, 242-43, who does not even suggest any other explanation.

[18] *National Intelligencer,* September 9, 1842.

in my view, assumed authority of Congress as a national legislature. . . ." Or, if it were regarded as a local operation of the District of Columbia upon which general powers had been conferred, it was even more obnoxious.

The details also he viewed with disfavor. In the first place, "It may . . . indulge in mere local discounts under the name of bills of exchange. . . ." In the second place, he found that it would neither relieve the currency situation, especially in the agricultural states, nor hasten the resumption of specie payments by the State banks, but rather to the contrary, and force them to "exist at the mercy of this national monopoly of brokerage."

After some other minor objections, he again rehearsed his regrets that he was unable to yield his opinions to the wishes of Congress. Many laws had been passed, all of which, with the single exception of the Bank, he had accepted. With a reiterated plea for delay, he closed by again affirming the steadfastness of his constitutional opinions on the matter in question and the absence of any other considerations in his course.[19]

Webster's influence was at once thrown in favor of the veto. The New York *Express* correspondent reported that "The Veto Message is regarded by the Whigs generally as conciliatory. The President clearly indicates his intention of throwing himself upon the arms of his political friends," as the Whigs were called in contradistinction to the Virginian clique.[20] But this attempt at conciliation failed. Most of the Whig papers took a very different tone. The public had been successfully kept in ignorance of what all the politicians at Washington knew, and so was ready to believe that Tyler had "vetoed his own bill." Meanwhile the Cabinet was rapidly approaching dissolution.

On the morning of Friday, September 10, the Cabinet met to discuss their position. It was reported, and generally believed, that Crittenden had resigned the night before. The inclination of the Cabinet, it was thought, was to throw up their places if their friends would advise or permit such action. They

[19] Richardson, *op. cit.,* IV, 68-72.
[20] New York *Express,* September 11, 1841, Washington correspondence, September 9, night.

felt deeply the slight of not having been consulted on the
veto, and also the insinuations of the *Madisonian* that a
Cabinet so out of harmony with the President should resign.
Tyler tactlessly gave point to these insinuations by giving the
Executive printing of the veto message to that press, although
Gales and Seaton were the official printers of the House, to
which it was addressed.

While Whigs generally were said to advise the Cabinet to
hold on, it was believed that Clay had advised resignation,
holding that the Cabinet could not ignore the slights put upon
them. He also recommended moderation, however, and preached
"no denunciation of the President." It was understood, though,
that the Clay men would state their reasons for offering the
Fiscal Corporation Bill for Tyler's approval. But changes in
the Cabinet were regarded as inevitable. Webster and Granger
might hold on, but the rest were earnestly bent on resigning.
Tyler was in good spirits, receiving at the White House, the
preceding night, many of the Opposition and some Whigs.[21]

As a matter of fact, four of the Cabinet members had come
to a determination to resign the previous evening at Badger's
house, where they were entertained at dinner. Granger was not
present, but Clay was, and Webster, perceiving, as he thought,
that it was an arranged meeting between Clay and the Cabinet,
presently took his departure. Some of the secretaries, if not
all, had scrupulously avoided discussing with Clay the matter
of resignation, fearing the use which might be made of the
fact. Ewing, indeed, was not aware that Clay was to be of·the
party. His presence was a blunder, and hard to explain unless
his counsel was desired. The evidence appears to establish the
fact, however, that he took no part in the decisive conference,
but was conversing with the family at the time.[22]

Already, that day, Yorke of New Jersey, a Whig, had
sought to introduce a resolution for adjournment, but met with

---

[21] New York *Express,* September 15, 1841, Washington "Occasional Correspondence," September 10; *National Intelligencer,* September 13, 1841.
[22] New York *Express,* September 18, September 22, September 25, 1841;
National Intelligencer, September 18, 1841; Ewing to Clay, November 1,
1843, Clay Papers. In the letter cited, Ewing specifically charges that
Webster "got up a report, which he knew to be false, and caused it to
appear in several papers devoted to his interest."

objection. The next day, Friday, he presented and carried a resolution for adjournment on Monday at eleven o'clock.[23] It was thought that some of the resignations had already been sent in, but it was only on Saturday morning, September 11, that the President received them. The four secretaries quitted their offices about noon.

By Saturday morning, however, Granger also had determined to resign, but was unwilling to take so important a step without consulting with the New York delegation in Congress, who had met the night before and adopted a resolution advising his resignation. While the House was in session, he called upon Fillmore, Greig, and Morgan, who informed him that the Whig members then in Washington concurred in his conclusion, and at Granger's request a written declaration to that effect was drawn up and signed by the delegation. Granger, accordingly, notified Tyler that his resignation would be presented on Monday. While the newspaper statements published at the time ascribe his action to distrust of the President's aims and unwillingness to coöperate with the remodelled Cabinet, in private conversation with Philip Hone, Granger himself declared that it was through dissatisfaction with Tyler's policy in regard to appointments rather than because of the veto.[24]

Webster called upon President Tyler on Saturday morning "to define his position." A few moments later, Ewing's letter of resignation was handed to the President. Webster recognized it, and, divining its offensive character, quickly asked, before its seal was broken, that it might be entrusted to his care for a few minutes. He hastened with it to his office and dispatched his messenger to Ewing with the request that he would see him immediately.

Ewing, who was just leaving his office, called at once upon Webster, whom he found at his table with the letter before him. Webster took it up as if weighing it in his hand, asking Ewing if he recognized it. Then he added: "It is a harsh paper. The President has not read a word of it. He feels kindly

---

[23] *Congressional Globe*, 27th Cong., 1st Sess., pp. 445-47.
[24] New York *Express*, September 15, September 22, 1841; *National Intelligencer*, September 16, 1841; Cincinnati *Gazette*, September 16, 1841; Tuckerman, *op. cit.*, II, 90-91, September 29, 1841.

towards you. He has authorized me to tell you so; and, as you are determined to resign, if you part in friendship he will give you your choice of the foreign missions. Think better of it and withdraw this letter." Ewing replied that that was impossible; his people must know why he had left the responsible position in which General Harrison with their concurrence had placed him. The reasons were set forth in the letter and he had made up his mind to abide by it. Webster then told him that he had determined to remain for the present. He asked Ewing to change one sentence containing an important fact which he could have learned only from Webster, lest it disturb the latter's relations with the President. With this request Ewing complied.

All this consumed only a few minutes. On his return to the President, Webster surrendered the letter in silence, then asked, "Where am I to go, Mr. President?" "You must decide that for yourself, Mr. Webster," responded Tyler. Webster instantly caught at this remark and said, "If you leave it to me, Mr. President, I will stay where I am." Upon this, Tyler rose and extended his hand, rejoining warmly, "Give me your hand on that, and now I will say to you that Henry Clay is a doomed man from this hour." Then ensued a frank and free conversation in which positions were clearly defined and the Cabinet crisis discussed. In the end, the nominations of the new ministers were sent to the Senate in the handwriting of the Secretary of State.[25]

The Virginia clique were in favor of an entirely new Cabinet, and especially opposed to retaining Webster, whom they regarded as a "Federalist." Their plan was to send Webster as minister to England, where he could still be employed to settle the Maine boundary dispute, while Upshur should succeed him at the State Department. But the resignation of the Cabinet afforded the President and Secretary of State an opportunity for clear understanding and alliance against Clay. In addition, Tyler realized the importance of retaining the

---

[25] New York *Express*, September 10, September 18, 1841. Letter of John Tyler, Jr., January 29, 1883, Tyler, *op. cit.*, II, 112, footnote; as private secretary to his father, he was present at the interview. "The Diary of Thomas Ewing," *American Historical Review*, XVIII, 112, an entry much later than the events related.

great Northern leader, with whom his personal contacts had always been pleasant. Hence it was that Tyler sternly opposed himself to all intimations of turning Webster out and appointing Upshur or anyone else Secretary of State.[26]

In his determination to remain, Webster acted upon the advice of the Massachusetts Congressional delegation. On Friday he had sent a single line to Peter Harvey: "Do the Whigs of Mass. think I ought to quit or ought to stay?" A majority of the Massachusetts delegation advised him to hold on, Adams being urgent. He believed Webster's retirement would abandon the country to war. Later, it appears, Adams was of another opinion.[27]

Webster, perhaps even Tyler himself, was anxious to retain Granger. It would mean a second Whig of unimpeachable orthodoxy in the Cabinet. It would also prevent the impending appointment of Charles A. Wickliffe, which undoubtedly would be interpreted as an open declaration of war upon Clay, with the latter shut out of all political profit in the Post Office. From Webster sources it is stated that this aspect of the appointment led Tyler to hesitate at the last moment, probably under pressure from Webster. But the impending adjournment of Congress allowed no delay, and the original program was carried to completion. Thus the action of the New York Whigs in forcing the resignation of Granger was a distinct defeat for Webster in his policy of moderation, and a corresponding victory for the ultras, alike for Clay and Wise. The Northern element in the Cabinet was weakened, Calhoun given influence over the patronage of the Post Office, and Tyler led to take a step which was inevitably regarded as a direct and personal retaliation against Clay.[28]

Already, on Monday morning, so many of the Whigs in Congress as yet remained in Washington had met in the

---

[26] Tyler, *op. cit.*, II, 102-121.

[27] Webster to Harvey, September 10, 1841, Webster, *Writings and Speeches*, XVI, 356; New York *Express*, September 15, 1841.

[28] New York *Express*, September 15, September 18, 1841. The appointment of Wickliffe was probably not so much a matter of necessity as the *Express* letter implies, for it was anticipated as a practical certainty by both factions in Kentucky. Wickliffe's connection with Calhoun was also clearly recognized. Letcher to Crittenden, September 8, 1841, Coleman, *op. cit.*, I, 164.

promised caucus and adopted an address or manifesto, prepared by the novelist-politician, John P. Kennedy, of Baltimore.[29] It asserted that the special session had been called to carry out the reforms which had been the issue in the election, though not a formal platform. These were a restraint of the executive power through limitation of the president to a single term, prohibition of interference by federal officers in elections, and "a voluntary self-denial" by the president in the use of the veto power; a revision of the tariff and the establishment of a national bank; and an economical administration of the finances. Tyler's professions of Whiggism in seeking the nomination, the character of the Cabinet, and his inaugural address had been taken as sufficient assurances that his accession would not endanger this program. Reviewing the work of the session, it insisted that the vetoes rested not upon constitutional scruples but upon a design to alter political alignments, and accused the President of inconsistency, disingenuously treating Clay's Bank Bill as identical with Ewing's and thus the President's own. But, it asserted,

In the midst of all these varieties of opinion, an impenetrable mystery seemed to hang over the whole question. There was no such frank interchange of sentiments as ought to characterize the intercourse of a president and his friends, and the last persons in the government who would seem to have been intrusted with his confidence on those embarrassing topics were the constitutional advisers which the laws had provided for him.

Since he had "voluntarily separated himself from those by whose exertions and suffrages" he had been "elevated to that office through which he reached his present exalted station," the Whigs could no longer be held responsible for executive action. In the future program of the party, first place was given to a reduction of executive power by further limitation of the veto, by the adoption of a single presidential term, by the separation of the purse and the sword through lodging the appointment of the Secretary of the Treasury in Con-

---

[29] New York *Express*, September 15, 1841; *Niles' Register*, LXI, 35-36; this meeting had been planned as early as September 6. Cf. Cincinnati *Gazette*, September 13, 1841, Washington correspondence dated September 6, 1841.

gress, and by restricting the power of removal "so as to render the president amenable for its exercise."

The rank and file of the party, even the workers, accepted the statements of the manifesto. The storm of disappointment and rage that broke out did not long lack guidance. Not alone was Tyler anathematized as a traitor and Webster denounced as a venal lover of office; the direction was positive as well as negative. From all quarters burst forth a cry for Clay—the one great leader of whom they could have no suspicion, "the Embodiment of Whig Principles."

Already, on Tuesday, the day following the manifesto caucus, a public meeting had been held in Baltimore which planned a great demonstration for the occasion of Clay's passing through Baltimore on his way home. A committee conveyed the invitation to Clay, who replied in terms which left no room for doubt.[30]

Clay was a candidate for the presidency in 1844, and had been accepted by a large, possibly a controlling, section of the Whigs in Congress. The platform was no less clearly indicated. There was to be no ambiguous silence as in 1840. The economic issues which the Whigs had inherited from the National Republicans, and which had been brought to the fore in consequence of the mild rule of Van Buren and the prostration of business produced by the panic of 1837, were to be left in the background. All on which the party could agree had been enacted into law, or in all probability would be at the coming regular session. The Bank had split the party in its control of the government, and even Clay dared not face the electorate again with that as the principal issue. The prudent plan, and the one which promised to be the most effective against Tyler, was to return to the general constitutional issue on which the diverse elements of the party had originally been drawn together and from which it had derived its name. Once more the issue was to be the curbing of the power of the President through restriction of the veto and assertion of the independence of his "constitutional advisers"; once more the Whigs were to rally in opposition to "Executive Usurpation."

[30] Clay to Robert Gilmor, etc., *Niles' Register*, LXI, 67-68.

CHAPTER VIII

THE OLD CHIEF

ARDENT ADMIRERS of Henry Clay did not wait for the final breach with Tyler to launch his presidential candidacy. The first veto was sufficient to reawake the slogan "Union of the Whigs for the sake of the Union" and also the demand for "Harry of the West." After the second veto, notices of new accessions to the Clay ranks crowded the columns of the Whig organs. By October 1, 1841, numerous papers in Mississippi, Tennessee, Virginia, Missouri and Illinois had declared in his favor, and such editorial pronouncements continued throughout the ensuing winter and spring. By May, 1842, it could be justly said, "The papers throughout the whole land—the north, the south, the east, the west, are nominating Henry Clay for the next Presidency."[1]

Agitation through mass-meetings started almost as early as the newspaper movement, beginning at Philadelphia within a fortnight of the second bank veto. Early in the winter, Clay was placed in nomination by a meeting in Orange County, North Carolina, and such demonstrations were numerous during the spring. By mid-June, 1842, they had occurred in Tennessee, Pennsylvania, Georgia, Indiana, Delaware, Louisiana and Ohio, and at New Orleans and New York City. Clay clubs were also in process of formation. Before August, 1842, over two hundred Whig newspapers had declared in favor of Clay. Between July, 1842, and July, 1843, he was nominated by Whig State conventions in Maine, Vermont, Massachusetts, New York, New Jersey, Pennsylvania, Delaware, Maryland, Virginia, North Carolina, Georgia, Mississippi, and Kentucky. Early in 1844, Indiana, Illinois, Alabama and Arkansas instructed their delegates to vote for him in the national convention, and his nomination seemed assured.[2]

---

[1] Columbia (Missouri) *Patriot,* September 4, 1841, May 23, June 4, 1842; Lexington *Intelligencer,* September 17, September 24, September 28, October 1, 1841.

[2] New York *Express,* September 18, 1841. Lexington *Intelligencer,* December 17, December 21, 1841; May 10, May 27, June 21, June 28, July 1,

Clay was not permitted to secure the nomination altogether without opposition, however. Those perennial candidates, General Winfield Scott and Judge John McLean, were eager to fish in troubled waters. In the fall of 1841, Scott's impatience got the better of him and he wrote a letter defining his position on the issues of the day which he had lithographed and sent about like a circular. He also coquetted with the political Abolitionists through Thaddeus Stevens, who by May, 1842, was advocating Scott's nomination since he was more favorable to them and their principles than any other man who had a chance of election. By this time the Scott movement had gained so much strength that the Clay press began to talk of the general as Clay's running mate. Scott resolutely declined to consider this, though now driven to the conclusion that Clay's nomination was inevitable if he survived. But, Scott wrote in May, "His health is low, and when an early hard-liver begins to break up there is no possibility of recuperation." He still cherished this hope three months later; and the misfortunes of the Whigs in the fall elections led him to hope also that Clay's friends would "not like to take the risk." After a trip to Pennsylvania in May, 1842, Tyler refused to let him "go reviewing again," and a Scott convention at Harrisburg in July was a failure. Stevens advised him "to remain on the turf and await events" as late as February, 1843; and only a twelvemonth later did the Pennsylvania Anti-Masonic organs take down his name and hoist that of Clay. But after June, 1842, the Scott candidacy was negligible.[3]

The McLean movement started after the Scott candidacy had spent its force and was little more than an attempt to defeat Clay. The defeat of Corwin in Ohio and Davis in Mas-

---

July 22, August 2, August 5, September 2, 1842; January 27, March 7, March 21, 1843. *Observer and Reporter,* July 1, 1843; January 1, February 10, 1844. Columbia *Patriot,* July 2, July 9, July 22, September 30, 1842.

[3] Stevens to Scott, October 28, 1841; February 15, 1843; Stevens to J. Blanchwell, May 24, 1842; Scott to Stevens, November 1, November 4, 1841; May 5, August 2, 1842; Stevens Papers. Nathan Sargent to Clay, August 6, 1842, Crittenden Papers. Lexington *Intelligencer,* March 22, April 8, 1842; November 15, 1842. *Observer and Reporter, passim.* Cincinnati *Gazette,* November 16, November 22, 1841. Columbia *Patriot,* November 27, 1841.

sachusetts in the fall of 1842 gave new hope to the anti-slavery Whigs who distrusted Clay. Consequently in November various Ohio politicians made overtures to McLean, who, they said, could carry every Western State except Illinois. Clay, they declared, had "no sympathies in common with the people"; he could not carry the West, and his nomination would assure the election of Van Buren. This whispering campaign was carried on unostentatiously during the winter and spring, and Clay did not learn of it until May, 1843, when he was informed that Webster's partisans in New York City were attempting to play the same game as in 1839. Although measures were taken to counteract their machinations, they so far persisted that in October no less a person than Leslie Combs wrote to McLean suggesting the vice-presidential nomination with a promise of the succession in 1848. The Judge very cavalierly rejected this offer, though by the spring of 1844 he had so far reconsidered as to write to his friends for advice. In the end, however, he held to his original position and his name was not presented to the convention.[4]

Nor would the admirers of "the god-like Webster" permit Clay's leadership of the party to go unchallenged, though circumstances made his candidacy a forlorn hope of those who wished to defeat Clay. After the dissolution of the Cabinet, the batteries of the Clay press were turned upon him but little less fiercely than upon the President. The ensuing session of Congress was so disastrous to the political prospects of both President and Secretary that, by the spring of 1842, the administration had not a single advocate in the Senate and only four or five in the House. Webster, regarded as its controlling spirit, had become almost universally odious. The appointment of Everett as minister to England had alienated Rives, who wanted the place. Almost everybody was questioning Webster's integrity. Rumors of impending resignation were

[4] C. Morris to McLean, December 19, 1842; March 9, 1844; Jesse B. Thomas to McLean, December 27, 1842; G. C. Bates to McLean, December 12, 1842; Combs to McLean, October 14, 1842; McLean to Combs, October 26, 1842; S. Whitworth to McLean, February 13, 1844; Herman Lincoln to McLean, March 16, 1844; McLean Papers. Clay to Letcher, May 26, 1842, Crittenden Papers. Clay to Clayton, May 27, June 21, 1842, Clayton Papers. Lexington *Intelligencer,* October 21, November 29, 1842.

current in September, but, instead, October brought his defense of Tyler at Faneuil Hall. That masterly oration drew blood, and only Clayton's promptness saved Clay from the imprudence of a formal reply.[5]

By the spring of 1843, however, the tide was beginning to run in Webster's favor, especially in Ohio. There one group of Whigs was reluctant to vote for a slaveholder, while another disliked Clay as a duellist. One still more numerous had been turned against a national bank by the catastrophe of the old bank under its Pennsylvania charter. The extreme partisan character of Clay's course repelled others. The Compromise Tariff was also a source of weakness, and the defeat of Corwin, closely associated with Clay, had seriously impaired his prestige. Webster was told that he was the only leader who could draw the various factions together and lead them to victory, and that by the purchase of an interest in the Cincinnati *Gazette*, that powerful press, already detaching itself from Clay and assuming a neutral attitude, could be swung to his support. The Clay press was trying in vain to whip up enthusiasm, and it seemed impossible for him to carry that state against any candidate except Calhoun.[6]

By July, 1843, the other aspirants were much concerned, and also puzzled, as to Webster's plans. Scott warned Crittenden that Clayton was negotiating for Webster to run for vice-president with Clay, and by fall that movement was in full swing. "The old Swiss is bought up again," declared Rhett. Webster's friends in New York made overtures to Clay through Peter B. Porter, stipulating, however, that the proposition should originate with Clay, but to this Porter peremptorily demurred. Clay, however, gave a chilly reception to a similar overture from another source, declaring that he believed that the Whig party had gained rather than lost by Webster's alienation. In this Ewing, whom he consulted, concurred, specifying Webster's intemperance and "his open

[5] New York *Express*, October 20, 1841; Cincinnati *Gazette*, November 29, 1841; Columbia *Patriot*, September 9, 1842; Lexington *Intelligencer*, October 11, November 4, 1842. Calhoun to Clemson, April 3, 1842, Jameson, *op. cit.*, p. 508. Clay to Clayton, November 2, 1842, Clayton Papers.

[6] Alphonso Taft to Webster, April 7, 1843, Webster Papers.

and gross immorality" as weakening him in "the strict community" where he lived, while recent anti-Catholic demonstrations there had made him unpopular among the Irish and Germans of Ohio.[7]

By the opening of November, however, the activity of the Webster partisans in New York City had been checkmated and the "god-like" statesman had disavowed the scheme. Early in 1844, he declined a proffered nomination from New Hampshire and definitely came out for Clay. In February, Mangum, closest to Webster of all the Clay leaders, gave a dinner at Washington at which Webster, Barrow, Crittenden, Choate, Rives and Scott were present. Mutual explanations were made, existing differences composed, and all the distinguished gentlemen definitely agreed upon the nomination of Clay. With the convention only three months away, it seemed impossible for any new obstacle to intervene between Clay and the long-sought goal.[8]

But the holding of the convention was itself an evidence of the opposition to Clay. Scott had insisted that the candidate should be nominated by a national convention, the first suggestion of which had been made in the eventful days of September, 1841. The answer of the Clay press was that if Henry Clay was to be the candidate of the Whig party, "let that party nominate him—not by concert, not by conference, not by delegation, but spontaneously from the heart." The Clay strategy was to carry on a whirlwind movement by means of county and state nominations through irregular mass-conventions, and then to declare that, since the party had spontaneously expressed its choice, a convention was superfluous. Such strategy could be attempted only with a party as inveterately opposed to organization and discipline as the Whigs, but it proved as successful for Clay in 1844 as when

---

[7] Columbia *Patriot,* July 22, 1843. Scott to Crittenden, July 8, 1843; P. B. Porter to Clay, September 25, 1843; Crittenden Papers. Clay to Clayton, October 10, 1843, Clayton Papers. Clay to Ewing, October 29, 1843, Ewing Papers. Ewing to Clay, November 11, 1843, Clay Papers. Rhett to Calhoun, October 7, 1843, Jameson, *op. cit.,* p. 886.

[8] Porter to Clay, November 6, 1843, Crittenden Papers. Columbia *Missouri Statesman* (hereafter cited as *Missouri Statesman*) January 5, February 16, 1844. St. Louis *Missouri Republican,* February 2, 1844. *Observer and Reporter,* February 14, 1844.

used against him in 1848. In both cases, however, the minority forced the holding of a convention.[9]

By June, 1842, however, it appeared that this strategy had been successful and that Clay was "fully and fairly the Whig candidate." Consequently in September the Clay press began to recede from its *non possumus* attitude toward a convention. In February, 1843, the matter was finally settled by the Whig Congressional caucus, which set May 3, 1844, as the date of the convention and fixed the number of delegates as that of the Senators and Representatives. Clay had acquiesced in the arrangement, but was far from happy. "What I apprehended, in the event of a National Convention," he wrote in the following May, on learning of the McLean movement, "is about to be realized—intrigues to supplant the favored Whig candidate. McLean, Scott, Webster will be, have been, all approached." But, as has been shown, the initial impetus of the Clay candidacy was sufficient to overbear all schemes, and he entered the national convention its predestined nominee.[10]

From all sides, also, came indications that the chances of success were splendid, with just one threatening element— the slavery question. The Democratic press, to be sure, made much of Whig losses in state elections, but the correspondence of the politicians tells another story. Even in the South, Clay had gained. Organization, always the weak point of the Whigs, seemed the one essential to success. New England was of course regarded as safely Whig, while reports from the Middle States gave Clay an immense advantage over Van Buren. The only real danger in New York, as in Ohio, came from the Abolitionists, who were strong and growing. Nine-tenths of them were drawn from the Whigs and were hostile to Clay.

[9] Columbia *Patriot,* December 2, 1843; Lexington *Intelligencer,* September 28, 1841.

[10] Columbia *Patriot,* October 23, 1841. Reverdy Johnson to Crittenden, September 15, 1841; Thos. W. Norton to Crittenden, February 8, 1842, Crittenden Papers. Mangum to Clay, June 15, 1842, Clay Papers. W. C. Preston to Waddy Thompson, July 10, 1842, Thompson Papers. Lexington *Intelligencer,* September 27, December 20, 1842; February 28, 1843. Clay to Clayton, November 1, 1841, May 27, 1843, Clayton Papers.

Ewing was seriously attempting either to break up their organization in Ohio or to hold them in line for Clay; but he saw in them an ultimate danger to the party, since they were moved by "a violent spirit of enthusiasm" which could not permanently be controlled.[11]

The Calhoun group of Southern leaders was equally convinced of Clay's success against their chief, owing to the schism between the northern and southern wings of the Democracy resulting from the policies of the Albany and Virginia machines. Against that consummation they saw but one chance —the raising of the Texas question, with a consequent weakening of Clay at the South. If this conviction became sufficiently strong with the Southern leaders, it might impel them to a course of action which would disappoint Granger's belief that Texas would be merely "glanced," and render abortive all Ewing's subtle schemes for breaking up the organization of the "Liberty Men."[12]

Meanwhile, Clay was carrying on as active a campaign as the political habits of the time permitted. At the close of the special session, he had hastened home to Ashland, avoiding so far as possible all public demonstrations, including the barbecue planned by his fellow-townsmen of Lexington. Even in declining, however, he made it clear that "Executive Usurpation" was to be the paramount issue of the campaign. Although rather ostentatiously avoiding the pomp and parade with which the Whigs sought to signalize his arrivals and departures, at Wheeling he yielded and a great concourse

---

[11] Jefferson *Inquirer,* November 11, 1843. W. Lumpkin to Calhoun, November 15, 1841; R. M. T. Hunter to Calhoun, September 19, 1843; F. W. Pickens to Calhoun, October 22, 1843; B. F. Porter to Calhoun, February 5, 1844; Jameson, *op. cit.,* pp. 832, 883-84, 889-90, 921-22. Alexander Porter to Crittenden, December 2, 1843; Clayton to Crittenden, December 9, 1843, Clayton Papers. Weed to Granger, March 15, 1844; Granger to Weed, December 31, 1843; Granger Papers. Selden to Van Buren, November 25, 1843; John Gragg to Van Buren, November 20, 1843; A. C. Hana to Van Buren, November 20, 1843; Van Buren Papers. Ewing to Clay, November 1, 1843, Clay Papers.

[12] Gadsden to Calhoun, January 27, 1844; Calhoun to J. E. Calhoun, February 7, 1844; Calhoun to Wharton, February 22, 1841; Jameson, *op. cit.,* pp. 567, 578, 917-19.

of people escorted him for six miles. Declining a public dinner, he nevertheless spoke twice. In his first remarks, "he cast reflections upon no one," but after supper he spoke on the veto-power.[13]

The exhaustion which Clay had pled in avoiding public entertainments was only too real, and the two months intervening before the regular session of Congress were none too long for his recuperation. Indeed, he contemplated resigning in November, but could not bring himself to so prompt a fulfillment of the agreement under which, it appears, Crittenden had resigned. It was understood that he was to quit in February, though his friends doubted his resolution. Crittenden was on hand in Washington from the opening of the session, but Clay kept him waiting a full month longer than he had expected, and then regretted having fixed the date so early, since the important questions had not been disposed of, as he had anticipated. Meanwhile, to the relief of Clay's friends, illness kept him silent. Nevertheless, he succeeded in holding the great body of the Whigs together under his banner.[14]

At last, however, on March 31, Clay delivered his "Valedictory." The galleries were overflowing before eleven o'clock and before twelve the lobbies and passages were "all crowded and choked up." The "morning business" was disposed of at half-past one, when, there being no question before the Senate, Clay rose and spoke for an hour and a half. The report published in the *National Intelligencer* was, as usual, quite different from the speech itself. Silas Wright thought it was "the prepreparation with the prunings," and "much better than the speech would have been." Wright thought the speech characteristic only in its egotism and very tame, arousing no enthusiasm in the audience; nor did he perceive any response to Clay's own deep feeling, which at many stages brought him to tears.

---

[13] New York *Express*, September 18, September 25, 1841. Lexington *Intelligencer*, September 14, September 18, September 24, September 28, October 1, 1841.

[14] Lexington *Intelligencer*, November 23, 1841. Cincinnati *Gazette*, November 24, 1841. Clay to Clayton, November 1, 1841, Clayton Papers. Crittenden to Letcher, January 9, 1842; Letcher to Crittenden, February 4, 1842; C. S. Morehead to Crittenden, January 2, February 9, February 23, 1842; Crittenden Papers. Calhoun to Duff Green, April 2, 1843, Jameson, *op. cit.*, pp. 507-8. Wright to Van Buren, April 2, 1842; Van Buren Papers.

Clay looked so old and careworn that Wright was sick and solemn in spite of himself.[15]

A hundred and fifty guests, chiefly members of Congress, united to honor Clay with a dinner on the ninth; and three days later his birthday was celebrated with a ball at the Assembly Rooms. About this time, Clay sat directly opposite Benton and Wright at a dinner given by the Russian minister, "his face clouded, his tongue silent, his air abstract and desolate." They both thought him reluctant to leave Washington and that he had resigned only at the insistence of his Kentucky friends and because he had so far committed himself to it before leaving home that he could not recede. He delayed his departure so long that only on May 2 did he arrive at Lexington. A reception committee met him at Maysville and accompanied him on the last stage of his journey, while at Paris many citizens of Bourbon County joined his escort. At the Fayette County line he was met by a great assemblage, which after an address, proceeded in a procession a mile and a half long to Ashland, the bells of the Lexington churches pealing as it passed through the streets.[16]

Two days later, Lord Morpeth arrived at Lexington and was a guest at Ashland during his sojourn. A fortnight later, Van Buren arrived, after visiting Mobile, New Orleans, Nashville and the Hermitage. Together with Paulding, his traveling companion, the "Little Magician" also became Clay's guest for four days. They may have talked politics, and even, as Calhoun suspected, agreed to fight it out on the old issues of the American System. Then, if ever, they came to an understanding on the subject of Texan annexation, but as to all this, no evidence has been found.[17]

Clay was far from happy in this comparative quiet, as his friends appreciated, though he bore up under "the affliction of retirement" better than they had expected. Excitement was necessary to keep up his spirits, and this was furnished

---

[15] Wright to Van Buren, April 2, 1842, Van Buren Papers.

[16] Lexington *Intelligencer,* April 19, April 22, May 3, May 6, 1842. Benton to Van Buren, April 14, 1842, Van Buren Papers.

[17] Lexington *Intelligencer,* April 26, April 29, May 6, May 24, May 27, 1842. Van Buren to Jackson, May 27, 1842, Van Buren Papers. Calhoun to Hunter, Jameson, *op. cit.,* pp. 548, 556, 564.

by a great barbecue given on June 9 at Lexington. It was
claimed that there were from three hundred to five hundred
carriages in the procession, while the crowd upon the grounds
was variously estimated at from fifteen to twenty-five thousand.
Of these two or three thousand were ladies, out of regard for
whom, as was usual at Whig meetings during this campaign,
no intoxicating liquors were allowed on the grounds. To this
vast audience Clay spoke for more than two hours, arraign-
ing Tyler and presenting the issues of the American System.[18]

The great anxiety of Clay's friends now was to keep him
from imprudent utterances. "He must hereafter remain a little
quiet, and *hold his jaw*," wrote the Rabelaisian Letcher. "In
fact he must be *caged*—that's the point—*cage* him. But he
swears by all the gods he will keep cool and stay at home. I
rather think he will be entirely prudent, tho' I have some occasional fears that he may write too many letters—still he is
quite a *handy man* with a pen, and all his letters have some
good reading in them." "I hope the speech he made at Lexington will prove *his last speech*," wrote Judge Alexander Porter
of Louisiana. Fifteen months later, a North Carolina Whig
protested, "If he would let himself alone, we should have less
trouble in electing him. He and Scott are both too fond of
their own epistolary style— . . . If St. Paul had been a
candidate for the Presidency, I should have advised him to
cut the Corinthians and not to let the Hebrews even see his
autograph."[19]

Nevertheless, Clay did not stick to his promise to stay at
home, and the Lexington speech was not his last. On September 29, he was present at a great barbecue at Dayton, Ohio,
accompanied by Crittenden, Governor Morehead and others.
The distinguished gentlemen had addressed a great crowd at
Maysville en route, and now the speechmaking lasted from
one o'clock to sundown, Clay speaking for two hours. Six days

---

[18] Lexington *Intelligencer*, June 10, June 24, 1842. Letcher to Crittenden,
May 19, 1842, Crittenden Papers.

[19] Letcher to Crittenden, June 21, 1842; Porter to Crittenden, July 21,
1842, Crittenden Papers. E. W. Johnston to Mangum, September 14, 1842,
Mangum Papers.

later another great barbecue at Indianapolis gathered a crowd said to have numbered eighty thousand to listen to his eloquence. Here he attempted to conciliate the Democrats by complimenting Benton on "the contempt and disdain with which he treats John Tyler," and by exclaiming of Jackson, "God bless the old hero!—I wish him no harm and, although he has injured me much, I would not, if in my power, soil a hair of his venerable head." A sycophantic correspondent reported to Van Buren, however, that the meeting had done Clay and his party harm rather than good, for the people were surprised at the bitterness he showed, and disappointed at "his old, careworn and broken appearance." According to this same gentleman, Clay's exclusive manners gave great offense to the democratic Hoosiers. At Indianapolis, they criticised him for dining in private with Governor Noble. At Madison, "the middling class of the Whig party" insisted on his going to a public house where all could meet him, and when he went instead to the home of a Congressman, after he had retired, "the disappointed masses revenged themselves by hooting and breaking the windows."[20]

At Richmond, Indiana, at the close of his speech, a Quaker named Mendenhall presented a petition praying him to emancipate his slaves. Clay's reply is published in his collected speeches as his official pronouncement on abolition, but as published cannot be more than a small portion of what he actually said. "We have not time to give even an outline of the answer of Mr. Clay," said the local newspaper, the Wayne County *Record.*

It was severe, yet courteous—gentlemanly and even mild yet withering as the scorching heat of the vertical sun. . . . Mr. Clay remarked that his [slaves] were as well shod, as well clad, as sleek and as fat, and pointing a finger significantly at the subject of his address, he believed they were as honest as him [sic], or any of his associates in the petition. After speaking about half an hour to Mr.

---

[20] Lexington *Intelligencer,* September 24, September 27, September 30, October 7, October 11, October 14, 1842. Columbia *Patriot,* November 11, 1842 (Indianapolis speech). Nathaniel West to Van Buren, October 12, 1842, Van Buren Papers.

Mendenhall, . . . in conclusion Mr. Clay invited him to go home, and attend to his own business . . . and if he had any means to spare, . . . to bestow them on the poor in his own neighborhood.[21]

By the middle of October, Clay had again "returned to the quiet and peaceful shades of Ashland," with his health much improved by his travels. Two weeks later he attended a great barbecue and "convention" at Frankfort, where he spoke for three quarters of an hour in response to a presidential nomination by the Whigs of his own state. A flow of eloquence from a dozen other speakers made up for the brevity of the candidate's remarks and the lack of alcoholic stimulants.[22]

Late in November Clay started for New Orleans, with some thought of proceeding to Cuba, ostensibly on business, but probably for the sake of his health as well. He spoke from the deck at Evansville, where nearly the whole population greeted him from the wharf. He was greeted by the mayor at Memphis, and escorted by the "Blues" to the hotel, where he held a three hour reception. Notice of his approach to Natchez, where he remained several days, was given by the firing of cannon, and he was honored by another military escort, a formal reception, and a ball, but he declined an invitation to a barbecue. At Vicksburg he was entertained in similar fashion.[23]

Clay's reception at New Orleans befitted the wealth and Whiggery of the southwestern metropolis. A deputation and an escort of five steamers bearing hundreds of citizens met him at Lafayette. As the fleet swept down the river, where the shipping was decorated and the wharves lined by huge crowds, salutes were fired from nearly all the vessels, including two of seventeen guns from two Texan warships. On approaching the city, he was greeted by a salute of a hundred guns from the Place d'Armes and the Poydras Street Wharf. Having passed the city and returned, he landed at that wharf, where waited the usual reception committee with its speeches of

---

[21] Lexington *Intelligencer,* October 11, 1842. The report of Clay's speech at Dayton also was censored; cf. Alphonso Taft to Webster, April 7, 1843, Webster Papers.

[22] *Ibid.,* October 14, October 28, 1842.

[23] *Ibid.,* November 25, December 2, December 6, December 13, December 20, 1842. Clay to Crittenden, January 14, 1843, Crittenden Papers.

welcome. He was then escorted to his stopping place, the home of Dr. Mercer, by a great procession headed by the Louisiana Legion and including civic dignitaries, foreign counsuls, fire engines, and all the state officers except the governor. It was said that the crowd which greeted him was the largest ever assembled in New Orleans at one time. That evening the New England Society gave a dinner in his honor at the St. Charles Exchange.[24]

Early in February he made a visit to Mobile, and on the sixteenth began a leisurely journey home, where he arrived on March 6. On the way he visited the Louisiana State Fair at Baton Rouge, and stopped at Vicksburg and Memphis, besides making a side trip to Jackson, Mississippi. Corwin saw him in New Orleans, travelled a hundred miles with him, talked politics, and reported to Ewing that the sugar men were all Whigs, but the cotton men were not so sure. Clay himself wrote to Crittenden and Clayton that the papers had not exaggerated the enthusiasm of his reception everywhere and that a confident spirit prevailed among the Whigs. But Van Buren was informed, regarding his visit to Mobile, that "The Whigs tried hard to make him the big man, but he can do no good for himself in Alabama."[25]

Clay's health was said to have been much improved by his sojourn in the south, and on April 10 he addressed the citizens of Lexington in vindication of the Whig party and in response to recent criticisms of his own political course. He was in reality replying to Thomas F. Marshall, recently Congressman from the district, who had gone over to the Democrats. A projected visit to Missouri was cancelled on the plea of private and professional engagements, and the candidate remained quietly in the vicinity of Lexington during the summer and autumn, playing the rôle of retired statesman. However, be-

[24] Lexington *Intelligencer,* January 3, January 6, 1843. *Missouri Statesman,* January 13, 1843.
[25] Lexington *Intelligencer,* February 21, February 28, March 3, March 7, March 10, March 14, 1843. *Missouri Statesman,* February 24, April 14, May 5, 1843. Corwin to Ewing, April 1, 1843, Ewing Papers. Clay to Crittenden, January 14, 1843, Crittenden Papers. Clay to Clayton, April 14, 1843, Clayton Papers. Wm. R. Hallett to Van Buren, February 16, 1843, Van Buren Papers.

tween July and November he wrote six letters designed for publication.[26]

Private affairs, indeed, were sufficient to absorb much of Clay's interest at this time. During the intervals of these political excursions, he devoted himself to agriculture at Ashland, preparing for an extensive venture in hemp-growing. In the closing months of 1842, his son Thomas failed for $50,000, Clay himself being creditor for half the amount. He gave preference to the other creditors, and so lost most of his money. A son-in-law in New Orleans was also in difficulties, again deeply involving Clay, which was one reason for his southern trip. These embarrassments doubtless had a good deal to do with his resumption of law-practice in the spring of 1843, though he wrote Clayton that it was to assist his son James, and also to be at his office in Lexington, "more accessible to perfect strangers who might be prompted by mere curiosity" to see him than he could be at Ashland. From some of his financial embarrassments he was thought to have been relieved by a generous bequest from Judge Porter of Louisiana, but it was later authoritatively stated that he had been left only his friend's diamond breast-pin.[27]

Two days before Christmas, Clay again arrived at New Orleans, remaining some two months, with occasional brief visits to Natchez and several places in the interior of Louisiana. Much of his time, however, was spent in the St. Charles Hotel wearing "that old snuff-colored surtout with the greasy collar" and "playing the 'farmer' to perfection." The material upon which he was working was, of course, the thousands of people from all the states trading on the Mississippi River, many of them men of fortune and influence, who thronged New Orleans during the business season.[28]

---

[26] *Observer and Reporter,* September 23, October 25, December 2, 1843. *Missouri Statesman,* April 29, 1843.

[27] Lexington *Intelligencer,* March 7, March 13, April 11, 1843. McCalla to Van Buren, January 11, 1843, Van Buren Papers. Clay to Clayton, August 8, 1842; April 14, May 27, 1843; Clayton Papers. Letcher to Crittenden, February 4, 1844, Crittenden Papers. *Missouri Statesman,* February 23, March 8, 1844. *Observer and Reporter,* March 2, 1844.

[28] *Observer and Reporter,* December 12, December 16, 1843; January 10, February 10, 1844. *Missouri Statesman,* February 10, March 22, 1844. J. Bragg to Van Buren, February 4, 1844, Van Buren Papers.

After a visit in Mobile, where a ball with eight hundred guests was given in his honor, he proceeded by way of Montgomery to Columbus, Georgia, where the Whigs staged a three-day demonstration in his honor. The Whig press reported that he was "received with the liveliest enthusiasm," but Forsyth reported to Van Buren that "as a popular demonstration, the whole affair was a failure, scarcely denied by Mr. Clay's friends." Thence, by way of Macon and Milledgeville, he proceeded to Savannah. Here he was greeted by a salute of twenty-six guns, and three thousand citizens on horseback escorted him into the city and to his lodgings at Senator Berrien's, where the reception committee was elaborately entertained that evening. The next day at noon, he spoke from the balcony of the Pulaski House. Devoting most of his speech to the Bank, he defended himself from the charge of inconsistency, rather hedged on the tariff, and strenuously denied that he was on an electioneering tour.[29]

He then proceeded by way of Augusta to Columbia, where he was for several days the guest of Preston, now president of the College of South Carolina. Accompanied by Preston and Wade Hampton, he reached Charleston on April 6, where he was received with salutes and escorted by a procession through decorated streets to the theater. He spoke for two hours, again denying that he was on an electioneering tour —he was just a plain farmer. He denied that the tariff of 1842 violated the principle of the Compromise Act of 1833, and urged a middle ground between free trade and prohibition, with concession to all interests. He insisted on a bank.[30]

Clay arrived at Raleigh April 12 at six o'clock. The city was illuminated in his honor, while the thousands who had come to hear him were camped in the suburbs. He was the guest of Governor Morehead, and on Saturday spoke from a platform at the Capitol. It was estimated that from ten to fifteen thousand Whigs were at Raleigh. He departed on the following Thursday, arriving that night at Petersburg, Vir-

[29] *Observer and Reporter,* March 13, March 16, March 27, April 3, April 10, 1844. *Missouri Statesman,* April 5, April 26, April 12, 1844. Berrien to G. W. Crawford, February 6, 1844, Berrien Papers. Forsyth to Van Buren, April 18, 1844, Van Buren Papers.

[30] *Observer and Reporter,* April 4, April 13, April 20, 1844.

ginia. Here he remained until late Saturday afternoon.
Thursday night he was tendered a handsome reception; Friday
he spoke at a barbecue which was followed by another reception and a gala performance at the theater. On Saturday he
saw the town and called on various citizens until the departure
of his boat for Norfolk. Being detained by fog, he did not
reach that city until Sunday morning, when he went to the
residence of Colonel Meyers and then attended church. The
end of the week found him in Washington.[31]

On Saturday morning the "Raleigh Letter" appeared in the
National Intelligencer, and that evening Van Buren's letter on
Texas appeared in the *Globe*. The following Wednesday Clay
was unanimously nominated for the presidency by the Whig
National Convention meeting at Baltimore. The three-years'
campaign had reached a triumphant consummation; as never
before, Clay stood forth as the unquestioned leader of a great
national party.

---

[31] *Ibid.,* April 24, 27, 1844.

CHAPTER IX

THE LONE STAR

To EVALUATE Clay's attitude on the annexation issue, it is essential to understand the relations of Kentucky, and its Whig leaders in particular, with the Lone Star Republic. Those relations had long been both intimate and sympathetic. The sympathy which Americans of that generation, and especially Westerners, felt for any people striving for independence, the special interest in the disintegrating colonial empire of Spain aroused by Clay's eloquent advocacy of the cause of the nascent republics erected on its ruins, sympathy for the peculiar grievances of the Texans—all contributed to their lively sentiments of friendship for Texas and hostility to Mexico. Most potent of all, however, was the presence of many of their own neighbors and friends, for hardly a county in Kentucky had failed to contribute settlers to Texas. This connection had combined with love of adventure to draw additional contingents during the Texan War of Independence, so that when annexation was proposed, it meant to Kentuckians merely reunion with a people whom they considered bone of their bone and flesh of their flesh.[1]

Crowded as were the news columns of the Kentucky press, they always had room for Texas items, even to devoting over a column to a summary, with extracts, of President Lamar's annual message of 1841. In the same issue with this, appeared another news item and an editorial expression of sympathy. Four weeks later, the same paper published a letter from Governor Boggs of Missouri to General Leslie Combs, telling of the failure of the Texan Santa Fé expedition and the capture of Combs's seventeen-year-old son, together with a

---

[1] D. H. Lewis to Calhoun, April 6, 1844, Jameson, *op. cit.*, pp. 935-38. Memucan Hunt to Mangum, March 27, 1844, Mangum Papers. *Observer and Reporter*, July 6, 1840. Stephen F. Austin, *An Address . . . Louisville, Kentucky, . . . 1836*, p. 1. The prompt publication of this address at Lexington is itself evidence of the intensity of local interest. For access to this extremely rare first edition, I am indebted to Dr. Alex. Dienst of Temple, Texas.

number of other Americans. From that time forward its columns overflowed with reports of the condition of the prisoners, denunciations of Santa Anna, and with letters from General Combs and the officials at Washington until the boy was released—because of his family and youth, as Santa Anna took care to anonunce—and in due time arrived in Lexington. Shortly thereafter it gave space to Franklin Combs's "Narrative," all the while continuing to clamor for the release of the other prisoners, even if armed intervention were necessary to effect it. The Tyler Administration was continually attacked as supine in its attitude. This paper was Clay's Lexington organ, and his Louisville organ, the *Journal*, joined in the demands. Later, for over a year, it ran as a serial Kendall's narrative of the expedition.[2]

When news was received of Vasquez's raid on San Antonio, the *Intelligencer* published the letters in an extra, a most unusual practice for those days. It was contained in a letter from Joseph Eve, the American charge d'affaires in Texas, a Kentuckian and intimate correspondent of Crittenden's, bringing tidings to friends in Kentucky of some of those who had gone to the front. Another letter, unsigned, concluded with an appeal from Albert Sidney Johnston, another Kentuckian then in the Texan military service, for aid from Kentucky. This last was reprinted in the first regular issue, and the *Intelligencer* reinforced Johnston's appeal by a vigorous editorial. "Whatever defeat and disaster may befall the gallant Texans in the onset," it declared,

we have no fears of the ultimate issue. They are fighting the battles of liberty, against a set of mercenary barbarians, and the God of battles will be with them and lead them on to victory. Nor will they need friends to aid them in their struggle for independence! Their brethren in this country will not stand idly by and see their fair land again reduced to Mexican subjugation. The valley of the Mississippi will send forth its hundreds and thousands, if need be, to aid their friends and their kindred in the young Republic . . . , and the wrongs which have been heaped upon their own countrymen, and the cruel indignities which American citizens are

---

[2] Lexington *Intelligencer*, December 3, 1841; December 31, 1841—March 29, 1842, *passim*.

now suffering in the Mexican capital will nerve their arms to deeds of valor, which will strike terrors into the cowardly hearts of the hireling soldiery of the miscreant who owes his life to the magnanimity of the gallant Texans.[3]

Two months earlier, General Combs had written from Galveston: "If Santa Anna gets possession of the Gulf, he will invade Texas by land and sea; and at the same time let loose the hordes of Indians upon the frontiers. Will Kentucky and her Western Sisters remain idle and inactive, while the women and children of *their youngest sister* are butchered by these modern Algerines, and her cities sacked, and her fields desolated? I cannot believe it."[4] Hearty, then, was the support which the Clay press gave to Texan agents who arrived in Kentucky in June and who were authorized to receive "any number of emigrants, armed and equipped for the service"— the invasion of Mexico. These recruits were to be sent in companies of not less than fifty-six, the Texan government engaging to confirm all their selections of officers. Contributions were sought to arm, provision, and transport them to New Orleans, beyond which transportation could be furnished by the government. These agents held meetings in Lexington, Georgetown, and elsewhere, prominent Whigs giving hearty support. Thus there can be no doubt that the Kentucky Whigs ardently sympathized with the Texans, whom they thought to be only temporarily separated from the United States.[5]

"The appetite for Texas was from the first a Western passion stimulated by no one more greedily than by Henry Clay. He had denounced the Florida Treaty for fixing the boundary at the Sabine, and held and preached the doctrine that we should have insisted upon our shadow of a claim to the Rio del Norte." So wrote John Quincy Adams in March, 1843, though he was convinced that the annexation movement then under way was a Southern conspiracy for the extension of slavery. It was Clay who, in 1836, reported from the Com-

[3] *Ibid.*, March 29, 1842.
[4] *Ibid.*, February 18, 1842; the italics are mine. Cf. also editorial of October 14, 1842.
[5] *Ibid.*, April 12, June 3, June 10, June 17, June 28, 1842.

mittee on Foreign Relations the resolution which authorized recognition of Texan independence. When the annexation question came to the front in 1837, the Texan representatives in Washington placed strong reliance on Clay's favorable attitude. On the eve of the adjournment of Congress, he sought to raise the question of American claims against Mexico, and they believed that he would take the lead for annexation should the Van Buren Administration hold back. "I cannot doubt that *he* is with us," wrote Grayson in October. Three months later, Hunt reported that, "In the course of a confidential conversation, which I had with Mr. Clay, a few days since, he assured me that he was friendly to the annexation of Texas, but that in his opinion, the time had not arrived when the question could be taken up in Congress with any probability of success."[6]

The exigencies of politics prevented annexation at that time, but Clay repeatedly found occasion to serve the interests of the Texan republic. When a commission was sent to England to borrow money, in 1839, Clay gave one of its members, Albert T. Burnley, letters of introduction to his relative, Sir Henry Clay, which secured him access to parliament and other public places, to Lord Ashburton, and to certain bankers. These letters placed him at once on a favorable footing with these influential men and gained for Texas a fair hearing as to credit consideration. In April, 1842, the Texan chargé d'affaires was seeking to verify certain rumors that Great Britain was furnishing Mexico with money and supplies for the subjugation of Texas. Clay had a personal interview with Lord Ashburton, then in Washington on a special mission, and with the resident minister, Fox, with both of whom he was on terms of intimacy. They spoke without restraint and with great apparent candor during the interview, and at its conclusion Clay immediately repeated their conversation to the Texan minister. As a result, the Texan government was

---

[6] Adams, *op. cit.*, XI, 348-49. *Congressional Globe*, 24th Cong., 1st Sess., pp. 453, 479, 486. Hunt to Irion, October 21, 1837; Grayson to Houston, October 21, 1837; Hunt to Irion, January 31, 1838; G. P. Garrison, ed., *Diplomatic Correspondence of the Republic of Texas* (3 vols. *American Historical Association, Annual Report, 1907-08:* 1907, vol. II, 1908, vol. II, pts. 1-2), I, 264-67, 287.

enabled to make a general and authentic denial of the rumors, which were doing much harm.[7]

Crittenden was quite as intimate as Clay with the Texan agents at Washington, frequently securing information for them and rendering other friendly offices with the American government. They were especially gratified by the appointment of his friend and fellow-Kentuckian, Joseph Eve, to the Texas mission. Eve made no secret of his personal desire that the United States should intervene to compel Mexico to make peace, and Sam Houston appealed to him as a friend for confidential information as to American sentiment toward annexation. Burnley also was one of Crittenden's intimate correspondents. But Crittenden had also a personal stake in Texas, for in 1842 his son George and other members of the Crittenden family were settled there. Early in 1843, George Crittenden was taken prisoner with the ill-fated Mier expedition and his father of course exerted all his influence to secure his release, or at least to ameliorate his imprisonment. At Lechter's request, Webster directed the American minister, Waddy Thompson, to do all that he could, unofficially, in his behalf, and Almonte, the Mexican minister at Washington, requested Santa Anna to release him. In January, 1844, when the annexation treaty was actually in train, Van Zandt, the Texan minister, specifically listed Crittenden and his colleague, Morehead, as ready to "support it beyond doubt."[8]

The capture of young Franklin Combs, of which mention has been made, took his father to Galveston to work for his release. Thence the "Kentucky Rifle" addressed fiery communications to the press, urging American intervention to force Mexico to make peace. But he also wrote a confidential letter to President Tyler, enclosing a Texan tariff which, as he pointed out, would adversely affect Ohio, Illinois, Indiana,

---

[7] Burnley to Clay, January 10, 1840; Crittenden to Burley, June 11, 1842; Crittenden Papers. Reily to Jones, April 14, 1842. Garrison, *op. cit.*, I, 552-53.

[8] Lexington *Intelligencer*, March 29, 1842; May 9, May 12, 1843. Houston to Eve, February 17, 1843; Eve to Jones, June 10, 1843; Garrison, *op. cit.*, II, 128, 190, 241. Eve to Crittenden, September 16, 1842; Crittenden to Mrs. Crittenden, February 5, 1843; Webster to Thompson, February 7, 1843; Crittenden to Letcher, February 24, 1843; Crittenden Papers.

Maine, New York and Massachusetts. But, he insisted, Texas was not to be blamed for this, since her petitions to Mexico for peace and to the United States for annexation had alike been spurned. She had at last turned to Great Britain and Belgium for loans, and Combs urged annexation before British influence was established. "I should be gratified," he concluded, "to have a hearing at Washington on this subject—I could make my views palpable to the touch of the most obtuse."[9]

By 1843, it had become evident that only an extension of either British or American influence in Texas could end the useless ravages of Mexican raids. Deep hostility toward Great Britain was traditional in Kentucky from the Revolution and the War of 1812. Therefore the press voiced bitter opposition to British intervention in Texas. Thus an additional ground was given for assuming that neither the Whig rank and file in Kentucky nor the Clay group of leaders would be averse to annexation. That consideration must have carried great weight in Tyler's mind when he contemplated raising the question of annexing Texas, whether his real motive was glory to himself or embarrassment to Clay. These anticipations, however, were rudely disappointed by Clay, who declared war on Tyler's annexation policy and sought to dispose of it before the formal opening of the presidential canvass. In this he signally failed, for he had incorrectly appraised the forces already aligned for annexation or ready to fall in with it. Thus he found himself committed to an opposition which agreed with the sentiments of neither himself, his chief lieutenants, nor his immediate constituency, and forced by consistency to take up a compromise position which pleased no one.

One of Clay's errors was in ignoring the attitude of the Calhoun men on this issue. That statesman seemed so completely out of the presidential race that the Clay men confidently expected most of his followers to support Clay in preference to Van Buren. Calhoun and his lieutenants, however, saw only ruin for the cause of State rights in another race between Clay and Van Buren on the issues of the American System.

---

[9] Combs to Tyler, February 5, 1842, *Observer and Reporter*, July 24, 1844. Originally published in the Democratic *Kentucky Yeoman*, this letter caused Clay's supporters much embarrassment.

They believed that Van Buren and Clay had agreed to suppress other issues. To prevent this, they were determined to force to the front the slavery issue in some form, either directly, or indirectly through the Texas question. This would also further Calhoun's dream of splitting the Democrats as Tyler had split the Whigs, along sectional lines, by which Calhoun hoped to be put forward as the Southern candidate for the presidency, and to throw the election into the House of Representatives as in 1824. Obviously, this offered every facility for a coalition with the Tyler men, and would so defeat Clay's plan of suppressing the Texas issue.[10]

There is reason to believe that Tyler anticipated opposition to annexation from neither Clay nor Van Buren, nor did he intend originally to make it an issue in the presidential campaign. His idea appears to have been that annexation would reflect "glory" on his administration and restore the popularity he had lost by the bank vetoes. He also seems to have anticipated no Northern opposition except from the radical anti-slavery element, and arguments were advanced to placate that opposition. With these expectations, the first intimations of annexation were thrown out in the autumn of 1841. The abolitionists, taking instant alarm, began a militant opposition. The original design of clearing the road for annexation by securing Mexican recognition of Texan independence met diplomatic obstacles. Webster, realizing the explosive potentialities of the scheme, was glad to absorb himself in negotiations concerning the northeastern boundary, and in March, 1843, assured Adams that "it never could be effected by him or with his consent." Thus, instead of being disposed of a year or more before the presidential canvass, the question hung fire until it must either be abandoned or become an issue in the campaign.[11]

[10] Crittenden to Letcher, December 10, 1843, January 28, 1844; Letcher to Crittenden, December 18, 1843; Coleman, *op. cit.*, I, 210-12, 215-16. Calhoun to Hunter, September 12, December 22, 1843, February 1, 1844; Jameson, *op. cit.*, pp. 549, 556, 564. Practically all of Calhoun's correspondence during this period might be cited for the general plan. Cf. Stevenson to Van Buren, October 17, 1843, Van Buren Papers.

[11] Adams, *op. cit.*, XI, 345-47. The general account of the development of the annexation policy is based in the main on the encyclopedia mobilization of evidence in Justin Smith's *Annexation of Texas*. Smith's appraisal

In the meantime, however, the whole political situation had changed. The long session of the Twenty-seventh Congress had dragged to its belated close with constantly increasing exacerbation between the majority and the Executive. The Whigs had contemptuously rejected Tyler's "Exchequer" plan. The President, stubbornly interposing his veto, had forced them to stand by the distribution compromise of the special session and make the hard choice between distribution and protection. These quarrels had culminated in Adams's violent report and Tyler's protest, after which no hope of reconciliation remained. Tyler's only recourse, therefore, was the creation of a third party.

More acute politicians than Tyler, such as Calhoun and Wise, had long foreseen the inevitability of this step, and also that its logical basis was an alliance of the "Impracticables" and the Nullifiers. This alliance, however, was postponed by Tyler's preference for a coalition with the Webster Whigs, in spite of the distrust of Webster and his principles felt by Tyler's Virginia advisers. By the close of 1842, however, there could no longer be any doubt of the Whig abhorrence of Tyler. So far from Webster's bringing him support from New England, that section seemed to be on the point of abandoning its "god-like" statesman. Webster's own interest, therefore, required that he should not linger at the State Department, once the northeastern boundary was settled; to be the negotiator of Texan annexation would manifestly be his complete ruin. At the same time, to remain in his position in order to obstruct Tyler's darling project would be unbecoming, in view of the President's past confidence and support. The withdrawal of Webster from the Cabinet cleared the way for the consolidation of the Southern bloc.

Tyler still hesitated to throw himself into the arms of Calhoun, but Wise audaciously took advantage of the "Peacemaker" catastrophe to force the coalition upon him. First tendering the State Department to Calhoun through McDuffie, as though by authority, he then wrested approval of his

---

of public opinion, however, neglects the press of the Ohio Valley. J. S. Reeves, *American Diplomacy under Tyler and Polk* also yielded valuable suggestions.

course from the unnerved President. Confirmed by the Senate without hesitation, Calhoun assumed office for the express purpose of consummating annexation. Two weeks after his arrival in Washington, the treaty was signed; ten days later, it was sent to the Senate.[12]

In the meantime, however, the new Secretary of State took a step which was scarcely compatible with a sincere expectation or even desire that the treaty should be ratified. On April 18, 1844, Calhoun addressed a note to Pakenham, the British minister in Washington, designed to initiate a general debate with the British Government on slavery. Pakenham did not accept the challenge, but Calhoun's letter, sent to the Senate before a reply was received, gave ample ground for an inference that the chief reason for the annexation of Texas was the preservation of slavery.[13]

Unless Andrew Jackson's judgment that the action was due to lack of "good common sense" be accepted, the most reasonable explanations all point to the consolidation of a Southern sectional bloc under the leadership of Calhoun. Intimations of Clay's opposition to immediate annexation had already leaked out and threatened to draw off the Southern Whig Senators whose votes were essential to ratification. By injecting the slavery issue without disguise, these votes might be whipped into line. Blair believed that the letter was written expressly to force Van Buren to come out against annexation. Clay thought the whole question had been brought up entirely for the purpose of disrupting the Whig Party. If such a sectional bloc could be formed, a Southern candidate, either Calhoun or Tyler, might be one of three before the House of Representatives. To the Calhoun clique, the situation of 1824 had become almost an obsession, either from sheer inability to grasp the idea of national political organization as developed by Jackson, Van Buren and Clay, or from the realization that only thus could a minority group hope to gain control of the government. Their positive and negative views admitted of no

[12] H. A. Wise, *op. cit.*, pp. 220-25.

[13] The Pakenham letter is exhaustively discussed by Smith, *op. cit.*, pp. 199-220. Reeves, *op. cit.*, pp. 150-55, probably under the influence of Von Holst, interprets Calhoun here as a slave to his logic. That is, he agrees substantially with Jackson.

compromise, while the national parties were built up on the principle of mutual concession. Therefore, the last hope of these inflexible doctrinaires lay in the disruption of the national parties. Their belief in the disruptive potentialities of Texan annexation was justified by the event.

The annexation issue definitely came to the surface in the autumn of 1843. The ground had been well prepared, however. In the preceding winter, Gilmer had written a letter on the subject, which had appeared in the newspapers and been used to draw from Jackson the letter destined to destroy Van Buren with the Southwestern Democracy. Early in the fall, also, *The Madisonian* began to publish bellicose editorials on alleged British intrigues in Texas. These were thought to have emanated from the pen of Upshur. As early as September, John Letcher warned Van Buren of the Jackson letter and of the plan of the Calhounites to defeat Van Buren and stampede the convention to Calhoun by that means. Early in October the game became apparent to Van Buren's friends in Virginia, and they ascertained that Tyler might be induced to bring the matter before Congress. Both Stevenson and Roane warned Van Buren of it, at the same time fishing for a statement of his position. "One thing is certain," wrote the former, "they will not let you remain quiet on the matter, & you will be forced to face the public."[14]

Meanwhile *The Madisonian* kept up its agitation while the *National Intelligencer* was again attempting to ignore Tyler's opinions and intention. Although there were rumors, early in November, of dissension in the Cabinet over a proposition to include in the annual message a recommendation of annexation, at the end of the month and so late as December 9, after the message had actually been sent to Congress, Cave Johnson made no mention of Texas in his reports to Polk. That same day, however, A. V. Brown confidentially warned Polk of the gravity of the issue. The message, he believed, was to be followed by a definite proposition, probably a treaty. The Whigs

---

[14] Letcher to Van Buren, September 23, 1843; Stevenson to Van Buren, October 3, 1843; Roane to Van Buren, October 17, 1843, Van Buren Papers. Scott to Crittenden, October 14, 1843, Coleman, *op. cit.*, I, 203-4; in the Crittenden Papers, undated, but really earlier, being alluded to in a letter of that date.

were mistaken in thinking that Tyler had said all he had to
say and had brought up the question only to make trouble.
They thought the question would die away if both parties
ignored it, but Brown urged that neither the Whig nor Democratic press of the Southwest should commit themselves against
annexation.[15]

Meanwhile, on November 29, Crittenden had warned Clay
of Tyler's forthcoming pronouncement on Texas and the possibility of a recommendation of annexation. It is a fair assumption that in this letter he expressed the views ascribed to the
Whigs by Brown, for those views are strikingly echoed in the
opening paragraph of Clay's reply, and except on that assumption it is hard to understand why Clay took the stand he did.
Clay replied hastily and in considerable excitement on December 5, sending off his rough draft just as he had dictated it
to his son.[16]

Clay wrote that he had received an inquiry from the editor
of an abolition paper in New York, to which he had returned no answer. Not that he was unwilling to announce his
opinion, but he did not think it right unnecessarily to present
new questions to the public. Those already before it were sufficiently important and numerous without adding fresh ones.
Nor did he think it right to allow Mr. Tyler, for his own
selfish purposes, to introduce an exciting topic to add to the
other subjects of contention which existed in the country. Since
Mexico asserted title to Texas, it could not be annexed without a war with Mexico, and nobody would think such a war
wise or proper. We had acknowledged the independence of
Texas, as we had a right to do for the sake of commercial and
other intercourse, "but that acknowledgment did not extinguish
or in any manner affect the rights of Mexico upon Texas."
The House of Representatives could do nothing prior to the
exercise of the treaty-making power by the President and the
Senate; and an annexation treaty could not secure a constitutional majority in the Senate. "Why, then, present the ques-

---

[15] Johnson to Polk, November 28, December 9, 1843; Brown to Polk,
December 9, 1843; Polk Papers. *Observer and Reporter,* November 15,
November 18, 1843.

[16] Coleman, *op. cit.,* I, 207-10.

tion?" It was manifestly "for no other than the wicked purpose of producing discord and distraction in the nation."

Taking this view of the matter, Clay thought that if Tyler should make such a recommendation, it would be best to pass it over, if possible, "in absolute silence." As for his reasons, first, the territory of the United States was already large enough. Secondly, for reasons already stated, it would be impracticable to accomplish annexation. Thirdly, "if Texas were annexed to the United States, the motive with those who are urging it would not be fulfilled. It would not now or ever give to the slaveholding section of the Union a preponderating weight. The other portion would continue to retain the ascendency, which would be ultimately increased by the annexation of Canada, to which there could be no objection if Texas were admitted into the Union."

Because of the examples of Florida and Louisiana, he would not dwell upon the very doubtful constitutionality of the admission of Texas. He would "regret very much, should the proposition come to a formal question, if the Whig party should, in a *body*, vote in the affirmative. Such a vote would be utterly destructive of it, without the possibility of securing Texas." Texas was destined to be settled by our race, would have our language and institutions, and would be a good neighbor. He thought there was no foundation for the fear that Great Britain had colonial designs in Texas, for it would excite the hostility of the European powers as well as the United States.

Clay thus advised three alternative courses of action: ignore the question, if possible; if this were not possible, dodge it; and, as a last resort, vote against it. When George Bancroft got wind of this letter, he at once reported it to Van Buren with the comment that it meant "Let me humbug the Northern abolitionists and then humor the South." In January, 1844, Van Zandt, the Texan minister at Washington, wrote that Crittenden, Morehead, Archer and Mangum desired to postpone the annexation question "in order that Mr. Clay may have the credit of effecting it," in the probable event of his election. They were, of course, following Clay's instructions in this, but Van Zandt also thought that they would "beyond doubt" support the treaty if it were then made. In June, on hearing of the defeat of the treaty, Preston wrote to Crittenden, "I am glad . . . and when Clay is in and Mexico consents, the matter can be renewed." This was from a man who had been in Clay's society for a week, scarcely ten days before he wrote his Raleigh letter. But indeed, before reaching South Carolina, Clay had determined on his course and so informed the Georgia politicians with whom he talked, some of whom advised against it. One of these was Alexander H. Stephens, who knew from conversations with him that he was really in favor of the admission of Texas, "if it could be done without endangering the Union," and who "believed that it would be a leading object of his Administration, if elected, to bring Texas in without violent agitation."[17]

Only by thus ascribing like Stephens the course adopted by Clay to "policy," and by recognizing with John Quincy Adams that the Raleigh letter merely pronounced against "annexation at this time,"[18] can we reduce all of Clay's Texas letters to that consistency dear to the politician and which in his final letter to Gales and Seaton he insisted that he had maintained throughout. Not merely do the five letters then become consistent with one another, but they also harmonize with Clay's earlier attitude toward Texas and with the long-cherished sentiments of his closest associates.

On December 9, the *Observer and Reporter*, which had now become Clay's Lexington organ, published a long editorial echoing the ideas of the letter of December 5, and on the fourteenth Clay departed on the tour which was to conclude with the publication of the Raleigh letter. The anti-Clay faction, however, did not submit to Clay's policy without a struggle. In the Kentucky legislature, Wickliffe of Nelson introduced resolutions approving the annexation of Texas. They received a favorable committee recommendation, and were tabled only by the close vote of fifty-three to fifty-eight after

[17] Bancroft to Van Buren, April 16, 1844, Van Buren Papers. Van Zandt to Jones, January 20, 1844, Garrison, *op. cit.*, II, 241. Preston to Crittenden, June 5, 1844, Crittenden Papers. M. L. Avery, ed., *Recollections of Alexander H. Stephens*, pp. 17-18.
[18] Avery, *op. cit.*; Adams, *op. cit.*, XII, 19.

a vigorous debate.[19] Although the Clay forces had won this first skirmish, Tyler now by a sudden stroke flanked them out of their advanced positions and set their backs to the wall—he presented an annexation treaty for ratification by the Senate. The question was no longer academic as Clay assumed, but highly practical and most alarmingly political.

Clay was at New Orleans disporting himself in his rôle of Kentucky farmer and courting the support of the planters there assembled, when news arrived from Texas which took him completely by surprise and which he could hardly believe—namely, that in some way it had been ascertained that forty-two Senators were in favor of the annexation of Texas, and had advised the President that they would vote for the ratification of a treaty to that effect, that negotiations had accordingly been started, and that a treaty would speedily be concluded. Clay's anxiety was pathetic. Relating to Crittenden this alarming intelligence, he besought him to write him at two points on his approaching journey and give him such information as he was at liberty to disclose. Especially alarmed was Clay by the reported attitude of the Senator, for, he wrote, "If it be true, I shall regret extremely that I have had no hint of it."[20]

It was March 25 when he again turned to this subject in his letters to Crittenden. "I received at Montgomery and Columbus both your letters relating to Texas, and I find that the subject is producing great excitement at Washington," he then wrote. "I have forborne hitherto to express my opinion with regard to it. I reserve for my arrival at Washington the consideration of the question whether it is not necessary to announce my opinions. I think I can treat the question very differently from any treatment I have yet seen of it, and so as to reconcile all our friends and many others to the views which I entertain. Of one thing you may be certain, that there is no such anxiety for the annexation here at the South as you might have imagined."[21]

This was written from Savannah. Clay then proceeded

---

[19] *Journal of the Kentucky House of Representatives, 1843-1844,* pp. 41, 371, 407-8.

[20] Clay to Crittenden, February 15, 1844, Crittenden Papers.

[21] Clay to Crittenden, March 24, 1844, Crittenden Papers.

through the Carolinas to Raleigh, where he wrote out and sent to Crittenden for publication the statement of his opinions. No evidence is available as to why he changed his mind about waiting until he reached Washington to do so. The letter was written the day before he left Raleigh for Petersburg, and he acted with the concurrence of three North Carolina leaders, Badger, Governor Morehead, and Stanly. He directed Crittenden to confer with Mangum, Berrien, Morehead of Kentucky, Alexander H. Stephens, and any other leaders he wished; and left to him the decision as to whether it should be published before or after his arrival in Washington. They were also authorized to make slight modifications in its phraseology.[22]

Two days later, from Petersburg, however, he wrote Crittenden a peremptory letter, insisting on its publication "not later than today or tomorrow week." Apparently feeling that Crittenden disapproved, he asserted complete confidence in the ground he had taken. He left to his friends merely the decision as to when the letter should appear; he could not consent to its suppression or unnecessary delay in publication. He thought public opinion everywhere sounder than at Washington. These ideas he repeated in more detail three days later from Norfolk, having meanwhile received a letter from Crittenden. He thought the Washington politicians much over-rated the favor of the South toward annexation. He advised the rejection of the treaty by the Senate, promptly, firmly, with dignity, and by a majority. Van Buren stood opposed, so they would occupy "common ground," and his present attitude made it necessary for Clay to break silence. If Van Buren changed his position, it would be "so much worse for him." The public mind was too fixed on the presidential question, the current "running too strong and impetuous to be now affected by Texas." Clay arrived in Washington on Friday, April 26, and the next morning his Raleigh letter appeared in the *National Intelligencer*. Crittenden had taken the extreme time limit set by Clay, and had even waited for his chief's arrival, to publish the momentous document.[23]

---

[22] Clay to Crittenden, April 17, 1844, Crittenden Papers.
[23] Clay to Crittenden, April 19, April 21, 1844, Crittenden Papers. Kendall to Van Buren, April 29, 1844, Van Buren Papers. Adams, *op. cit.*, XII, 19.

This very long statement rehearsed the ground of the letter of December 5, with such changes as the negotiation of the treaty necessitated. It also made the additional charge that speculators were lobbying in the interest of ratification. While carefully avoiding the pronouncement of any attitude of permanent opposition to annexation, it expressed decided opposition to immediate annexation. The whole argument is well summed up in a single sentence:

I consider the annexation of Texas, at this time, without the assent of Mexico, as a measure compromising the national character; involving us certainly in war with Mexico, probably with other foreign powers; dangerous to the integrity of the Union; inexpedient in the present financial condition of the country; and not called for by any general expression of public opinion.[24]

In that evening's *Globe* appeared Van Buren's letter, also taking ground against immediate annexation. This cast a damper on the high spirits of the Southern Democrats, who had been gleefully confident of riding rough-shod over Clay at the South.[25] Immediately there rose the cry of collusion, suspicion of which has never been dispelled. There can be no question but that each candidate believed that the other would take the ground he did, and that he could therefore safely publish his own opinion. Yet not only is it impossible to find definite evidence of agreement, but the circumstantial evidence supporting that view is at least balanced by other circumstantial evidence to the contrary.[26] But agreement or no agreement, the significant fact is that both believed that their letters would neutralize annexation as a party issue and definitely eliminate it from the presidential campaign.

[24] *Observer and Reporter,* May 8, 1844.

[25] Johnson to Polk, April 29, 1844, Polk Papers.

[26] The Van Buren Papers from December to April are full of letters bearing on the formulation of the "Hammett Letter" in which Van Buren stated his views. Those of Wright and Butler are most significant, and also deal with the abortive attempt of J. C. Spencer, Tyler's Secretary of War, to negotiate such an agreement. He was rebuffed by Van Buren's friends, and I have found no evidence that he even approached the Clay men.

CHAPTER X

THE EMBODIMENT OF WHIG PRINCIPLES

CLAY ENDED his Southern tour confident, if not elated. He believed that even the tariff had been made acceptable to the South by his presentation.[1] The publication of Van Buren's letter on Texas, taking ground identical with his own against immediate annexation, seemed to have extinguished the firebrand kindled by Tyler. Four days after the publication of the Raleigh letter, on May 1, the Whig convention in Baltimore unanimously nominated him by acclamation. The next day a "ratification convention" of "Young Whigs" confirmed the action of the national convention amid the greatest enthusiasm. Even Webster participated in the demonstration; the Whig party seemed united and confident as never before.[2]

The Raleigh letter, in view of Van Buren's stand, appears to have satisfied both the Northern and the Southern Whigs. Such of the former as were not opposed to annexation were happy to see Tyler's plans defeated, and could well afford to let the future take care of itself. The politicians were pleased that a check had been given to the growth of the Liberty party. The Southern Whigs were equally delighted to see "Captain Tyler headed" on this issue also, and took opposition to annexation "at this time" literally to mean "not just yet."[3]

By the end of May it was generally understood that there was practically no hope of ratification, and on June 8 the treaty was officially rejected. Yet still the question would not down as a political issue. Exactly a month after the publication of Clay's and Van Buren's letters on annexation, two other conventions met. One, composed mainly of federal officeholders, nominated President Tyler and adjourned. The other represented the "unterrified Democracy." The Democratic con-

---

[1] Clay to Crittenden, April 21, 1844, Crittenden Papers; B. W. Leigh to Mangum, April 22, 1844, Mangum Papers.

[2] *Missouri Statesman*, May 17, May 24, 1844, *Niles' Register*, LXVI, 146.

[3] *Observer and Reporter*, June 26, 1844, which is quoting Albany *Evening Journal*. Preston to Crittenden, May 4, June 5, 1844, Crittenden Papers.

vention, under Southern leadership and over the protests of Van Buren's representatives, adopted the two-thirds rule by a vote of 148 to 112. After seven ballots, with votes distributed among seven candidates, the convention turned from Van Buren and Cass, who had been leading, and nominated James K. Polk, who had been a candidate for the second place. The abandonment of Van Buren, the choice of "Young Hickory," and the platform declaration for the "re-annexation of Texas at the earliest practicable period," showed that in spite of the efforts of Clay and Van Buren, the issue raised by Tyler was to dominate the campaign.

In Kentucky, disaffected Whigs like the Wickliffes and Thomas F. Marshall were exploiting the Texas question to shake Clay's leadership and had ventured to raise the standard of revolt in Lexington itself. They attempted to identify Clay's opposition to annexation with abolitionism. In this they were aided by the imprudent utterances of Cassius M. Clay, who had constituted himself the champion of his famous, though distant, kinsman. Clay was forced eventually to repudiate this championship, thereby suffering considerably among the anti-slavery Whigs.[4]

The Kentucky Democrats early took strong ground for annexation and unhesitatingly abandoned Van Buren upon publication of his letters. With the nomination of Polk upon an annexation platform, they began to prosecute their campaign more vigorously than ever, reinforced by the disgruntled Whigs. "They have raised money, published pamphlets, and scattered them in the log cabin of every voter in the hills," declared the *Observer and Reporter*. "Their emissaries are traversing the State, . . . publishing the most unblushing lies gratis, leaving no means untried, to prejudice the uninformed against our cause. Regular electors, state candidates—stump orators of every grade—democrats, locofocos and apostate renegades from the Whig cause to Tylerism, have united their weakness in one common effort, and are moving Heaven, Earth, and *Texas*, to effect their unholy purposes." Abandoning principles and other issues, "Like the ass with the lion's skin, they have

---

[4] *Observer and Reporter,* March 30, April 3, April 6, May 15, June 1, September 4, October 9, 1844.

covered up the deformity of body and limb, ears and all, of
Locofocoism, with Texas."[5] The annexation issue was so over-
whelmingly popular in Kentucky as to offer hope of carrying
the state even against "Harry of the West" himself.

The tactics of the Whigs to meet this onslaught confirm
this view. Toward the end of March, the *Observer* asserted that
the Kentucky Whigs had thought of annexation as a future
and not as a present issue, and that they regarded Tyler's
procedure as high-handed, unauthorized, and unconstitutional.
It warned them against attempts to link opposition to annexation with abolitionism—slavery was guaranteed by the Constitution and not dependent on the annexation of Texas. It
claimed that Tyler and the Democrats had raised the question
to forestall the election of Clay, which was certain unless some
question was presented to spread discord in the Whig party.
This was clearly the purpose of the Texas question. But, it
said, the people desired no new issues. Early in April, it was
belittling the annexation meetings and urging those Whigs who
favored annexation to oppose it at this time, but the editor
thought that "as much unanimity in opposition to the annexation of Texas exists among them, and indeed more, than
could be expected upon such a question." In commenting on the
Raleigh letter, it declared that even those Whigs who favored
annexation objected to its introduction into the campaign,
preferring that it should "be presented at a time when the
public mind is less excited." Down to the first week of June,
it persisted in this course, anxious that the treaty should be disposed of as soon as possible in order to prevent any political
consequences. "There is scarcely a Whig who favors annexation," it declared, "who is not of the opinion that the time
selected by Mr. Tyler for the presentation of this question to
the Senate, is most unpropitious, and they are equally unanimous in the opinion that it would be far better to leave it to the
next Administration to settle this important question."[6]

After the nomination of Polk, however, the *Observer*, while
continuing to insist that the annexation of Texas had nothing

---

[5] *Observer and Reporter*, May 11, June 19, 1844. Kendall to Van Buren,
May 13, 1844, Van Buren Papers.

[6] *Observer and Reporter*, March 27, March 30, April 3, April 6, April 8,
June 12, June 26, 1844.

to do with slavery, took its cue from the New York *Evening Post* and began to insist that "annexation at the earliest practicable period" did not mean immediately. This was on June 12. But the issue could not thus be neutralized, so two weeks later the *Observer* published with approval a letter from New Orleans which said: "The feeling is gaining ground that enough has been said, and done upon the Texas annexation subject until Clay is elected. The subject then they [the Southern Whigs] expect will very soon be brought before the American people upon its merits, and will soon be disposed of as it should."[7]

In the issue of July 3, a whole page was devoted to a letter from George Robertson, the great Kentucky jurist of the period, on the subject of Texas, but the Chief Justice's exposition was far more political than legal. The agitation was denounced as premature, for it could lead only to war and to internal commotion. They should wait until Clay was president or the time more favorable, and not be rushed by the South Carolina Hotspurs and their Nashville Convention. "The destinies of many of my kindred and friends," he added, "are identified with those of Texas."

That same day, a great Whig mass meeting and barbecue was held at Lexington. Clay refused to appear on the grounds, but many Whigs called on him at Ashland. Ewing was present and Crittenden was the speaker of the day. Robertson presented the resolutions. The first endorsed Clay and Frelinghuysen; the second pledged the meeting to the principles they represented. The third was, "that the question of the annexation of Texas to the United States, *as lately gotten up*, is now agitated by designing politicians for the delusive purpose of diverting the people, at the approaching Presidential election, from a proper consideration of the radical and far more important domestic questions which should alone decide that momentous trial of popular virtue and intelligence." The fourth condemned Tyler's methods in negotiating the treaty, and the fifth approved its rejection as a sectional document. The sixth declared the Union as it was preferable to any other Union,

[7] *Observer and Reporter,* June 12, June 19, June 26, 1844.

the seventh repudiated the Nashville Convention, the eighth condemned the secession threats of South Carolina, and the ninth pledged support of the Union against all attempts at dismemberment.[8]

Two days before, Clay had written his first "Alabama Letter" to the editor of the Tuscaloosa *Monitor*. Although leading Whig journals of the "Cotton Kingdom" had given the Raleigh letter an interpretation not unfavorable to future annexation, the more definite promise of the Democrats was having its effect. Leading Whigs came out for immediate annexation, and late in June the Georgia Whig convention adopted resolutions introduced by Alexander H. Stephens definitely pronouncing in favor of future annexation. It is also clear, from the editorial policy of the *Observer and Reporter,* that only by the assertion that annexation was merely to be postponed were the Kentucky Whigs able to meet the onslaught of the Democrats. The Southern firebrands were even threatening to make the annexation issue a prelude to agitation for secession.[9] It was under these conditions that Clay wrote.

This letter was at once a patriotic and a politic document. While confessing that he had no personal objections to the annexation of Texas, an admission made much of by his opponents at the North, he in reality merely defined more clearly the position of the Raleigh letter. He was still trying to neutralize the annexation issue, just as in the preceding December. Then he sought to dispose of it as outside the range of immediate issues, now, because of the strenuous objection of a part of the Union, the North. His denunciation however was not devoted to the Northern extremists, but to those of the South, and since they would couple slavery with Texas, he in turn invoked the interests of slavery in the border states to defeat secession and maintain the Union. This letter of Clay's, often denounced as truckling to the South and a bid for votes, rings true to his real sentiments. So far from truckling to either section, it was a courageous and farsighted presenta-

---

[8] *Observer and Reporter,* July 6, 1844. The italics are mine.
[9] *Niles' Register,* LXVI, 224, 230, 313, 326, 404-6.

tion of the position of Kentucky, anticipating the dilemma in which she was placed by the Hotspurs sixteen years later. In it Clay also recognized what the Southern leaders failed to take into account in 1861, that any issue which could crystallize sectional sentiment in the South would do the same at the North, and that the South would face not a group of individual radicals but the whole section consolidated by danger to the Union.[10]

Therefore, in July, the rallying cry of the Kentucky Whigs once more became "The Union of the Whigs for the sake of the Union," while it was declared that the new issue presented by the Democrats was "Polk and Texas or Disunion." This was supported by numerous quotations from Hotspur resolutions. At the same time the Kentucky Whigs endeavored to prevent a complete breach with their brethren of the Lower South by showing that they might just as reasonably go for "Clay and Texas without disunion." Polk is for the annexation of Texas at "the earliest practicable period," said the *Observer*, "but when is 'the earliest practicable period?' It is, I suppose, when we can define the boundary of Texas, and obtain the consent of Mexico, which is precisely the ground taken by the Whigs, when first the subject was broached."[11]

At this juncture, the Frankfort *Kentucky Yeoman*, a rabid Democratic sheet, published Leslie Combs's letter to Tyler, written from Galveston in 1842, urging annexation. Coming from one of Clay's chief lieutenants, it could not but have great political effect, and Combs was forced to explain how he reconciled these views with support of Clay. "I am decidedly in favor of the measure," he wrote, "as one of great National importance whenever it can be accomplished consistently with the Constitution and national honor. . . . But what has the *immediate* or remote annexation of Texas, to do with the vital issues now dividing the American people into two great parties?" Those issues were the protection of American labor, the distribution of the proceeds of the public lands to the

---

[10] Clay to S. F. Miller, July 1, 1844, *Observer and Reporter*, August 7, 1844.

[11] *Observer and Reporter*, July 20, 1844.

states, a sound national currency, and the limitation of the executive power.[12]

Just a week after Combs made this rather lame attempt to explain his attitude, Clay wrote his second "Alabama Letter."[13] In this letter he frankly avowed that he had no personal objection to annexation—would even be glad to see it, could it be effected without the national dishonor, foreign war and domestic dissension involved in its immediate consummation. Slavery was a temporary institution which should not prevent a permanent acquisition, and should the question come before him in the event of his election, he would be governed by the state of facts and public opinion existing at that time, but above all by the paramount duty of preserving the Union.

This was again, when all allowances are made, a courageous pronouncement of a moderate position, and in consequence seriously open to attack by the extremists on both sides. For all its courage, moreover, the logic of the letter was not convincing. To declare that slavery and Texas had no legitimate connection was simply to refuse to recognize the fact that everyone who had any positive opinions on the subject did link the two issues. It was the growth of slavery that had created an opposition at the North which had not existed twenty years before; it was slavery which had whetted Southern desire for annexation. It was as a means of raising the slavery issue, by his own confession, that Calhoun had favored the injection of the annexation question into the campaign; and just as the raising of that issue was to the political advantage of Calhoun, in his geographical position, so it spelt political ruin to Clay, situated as he was in a state which was divided within itself on slavery. Just as Calhoun saw in the slavery issue a means of welding a Southern party which would enable him to emerge from his political isolation, so Clay saw in it the dissolution of the party to whose creation he had devoted his highest talents. Just as Calhoun saw in the formation of a Southern

---

[12] Combs to Tyler, February 5, 1842, March 19, 1844; same to Editor of Frankfort *Kentucky Yeoman,* July 20, 1844; *Observer and Reporter;* July 24, 1844.

[13] Clay to Thos. M. Peters and John M. Jackson, July 27, 1844, *Observer and Reporter,* August 28, 1844.

sectional party the first step toward the disruption of a Union which would not accept his leadership and which he believed no longer beneficial to his section, so Clay saw in it the failure of the nationalism which was the basis of his leadership and the ruin of the Union, love of which, he truly said, was the key to his whole political career.

The "Alabama Letters" were of prime influence on the campaign, seriously damaging the Whig cause at the North.[14] Yet when Kentuckians in general felt so warm an interest in Texas, Clay, whose power was based upon his perfect representativeness of his state and its people, must also have sympathized with these aspirations. To have been hostile to the annexation of Texas would have meant that he had become wholly separated in feelings from his own people and had approximated to the sentiments of New York.

Once more Clay spoke out on the annexation question, in a final letter addressed to the editors of the great national organ of his party.[15] "I wish now distinctly to say," he wrote,

that there is not a feeling, a sentiment, or an opinion expressed in my Raleigh letter to which I do not adhere. I am decidedly opposed to the immediate annexation of Texas to the United States. I think it would be dishonorable, might involve them in war, would be dangerous to the integrity and the harmony of the Union, and, if all these objections were removed, could not be effected, according to any information I possess, upon just and admissible conditions. It was not my intention, in either of the two letters which I addressed to Alabama, to express any contrary opinion. . . . In my first letter to Alabama, . . . I thought that my meaning was sufficiently obvious, that I had no personal, private, or individual motives for opposing, as I have none for espousing the measure, my judgment being altogether influenced by general and political considerations. . . . In my second letter to Alabama, assuming that the annexation of Texas might be accomplished without national dishonor, without war, with the general consent of the States of the Union, and upon fair and reasonable terms, I stated that I should be glad to see it. I did not suppose that it

---

[14] Weed to Granger, March 11, April 8, September 3, 1844, Granger Papers.

[15] Clay to Gales and Seaton, *Niles' Register,* September 23, 1844, LXVII, 74.

was possible I could be misunderstood. Nothing was further from my purpose than to intimate any change of opinion as long as any considerable and respectable portion of the confederacy should continue to stand out in opposition to the annexation of Texas. In all three of my letters upon the subject of Texas, I stated that annexation was inadmissible except upon fair and reasonable terms if every other objection were removed. . . .

Of course, the Democrats took advantage of Clay's repeated pronouncements to charge him with inconsistency. His letters were garbled, distorted, ridiculed in the manner customary in such circumstances. Yet for all that, they seem to have gone far to accomplish Clay's original purpose, the neutralization of the annexation issue, which, in the latter part of the campaign dropped into the background in those sections where annexation was most favored. Having shown that Clay's opposition was restricted to "immediate" annexation, it was not difficult to claim that annexation "at the earliest practicable period" also did not mean immediately. The *Observer* took advantage of a confidential circular of William Cullen Bryant and other anti-annexation Democrats, urging repudiation of the annexation issue, again to show that the two candidates were occupying practically identical ground. That was early in August, just before the Texas question was dropped to be replaced by other issues. Thus what was done in New York to reconcile anti-slavery men to Polk, was used in Kentucky to reconcile pro-slavery men to Clay. Having triumphantly squared the circle, the issue was treated as closed.[16]

The issues now stressed involved for the most part Clay's personal character and state politics. Not only on the annexation issue was Clay charged with inconsistency; even on the tariff he did not escape.

> " 'He wires in and wires out,
> And leaves the people still in doubt,
> Whether the snake that made the track
> Was going South, or coming back.'

How appropriately true the above lines are when applied to the course of Mr. Clay on the tariff," wrote a Missouri editor

---

[16] *Observer and Reporter,* August 3, 1844.

of Democratic faith; and he proved his point by two parallel columns of contradictory pronouncements alleged to have been culled from the letters and speeches of Henry Clay.[17]

The note struck by John Randolph eighteen years before in charging a "coalition between the Puritan and the blackleg" was repeated in tiresome iteration as the Democratic press compared Clay with his running-mate, the ultra-respectable Frelinghuysen of New Jersey. Duel and prayer-meeting, card-table and altar, slave-owner and abolitionist, so the points were made and elaborated in crude detail. These same lurid aspects of Clay's character and career were also made to do service for a similar comparison with his rival, the straight-laced Polk.

The Democratic candidate, they asseverated, was a man of irreproachable moral character; the gambling table had not seen him robbing his infatuated or half-intoxicated fellow-man of his money or property; the brothel had never resounded with the noise of his profligate mirth and obscene jest. Polk was not loaded down with the guilt of murder, meditated or accomplished; no widow and orphans, like those of Jonathan Cilley, wept the loss of a husband and father slain under his counsels. He had not been the first to provoke the violation of a law to prevent duelling, voted for by himself, nor had he been put under bonds to prevent his headlong passions rushing him into the penitentiary under that law. Polk had not violated constitutions and oaths of office by attempting to kill members of legislative bodies for words spoken in debate, as Clay had tried to kill Humphrey Marshall and John Randolph. Neither was he chargeable with the crime of violating the Constitution and his oath by acting in a legislative body with the perfect consciousness that he had not the constitutional qualifications, as did Clay in the Senate of the United States.

He had not, like Henry Clay, abused the frontier settlers as a "lawless rabble," no better than thieves, pirates and robbers, denying them the privilege of buying wilderness lands which they by hard work had made "to bloom as the rose," while willing to aid profligate debtors to wipe out all their debts by a bankrupt law. Neither had he refused to the poor

---

[17] Jefferson *Inquirer*, April 25, 1844.

Irishman or German, or other emigrant from the Old World, the privilege of making a lot of waste land valuable by his labor and buying it at the government price. He would not, like Clay, permit foreign bankers to purchase all the bank corporation stock in the country and become owners of a National Bank, to control the value of property and the wages of labor—to keep the moneys of the Treasurer, corrupt public men, and govern the government. Polk had none of Clay's haughty contempt for the laboring millions which would induce him to rank the laboring man below the Negro slave.

He had not, like Clay, when instructed by his constituents to give a vote for a president or for the repeal or passage of a law, set himself up as their master, haughtily answering, "I will not," and insulting them with imputations of "cruelty and inhumanity" for making the request. He had not gotten up a scheme to destroy a prominent rival, refused to make himself publicly responsible for matters which he was privately spreading far and wide to that rival's injury, been denounced and defied by him as an intriguer who dared not put his name to imputed slanders which he was not too honorable to propagate, and then, with a view to personal aggrandizement, rushed into the arms of that rival, as Clay did into those of Adams, and made common cause with him against old friends and in support of principles he had repudiated and denounced.[18]

Certain Pennsylvania and Ohio papers produced some original and highly curious charges. An extra sheet, in German, declared that Clay, if elected president, would hang all "Dutchmen" who offered to vote in elections. This was adorned with a wood-cut representing Clay hanging three "Dutchmen." Another asserted that he was in favor of the "Dutch" and Negroes intermarrying, and would, if elected, compel every "Dutchmen" to marry a black wife. A handbill contained a forged letter from Clay to the leader of the recent anti-Catholic riots in Philadelphia, congratulating him that a goodly number of churches had been burnt and regretting that all of them had not been demolished. It was further alleged that Clay had killed Jonathan Cilley and John Randolph with

---

[18] *Missouri Statesman*, August 2, 1844; Jefferson *Inquirer*, September 26, 1844.

his own hand, and that he once ran a foot race over the Washington race course for a purse of a thousand dollars.[19]

Such was the character of the attacks on Clay. The Whigs were not backward in the war of mudslinging; but Polk was a far less vulnerable target. He was protected by the comparative obscurity which gave point to the sneer of "Who is James K. Polk?" In the autumn a controversy raged for several weeks over Polk's grandfather: was he a Tory as the Whigs charged, or a signer of the "Mecklenburg Declaration of Independence," as the Democrats claimed? But the Democrats were easily entitled to a decision in this contest of scandal.

At last November came, and with it the bitterness of defeat for Clay. Having started out to neutralize the annexation issue, he refused to admit that he had failed in the attempt. He insisted that his defeat was due to "a most extraordinary combination of adverse circumstances." If there had been no native party, or if all its members had been truer to its own principles, or if the recent foreigners had not been all united against him, or if the foreign Catholics had not been arrayed on the other side, or if the Abolitionists had been true to their avowed principles, or if there had been no frauds, he declared he would have triumphed. Leslie Combs, however, insisted that "the Texas question was the *only one* made and openly advocated everywhere, by the Locofocos, and upon it all our losses in the South and West occurred." The Whigs, he said, had "opposed Tyler's treaty mainly because of its secrecy and the people's ignorance of its negotiation. But the people have been appealed to and have elected a mere *Tom Tit* over the old Eagle." Kentucky, he declared, was saved only by Clay's personal popularity.[20]

Combs's ardor for annexation may have biased his judgment; but J. C. Spencer, who as Secretary of War had opposed his chief on that issue, also testified to its decisiveness, though from the opposite angle. The final result had turned on the electoral vote of New York, where both parties made mighty efforts, producing "a monstrous poll." Harrison's majority

<hr>

[19] *Missouri Statesman*, November 22, 1844.
[20] Combs to Clayton, November 30, 1844; Clay to Clayton, December 2, 1844; Clayton Papers.

had exceeded 13,000, and Clay received 6,594 votes more than Harrison, yet Polk carried the state by a plurality of 5,021. Birney, the Liberty candidate received 15,875 votes. "You will perceive," wrote Spencer, "that the abolition vote lost you the election, as three-fourths of these were from Whigs converted into abolitionists." The foreign vote and "the utter mendacity, frauds and villainies of Locofocoism" also contributed to the result.[21]

Until the last weeks of the campaign, beyond all question, interest centered on the Texas question. Striking evidence of the potency of the issue even among Clay's warmest supporters has been presented. Far as Clay went toward a pledge of annexation, his opponent stood for it unequivocally. Slight as may have been the difference between their sentiments and intentions, that margin must have won for Polk many who had Combs's enthusiasm for annexation without his intimate relation to Clay. Thus, so far as the South was concerned, it can hardly be questioned that Clay's conservative position on annexation lost many votes which normally would have been Whig. As for the North, it has always been admitted that the defection of the Liberty men cost Clay the electoral vote of New York, and with it the election. Thus, had it not been for the annexation issue, conceding to Polk every Southern State he actually carried, Clay would still have been elected.

---

[21] Spencer to Clay, November 21, 1844, Clay Papers.

CHAPTER XI

THE SAGE OF ASHLAND

HENRY CLAY was as temperamental as a prima donna. His defeat by an antagonist whom he despised was altogether unexpected and overwhelming. The same temperament that made him over-sanguine when skies were fair and dictatorial when sailing full before the breeze now sent him down into the depths of despondency. The letters of his friends, intended to pour the balm of unaltered admiration upon his wounds, only made them smart the more. As for the next campaign, neither he nor his most devoted adherents dared to look forward another four years, for the "Sage of Ashland" was already an old man. Indeed, the disaster for the moment paralyzed even his invincible youthfulness. When the Kentucky electors, after casting their fruitless ballots, made pilgrimage from Frankfort to Ashland, his response to their address was in effect a valedictory.[1]

Soon, however, under the influence of flattering surroundings, his buoyancy returned. The genial influence of Southern social life, the applause and adulation amid which he moved at Ashland, at the Virginia springs, at New Orleans, and even at the national capital, dispelled the chill of realized age, convinced him of the unchanging regard of the public, and restored his hopes in all their sanguine influence. Tributes of one kind or another poured in from all parts of the Union, and soon he was awaiting in complacent cheerfulness the call to leadership in 1848. In response to all tributes he made characteristic reply, plainly indicating that he had already selected the restoration of the tariff of 1842 as a leading issue of the next campaign.[2]

---

[1] *Observer and Reporter*, December 10, 1844.

[2] Calvin Colton, *Last Seven Years of Henry Clay*, pp. 41-44. F. W. Seward, *Seward at Washington*, I, 782, 798. Horace Greeley to Clay, November 15, 1846; John Davis to Clay, November 13, 1846; Clay Papers. J. B. Mowrer to McLean, June 11, July 13, 1846; Whittlesey to McLean, August 31, 1846; J. L. Williams to McLean, December 16, 1846; McLean Papers. Cralle to Calhoun, September 23, 1845, Jameson, *op. cit.*, pp. 1052-

Not so, however, the leaders of the Whig party and various aspirants for the nomination. The meeting of Congress in the winter of 1845-46 was accompanied by not a little president-making at Washington. Under the lead of Clayton, Crittenden, and Mangum, Clay was pronounced out of the running and consideration was given to a ticket consisting of General Scott for president and Corwin for vice president. A "Life" of the General was given to the press and he was fully launched in the race. However, an unfortunate correspondence with the Secretary of War, Marcy, laid him open to ridicule, while his undissembled jealousy of General Taylor created antagonism which offset his hostility to the Polk Administration. Therefore, his chances steadily dwindled until the spring of 1848, when he again began to be talked of as a "compromise" candidate.[3]

As Scott lost favor with the party leaders, they turned to Judge McLean. The judge had been keeping a watchful eye on developments, both at Washington, and, through numerous correspondents, at other centers of political activity. During the second winter of Polk's administration he was quite happy. He was manifestly the head of a party, and Mangum was being considered as his running-mate. But the blossoming of a Corwin presidential candidacy and the support it received from the Ohio delegation in Congress boded ill for the judge.[4]

The strategy of the McLean campaign was to hold him in reserve as a "compromise" candidate, conciliating all the other candidates so far as possible in the hope of securing "second-choice" votes when the delegates found it hopeless longer to support their favorites. This compromise position, however, on the eve of the convention, fell to Scott, and the judge's managers did not allow his name to be presented.[5]

---

53. Berrien to Crawford, November 9, 1846, Berrien Papers. Maysville *Eagle,* May 25, July 6, July 8, 1847. *Observer and Reporter,* April 7, April 24, 1847. *National Intelligencer,* April 27, 1847.

[3] Seward, *op. cit.,* I, 770-73, 782. Silas Reed to McLean, October 26, 1846, McLean Papers.

[4] Seward, *op. cit.,* II, 37-38. *Niles' Register,* LXXIII, 126.

[5] *Niles' Register, loc. cit.* Whittlesey to McLean, July 11, 1845; H. J. Cranston to McLean, April 27, 1846; Mowrer to McLean, August 8, October 30, December 21, 1846; Wm. Miner to McLean, October 11, 1846; McLean Papers.

In the early presidential speculations, there were some who turned to Clay's closest friend, Crittenden, as appropriately his heir-apparent. Outside Kentucky, these were generally devotees of Clay; within the state, disgruntled local leaders, whose suggestions to him did not lack incitements to jealousy of Clay and revolt against his leadership. Crittenden plainly doubted Clay's availability as a presidential candidate and was not unwilling to be considered for the nomination himself. He would not permit his pretensions to be openly advanced in Kentucky, however, so long as Clay had not signified his intention not to make the race.[6]

The restiveness of the lesser chiefs made Kentucky a fertile seed-bed for the Taylor candidacy. General Taylor paid little heed to the early suggestions of his availability. Only in response to his relative and long-time friend, Crittenden, did he, in the winter of 1846-47, agree to accept the presidency if elected by the people: He would be the president of the nation, not of a party. This statement came in response to a letter borne by Thomas L. Crittenden, who joined the general's staff, and suggests that Crittenden was the inventor of the "non-partisan" strategy which was the most significant feature of the Taylor campaign.[7]

The Taylor candidacy cut little figure in Washington during the session of 1846-47. But with the news of Buena Vista came a startling change. A glorious victory snatched from the jaws of anticipated disaster made Taylor the unrivalled hero of the war. Within a fortnight, papers from Louisville to New York, from Saint Louis to Baltimore, were hoisting the general's flag. His suport, however, came not alone from newspapers; as fast as they could be organized, great meetings

---

[6] Crittenden to Kinkead, January 10, 1847; W. J. Graves to Crittenden, February 16, 1845; Jos. L. White to Crittenden, September 29, 1845; Anthony Butler to Crittenden, June 15, 1846; G. B. Kinkead to Crittenden, January 2, 1847; G. W. Williams to Crittenden, January 7, 1847; Crittenden Papers. For the relations of Clay and Crittenden, cf. C. M. Clay, *Life, Memoirs, Writings and Speeches,* I, 213-14, 216.

[7] Harriet A. Weed, ed., *Autobiography of Thurlow Weed,* pp. 571-73; *Niles' Register,* LXX, 256; LXXI, 20-21. Mowrer to McLean, June 11, July 13, 1846; Harvey to McLean, October 12, 1846; McLean Papers. Taylor to Crittenden, September 15, October 3, December 10, 1846; January 26, May 15, 1847; Crittenden Papers.

in various cities nominated Taylor for the presidency. Within a week the Kentucky movement for Taylor got under way, significantly enough in Mason County, the home-nest of the Marshalls, Clay's foes for half-a-century.[8]

In this movement every element hostile to Clay participated, regardless of their own past enmities. Cassius M. Clay hesitated not to coöperate with Thomas F. Marshall and the Wickliffes, while on every hand the latent opposition flared up with vengeful fervor. Beside these open foes of the "Old Chief" were ranged a group who conspicuously posed as his friends. Hated by their new allies only less than Clay himself, they dared not overtly repudiate his claims lest they be caught between the hammer and the anvil, for the rank and file of the party, lacking the personal grievances of the leaders, were unshaken in their allegiance to "Harry of the West."

These men, his trusted lieutenants in Kentucky and the union, professed to admire and love Henry Clay as much as ever. They preferred him for president to any other man. Could they by any exertion of theirs make him president, they would gladly do so, and so long as his flag was in the field they would fight under it against any and all foes. *But* his flag was not in the field, for he had said he would emerge from his retirement only at the unanimous call of the country, a call which the number and implacability of his enemies made it hopeless to expect. He was only waiting for the proper time to announce his recognition of this and to declare his unwillingness again to subject himself to all but certain defeat. Under these circumstances, Mr. Clay was glad for his friends to turn to a more available candidate—and that candidate was General Taylor.

This, in substance, was the "Judas kiss," "the Brutus stab," repeated over and over again in the correspondence of the time, in letters written by the Taylor leaders and in their conversations. It was based essentially on the idea that any positive move in Clay's favor could be headed off, at any rate until the Taylor organization was so perfected that Clay himself would

---

[8] Maysville *Eagle,* April 6, April 8, April 10, April 13, April 20, 1847; *National Intelligencer,* April 15, 1847; *Observer and Reporter,* April 17, April 21, 1847.

see the hopelessness of opposition and would refuse to allow his name to be used. If this strategy was successful, Clay would be relegated to permanent retirement and the path to political advancement opened to younger men, without their laying themselves open to his vengeance at the hands of the rank and file of the Kentucky Whigs.

The political practices of the time and his valedictory to the electors prevented Clay from making any overt initiatory move. His admirers in New York and elsewhere, who wanted to move for him, in seeking to learn his wishes turned naturally to Crittenden and his other Kentucky friends, only to receive these "croakings" in reply. The peculiar relationship of the "croakers" to Clay enabled them to carry out the first objective of their plan; but Clay, with characteristic audacity at last upset their calculations by the unprecedented act of announcing himself as a candidate. Their wrath and dismay at being forced to an open conflict with the "Old Chief" is almost ludicrous, but they were too far committed to draw back and they had already secured the Kentucky delegation for Taylor —a decisive factor in the contest.

Under this highly capable leadership the Taylor movement in Kentucky was rapidly organized. Mobility and adaptability characterized the campaign. Where Taylor Whigs could control, it was a Whig movement; where they were in the minority, it became non-partisan. Thus, by the autumn of 1847 it had swept through the outlying districts and finally inundated the Bluegrass. Only in Bourbon and Fayette did Clay's friends resist the tide. Without orders from the "Old Chief," bewildered by the inactivity of Crittenden and the other Congressional lieutenants of Clay to whom they were wont to look for instructions, lacking leadership and organization, their numbers and loyalty proved ineffective against the determined and well-led Taylor forces. So, when the crisis came, in February, 1848, Clay's foes controlled both the Whig legislative caucus and the state convention.[9]

---

[9] Maysville *Eagle,* April 29, May 6, May 18, May 20, June 1, June 6, June 10, June 26, July 6, September 16, September 18, October 7, 1847; *Observer and Reporter,* April 24, April 28, May 5, May 12, May 19, June 16, June 30, July 10, August 7, August 8, August 18, September 15, September 22, September 25, September 29, October 13, October 20, Novem-

The guiding spirit of the Taylor movement in both Kentucky and the Union was Crittenden. If he did not devise the "croaking" campaign, he at least became one of its leading exponents, for it was admirably adapted to the necessities of his own political situation in Kentucky. The Clay leaders grew more and more suspicious of him during the spring and summer of 1847, though he avoided all their efforts to "smoke him out." About the middle of September, however, a New York supporter, who had recently visited Kentucky and the West, warned Clay of Crittenden's relation to the Taylor movement. Without demanding an explanation, Clay sent the letter to Crittenden, who evidently replied to Clay's satisfaction, for Clay thereupon closed the correspondence by assuring Crittenden that he did not share those views. Repeatedly, both abroad and since his return home, such statements in regard to Crittenden's course had been made to him, but to all these he had represented Crittenden's conduct substantially in accordance with his own account of it.[10]

After Buena Vista, the Taylor movement became widespread, not only in Kentucky but in the Union.[11] Ostensibly popular and non-partisan in character, it really was carefully directed by highly skilled professional politicians whose general staff, composed of members of Congress, had its headquarters at Washington. From the first, controversy raged over the General's party affiliation, but by July, 1847, the Democratic press had practically conceded him to the Whigs, and on July 1, he was nominated by the Whig convention of Georgia. This triumph was the work of Alexander H. Stephens, who in December, 1846, had organized a Taylor club among the members

---

ber 6, November 27, 1847; Frankfort *Kentucky Yeoman,* August 19, October 14, 1847.

[10] Clay, *op. cit.,* I, 216. Gen. Z. Taylor to Col. J. Taylor, May 9, 1847; Col. J. F. Taylor to Gen. Z. Taylor, September 8, 1847; Taylor Papers. Archer to Crittenden, September 22, 1847; Taylor to Crittenden, November 15, 1847; same to same, January 3, 1848; Clay to Crittenden, September 21, September 26, 1847; Crittenden Papers. Harvey to McLean, September 20, 1847; Dowling to McLean, October 30, 1847, McLean Papers. Avary, *op. cit.,* pp. 21-22.

[11] Maysville *Eagle,* April 24, May 4, May 8, May 13, June 1, June 15, July 1, July 10, 1847; *Observer and Reporter,* April 24, May 15, June 16, 1847; *Niles' Register,* LXXII, 128, 294, April 21, July 10, 1847. Harvey to McLean, April 24, 1847, McLean Papers.

of Congress. Calling themselves the "Young Indians" and working in close coöperation with Crittenden, they originally were
only seven in number—Stephens and Toombs of Georgia,
Ballard Preston, Flournoy and Pendleton of Virginia, Lincoln
of Illinois and Truman Smith of Connecticut. This group, with
later accessions, became Crittenden's staff in conducting the
Taylor campaign.[12]

By the autumn of 1847, however, the first flush of enthusiasm over Buena Vista had passed, and Whigs were beginning to ask themselves what kind of Whig their prospective
candidate was. The answer was not encouraging, for the most
consistent characteristic of the General's letters was their persistent assertion that he would be the president of the nation,
not of a party, and that he would not be bound by any
pledges. This non-partisanship extended beyond profession;
he even accepted Democratic nominations as graciously as
Whig. Accordingly, Northern Whigs, who were deeply concerned for the Whig economic program as well as for the spoils
of office, and who disliked voting for a slaveholder anyway,
became increasingly cool toward the Taylor candidacy.[13]

As the Mexican war drew to its close, discussion of the
Wilmot Proviso took on ever-growing earnestness. The question of the annexation of New Mexico and California became
the most vital aspect of the peace terms, and, in consequence,
the slavery issue more, and more cast its shadow over the
presidential canvass. The extreme slavocrats of the Lower
South distrusted Clay, who had never outgrown the Jeffersonian anti-slavery views popular in his youth. Taylor's attitude
was unknown, but he was a Louisiana sugar-planter on a large
scale and not addicted to academic speculation. Therefore they

---

[12] Maysville *Eagle,* April 27, May 20, May 27, June 5, July 17, 1847;
Observer and Reporter, April 28, May 1, May 8, May 22, June 19, 1847;
Niles' Register, LXXII, 294, July 10, 1847; Frankfort *Kentucky Yeoman,*
April 22, April 29, 1847. Hickman *Standard,* July 22, 1846. Avary,
op. cit., pp. 21-24.

[13] Frankfort *Kentucky Yeoman,* October 28, 1847. Maysville *Eagle,* July
10, 15, 27, August 12, September 28, 1847. *Observer and Reporter,* July 24,
31, August 14, 25, September 4, 1847. Letter of Taylor, August 16, 1847;
Taylor Papers.

assumed that his views were acceptable and the Taylor candidacy began to assume a definite sectional aspect.[14]

By the same reasoning, the anti-slavery Whigs of the North arrived at a determination to prevent Taylor's nomination if possible. For this purpose, the candidacy of Henry Clay seemed the handiest means. Clay, who honestly believed that he did not wish again to be a candidate, nevertheless viewed the early phases of the Taylor movement with extreme distaste. He found Taylor even more exclusively a "military hero" than Harrison, and his candidacy a repudiation of the original anti-Jacksonian principles of the party. He especially resented the haste with which Kentucky had espoused Taylor's cause, apparently acquiescent in his own valedictory. His own state need not forestall an outside call to him by complete committal to a rival, for, up to Buena Vista, he had believed that the mass of the Whig party were determined to bring him forward again.[15]

The opening of the year of 1847 found Clay in New Orleans. While here he responded to a toast at the celebration of the landing of the Pilgrims by the local New England Society, and spoke at length at a great meeting for the relief of famine-stricken Ireland. The Irish had voted against Clay almost en masse, so this speech was given wide publicity. He visited an agricultural fair at Baton Rouge, and in February made a short visit to Mobile, accompanied by Ex-Governor Jones of Tennessee. It was cheerfully reported here that he looked not over fifty years old. Again there was pointed comment on his excellent health and youthful appearance when he reached home at the end of March.[16]

[14] Chase to Sumner, December 2, 1847, E. G. Bourne, *Diary and Correspondence of Salmon P. Chase* (*American Historical Association, Annual Report, 1902,* Vol. II), pp. 125-27. Seward to Weed, December 14, 1847; Seward, *op. cit.,* II, 59. *Observer and Reporter,* October 9, December 1, 1847. Frankfort *Kentucky Yeoman,* December 3, 1847.

[15] Clay to Daniel Ullman, May 12, August 4, 1847; Colton, *Private Correspondence,* p. 545. Clay to Crittenden, September 26, 1847; Crittenden Papers. Harvey to McLean, June 13, 1847; McLean Papers.

[16] *Observer and Reporter,* January 20, January 23, January 27, February 20, February 24, March 6, 10, 27, 31, 1847. Colton, *Last Seven Years of Henry Clay,* pp. 45-50.

Hardly had he recovered from the fatigue of his journey when news was received of the death of his son and namesake, slain at Buena Vista. This compelled the cancellation of a projected visit on legal business to Philadelphia. His domestic affliction combined with advancing years and declining strength to turn Clay's mind to serious thoughts upon religion; and on June 22 he was privately baptized at Ashland after the forms of the Episcopal Church. His morals and mode of life had been used against him in the campaign of 1844. While it would be most unjust to ascribe Clay's action to political motives, his supporters in the press did not hesitate to advertise the fact of his baptism and to use it to anticipate renewed attacks on his character. Late in July, accompanied by Dr. Mercer of New Orleans, he left Ashland for the White Sulphur Springs and watering places on the coast.[17]

At the Springs, Clay was "the observed of all observers," his morning hours being devoted to the reception of many visitors. After a stay of about a fortnight he departed for Cape May and Newport. At the Relay House, near Washington, he encountered Benton, and the people in the cars were astonished at the cordiality of their greeting. On his arrival at Baltimore, hundreds of friends thronged Barnum's Hotel to see him. He declined a special train to Philadelphia, where his stay was marked by ovations whenever he appeared in public—at the depot on his arrival, after the church service on Sunday, and again on his departure. Saturday night he was serenaded and forced to speak.[18]

He arrived at Cape May by special boat Monday evening, and the next morning was given a reception in the Public Hall or Saloon. Following upon this, the gentlemen escorted him to the bathing beach. At first he was somewhat surprised and astonished at the novelty of his situation, but he quickly entered into the spirit of the fun, became delighted, swam on top of the breakers, ducked the ladies and was ducked in turn,

---

[17] *Observer and Reporter,* March 31, May 1, June 30, July 24, August 21, 1847. Maysville *Eagle,* July 6, 1847. Colton, *Last Seven Years of Henry Clay,* pp. 53-54.

[18] *Observer and Reporter,* August 8, August 14, August 25, August 28, 1847.

and finally left the surf with reluctance. There was great scrambling among the ladies to grasp his hand in the water, and he displayed such life and agility that one could hardly believe him more than forty-five. A day or so later he again displayed his gallantry and agility by leaping from a runaway carriage with a young lady in his arms.[19]

He was waited upon by invitation committees from New York, New Haven, Philadelphia and elsewhere, and Boston appointed a similar committee of forty-six, headed by Abbot Lawrence. Clay, however, declined all invitations and on Thursday it was announced that he would return home the following week by the most direct route.[20] The visit of the New York delegation, a hundred and twenty-five strong, was the climax of the tour. Clay excused himself from visiting New York on the plea that his trip was in search of health and relief from sorrow; he had visited Philadelphia only because he had learned at Baltimore that it was the best route to Cape May. There was a dinner in the afternoon, without toasts or speeches out of regard for Clay's grief, followed by a meeting on the lawn addressed by Mayor Swift of Philadelphia.[21]

On Monday, the Philadelphia delegation accompanied Clay to New Castle, where there was an ovation at the wharf. After visits to Chancellor Kensey Johns and to Clayton, Clay arrived at Baltimore by boat from Frenchtown at eleven-thirty Tuesday night and went to Barnum's City Hotel. The crowd would not leave until he appeared, but he did not speak because of the lateness of the hour. He left Baltimore the next morning

---

[19] *Observer and Reporter,* August 28, 1847.

[20] The reason for this abrupt change of plans was probably the receipt of news of the Taylor meeting at Lexington. *Observer and Reporter,* August 7, August 18, 1847.

[21] "Previous to Mr. Clay's departure from the Columbia House, and while most of the gentlemen were engaged in paying the last attentions to the New York delegation, a curious scene was occurring in the parlor. The veteran statesman . . . had bargained with a few fair Philadelphians to exchange some clippings from his hoary locks for the nectar from their lips. The trade was carried on with such earnestness that there was danger of his needing a wig to cover his losses while the kisses he took in exchange caused innumerable heart-burnings to jealous lovers who accidentally were attracted to the spot." Maysville *Eagle,* September 2, 1847, quoting New York *Herald.*

at seven o'clock, out of regard for his health, leaving from the Outer Depot to escape the crowd. At this point Dr. Mercer, who had made a visit to New York, rejoined him.[22]

It was necessary to go by the White Sulphur to pick up Mercer's family which had been left there. In spite of extreme haste, his route up the Shenandoah Valley in an extra mail coach was a triumphal procession. Everywhere he was greeted by demonstrations, sometimes of a non-partisan character, even in the heart of that "Tenth Legion of Democracy." He reached the Springs August 28, and was home at Ashland the 19th of September.[23]

Throughout the trip Clay's speeches had been absolutely colorless. He had escaped making any extended address and his occasional remarks sedulously avoided political discussion, keeping tenaciously to the neutral ground of personalities. Ever the introductory reference, if not the burden of the theme, was the death of his son and the unbearably sorrowful associations of Ashland from which he had fled.

Clay men outside of Kentucky were not so circumspect as the "Old Chief's" immediate staff in waiting for permission to move in his favor. During July and August, in East Tennessee, in Ohio, at Philadelphia and at New York, the Clay candidacy began to be openly advanced by various newspapers and by public meetings. A great meeting at Lebanon, Ohio, declared that "No man who is not a thorough Whig, approved by a Whig National Convention, can receive our support for the Presidency, now or hereafter." This, indeed, became the rallying-cry of the Clay men, in obvious reprisal for the "non-partisan" methods used in launching the Taylor candidacy. Among the papers which undertook to speak for "Whigs who have not yet given up hope that Clay may be the next President," was the New York *Tribune*, which henceforth consistently advocated the nomination of Clay, and Greeley actually became a sort of eastern manager for the Clay candidacy.[24]

---

[22] *Observer and Reporter,* September 1, 1847.

[23] *Observer and Reporter,* September 15, September 22, 1847.

[24] *Observer and Reporter,* August 7, August 21, August 25, August 28, September 11, September 29, 1847; *Niles' Register,* LXXIII, 19-20. Maysville *Eagle,* September 27, 1847.

The *Courier and Enquirer* at once accepted the challenge; and link-

The "firm of Seward, Weed and Greeley" had not yet dissolved, although they appeared to be pursuing divergent political aims. Weed had proposed Taylor as a candidate immediately after Resaca de la Palma, but the General's "presidential letters" considerably cooled his enthusiasm. Seward's winter sojourns at Washington and summer tours to Cleveland, Detroit and Chicago, to Cincinnati, Lexington, Vandalia, St. Louis, and New Orleans ear-marked him as an aspirant for national honors, although he showed no eagerness for the vice-presidency, for which he was frequently mentioned. Toward the various presidential candidates he preserved a masterly neutrality and many observers believed his real object to be the presidential nomination in 1852.

But more than one mention of him is to be found as a presidential possibility for that very year, and McLean's New York manager at length became convinced that this was the explanation to Greeley's "turning and twisting." This, indeed, is the only clue which reduces the manoeuvres of the three to one consistent course of action such as their relationship presupposes. Seward discouraged the early Scott candidacy. Weed brought out Taylor when only Scott and McLean were in the race, but just before the convention was linking Seward's name with Clay's. Greeley, inveterately opposed to Taylor, pushed Clay until he seemed in full flush of success. But at this point he suddenly began to declare his cause lost, to insist that a compromise candidate must be found, and to coquette with the McLean men. Every move of the three tended to check the progress of the candidate leading at the moment, to balance their strength, and to produce a deadlocked convention which might make possible the nomination of Seward as Polk had been nominated by the Democrats four years before.[25]

---

ing Greeley's pronouncement in favor of Clay with Weed's earlier declaration that Taylor was losing ground, asserted that "the object of these movements . . . is not to secure the nomination of Mr. Clay, but simply to prevent the nomination of Gen. Taylor." *Niles' Register, op. cit.*

[25] J. B. Mowrer to McLean, August 17, September 6, September 13, October 4, October 11, 1847; January 29, February 13, February 14, March 27, April 3, April 10, April 17, April 19, April 20, April 24, May 8, May 11, May 15, May 22, June 5, 1848; Dowling to McLean, October 30, 1847; February 26, April 26, May 12, 1848; James Harvey to McLean,

Thus, as the summer drew on to autumn, Clay was definitely put forward as a candidate, and in the North his candidacy largely neutralized that of Taylor. The Clay boom received its initial impetus from Taylor's ill-advised letters. These offended strongly partisan Whigs by their no-party attitude, while the independent-minded were alienated by the idea that he either had formed no opinions on the leading questions of the day, or was willing to compromise them for general support. By September, the Taylor movement in Ohio had all but run its course. Clay's own movements also brought him before the public, which was, perhaps, already tiring of the General. The Clay press came out flatly for a National Convention, and, much to Taylor's disgust, this became the definite demand of the Northern Whigs.[26]

September 20, 1847; E. M. Huntington to McLean, January 3, 1848; Elisha Whittlesey to McLean, April 12, 1848; D. B. Ogden to McLean, January 25, 1848; Caleb B. Smith to McLean, May 1, May 28, 1848; McLean Papers. Jas. S. Wendell to Clay, March 11, 1848; T. B. Stevenson to Clay, June 19, 1848; Sylvester Schenck to Clay, December 24, 1849; Clay Papers. E. J. Towne to Weed, March 13, 1848, Weed Papers. Albany *Evening Journal* editorials quoted in New York *Tribune*, February 28, May 18, 1848; Seward's correspondence with Weed and Mrs. Seward, January 1, 1845—June 10, 1848; Seward, *op. cit.*, I, 770-74, *passim*, and II, 37-70, *passim*. Richmond *Whig*, quoted in New York *Tribune*, January 29, 1848. *Observer and Reporter*, September 11, 1847. *Niles' Register*, LXXIII, 20, September 11, 1847. See also Waddy Thompson to Crittenden, February 9, 1848, Crittenden Papers; Gen. Z. Taylor to Col. J. P. Taylor, May 15, 1848, Taylor Papers; and C. M. Clay to Henry Clay, April 13, 1848, *Observer and Reporter*, April 22, 1848. It is significant that Greeley began to consort with Mowrer, who was McLean's New York manager, just at the time, January, 1848, when Clay's prospects were brightest.

[26] Gen. Taylor to Crittenden, September 15, November 15, 1847; Boyd McNairy to Crittenden, November 23, 1847; Stevenson to Crittenden, September 7, 1847; Archer to Crittenden, September 22, 1847; Burnley to Crittenden, April 4, 1848; Crittenden Papers. Dowling to McLean, October 30, 1847; Harvey to McLean, October 28, 1847; Mowrer to McLean, September 13, October 4, October 11, October 25, 1847; McLean Papers. McLean to Ewing, October 6, 1847, Ewing Papers. Calhoun to Clemson, September 6, 1847, Jameson, *op. cit.*, II, 737. Seward to Mrs. Seward, October 14, October 19, 1847, Seward, II, 55, 56. *Observer and Reporter*, September 18, October 23, November 16, 1847, quoting New York *Tribune;* also November 6, 1847; Frankfort *Kentucky Yeoman*, October 21, October 28, 1847; Maysville *Eagle*, November 9, 1847. *Niles' Register*, LXXIII, 126, October 23, 1847.

CHAPTER XII

OLD ROUGH AND READY

ONLY THE imperative compulsion of mental or physical disability can change the habits of a life-time, and forty years of leadership had made the atmosphere of politics the very breath of life to Henry Clay. To the end of his life there was no diminution in his mental powers, while the comparative retirement in which he had lived since his resignation from the Senate in 1842 had recuperated his health almost beyond belief. He was no longer obliged to avoid the press of crowds as in 1843. Instead, he revelled in human contacts as in the exuberant vigor of twenty years before. Therefore the peculiar character of the Taylor campaign and the general situation which had developed by the autumn of 1847 presented an irresistible provocation to Clay to make some move to checkmate the "croakers" and place himself definitely before the public as a candidate for the Whig nomination.

The policy of the Polk Administration in seeking to end the Mexican War with territorial acquisitions offered a theme far removed from mere party discussion and springing logically from Clay's annexation stand in the previous presidential contest. Accordingly, on November 13, 1847, Clay addressed a great meeting at Lexington, presenting certain resolutions which embodied his views on the war and the terms on which peace should be made. They raised a definite issue on a paramount question of national policy, and so, in effect were an avowal of his candidacy and an assumption of the party leadership.[1]

Opening with an indictment of the character of the war and the method by which it was brought on, Clay insisted that Congress alone could constitutionally declare its objects, which the President then was obligated to try to obtain by force and diplomacy. We could conquer and annex all of Mexico,

[1] Frankfort *Kentucky Yeoman,* November 5, 1847. Leonidas Jewett to McLean, December 7, 1847; McLean Papers. Burnley to Crittenden, December 12, 1847; same to same, September 23, 1848; Crittenden Papers.

but at great cost of men and money and at the risk of establishing imperialism. Two such great countries with populations so incongruous in race, language, religion and laws could not be united—permanent military government or extension of political privileges would be alike disastrous. We had no need of Mexican territory, for our own was sufficient for many times our population, with every desirable diversity of climate and soil; while we should create a great debt and forfeit the good opinion of the world. We might, however, acquire the harbor of San Francisco, which would be valuable for our future commerce, by purchase through the assumption of some of our citizens' claims on Mexico.

We were now continuing the war, Clay insisted, for the narrow strip between the Nueces and the Rio Bravo and the "barren province of New Mexico, with its few miserable mines," as indemnity for the expenses of the war. He would have them adopt a resolution disavowing any desire to acquire territory, for he had ever regarded slavery as a great evil, and would rejoice if it could pass, with due regard to "all circumstances affecting the security, safety and happiness of both races." Every state had the "supreme, uncontrolled and exclusive power . . . without any outside intervention" to deal with this question. Nearly fifty years ago he had vainly advocated gradual emancipation for Kentucky, and had since been active in the Colonization Society. These policies were very different from those of the Abolitionists, who had both hindered the cause of emancipation and produced sectional discord.[2]

The impression of this speech on the reading public was as great as that upon its hearers. The applause was all but unanimous. The Clay resolutions became the Whig platform on the war and its issues, were adopted by the Whig meetings everywhere, and became the chart by which Whig members of Congress and state legislatures governed their course. In the whole union, only two Whig newspapers, the New York *Courier and Enquirer* and the Nashville *Whig*, most militant of the Taylor press, failed to applaud it warmly. Although it did not go far enough to suit Seward, the Auburn *Advertiser* declared that

---

[2] *Niles' Register*, LXXIII, 197-200. (November 27, 1847) from *Observer and Reporter*.

"The last objection to Mr. Clay, on the score of principle is now removed," and Weed's *Evening Journal* remarked that "If that speech, as a whole, realized the expectations which the Telegraphic sketch has raised, it settles the Presidential question !"[3]

Clay had come forward as the spokesman of the Whig Party, and the party had acknowledged the voice of its great leader. Everywhere, except in the South, his candidacy swept over the country. In New York quite three-fourths of the regular Whigs favored Clay, and in the metropolis his friends controlled both the Whig committees. There can be little question that a majority of the Whig voters everywhere preferred Clay to all others and would gladly have risked defeat under his leadership.[4]

The politicians, however, were eager for the spoils of office and determined to win at all costs. It was impressed upon them by the "croakers" that Clay was unavailable, and it is indeed doubtful if he could have drawn many democratic votes. Taylor seemed able to do that very thing; and for that reason they supported him, accepting the private assurances of Crittenden and other insiders that he would give them a Whig administration. Few Whig papers dared avow an actual preference for Taylor; while they would prefer Clay as president, they were bound to prefer Taylor as candidate. It was in confirming this impression that the progress of the Taylor movement in Kentucky was highly damaging to Clay. The apparent hold of Taylor on Clay's own state was now the

---

[3] L. J. Glenn to Howell Cobb, December 1, 1847 (misdated 1848), U. B. Phillips, *Toombs, Stephens and Cobb Correspondence (American Historical Association, Annual Report, 1911,* vol. I), p. 89; Seward to Mrs. Seward, *op cit.,* II, 57-58; *Observer and Reporter,* December 1, December 4, 1847. Leonidas Jewett to McLean, December 7, 1847; McLean Papers.

[4] Weed, *op. cit.,* p. 575. Dowling to McLean, December 7, 1847; D. H. Whitney to McLean, December 15, 1847; McLean Papers. I am compelled to this conclusion in spite of the claims of some of McLean's correspondents that Clay's support was confined to the aristocracy, the masses being hostile to him. Cf. Mowrer to McLean, December 13, 1847.

By spring, even in the South, there was a decided reaction in Clay's favor. Toombs to Jas. Thomas, April 16, May 1, 1848, Phillips, *op. cit.,* pp. 103-5; "Mr. Clay has not five friends of his nomination in both branches of Congress; but eight-tenths of them are afraid to open their lips upon the subject to the public." *Ibid.*

strongest argument left to the Taylor men outside the Lower South, and Clay's efforts were therefore bent to destroy that impression.

In October a committee of Lexington Whigs loyal to Clay, headed by the distinguished George Robertson, had issued a confidential circular denouncing the methods and character of the Taylor campaign in Kentucky. It declared that the meetings were not representative of the Whig party in either size or composition—"They were composed of some well-meaning Whigs, some doubtful Whigs, and a few locofocos." In the midst of the enthusiasm produced by Clay's speech, this circular was published by a native American paper. It stung the radical Taylor men to such fury that they began to demand a public demonstration of their control, to the dismay of the cautious Crittenden and Letcher, whose personal ambitions would be endangered by an open break with the "Old Chief." If only Clay would decide once for all what he was going to do! In spite of the opposition of these leaders, the lesser leaders began to arrange for a Taylor meeting at Frankfort in February, the evident purpose of which was a nomination of the General. Some desired even an earlier nomination by the legislature.[5]

The day after Christmas, Clay departed for Washington where he arrived January 10, greeted at the station by a wildly cheering crowd. He had spent the two week-ends at Cumberland and Baltimore, and the intervening week in visiting friends in Berkeley County, Virginia. He was ostensibly at the capital in connection with a suit before the Supreme Court. Clay's presence at the marriage of Benton's daughter to a brother of Mrs. James B. Clay gave new evidence of the rapprochement between those statesmen. The next evening he delivered a great address on retiring as president of the American Colonization Society.[6]

---

[5] *Observer and Reporter,* November 20, 1847. G. W. Williams to Crittenden, November 25, 1847; Letcher to Crittenden, December 23, 1847; January 1, January (?), 1848, January 20, 1848; J. S. Helm to Crittenden, January 11, 1848; W. J. Graves to Crittenden, January 21, 1848, Crittenden Papers.

[6] *Observer and Reporter,* December 29, 1847; January 12, January 15, Clay to Jas. B. Clay, January 16, February 1, February 21, 1848; Colton, *Private Correspondence,* pp. 553, 556, January 26, February

From his arrival in Washington, he unofficially took command of the Whig opposition in Congress, with the result that both Clay and Taylor men began to act with some system. At his first interview with his friends, in reply to a query from John Minor Botts as to the course the Whigs should take in relation to the war, he advised them to pass the resolution introduced by Alexander H. Stephens. He produced a great impression in Washington, especially by his appearance of health, looking better than ten years previously. Just before his departure from Lexington, the New York *Herald* reported that a poll of the Whigs in Congress showed ninety for Clay, sixty for Taylor, nineteen for Scott, five Abolitionists, and J. Q. Adams for nobody. A month later he was said to have gained ground since his arrival. Taylor himself was informed that there had been a great falling off among his friends in Congress, many having dropped him or become silent or indifferent.[7]

Clay had come to Washington practically determined on withdrawing his name from consideration. He was assured, however, that such action would lead to a prostration of the Whig Party, especially in the free states, and that Taylor could not be supported in his noncommittal position—indeed, some doubted if he could draw the full Whig support even if he assumed distinct Whig ground. Clay therefore suspended any definite action. His friends generally approved his passive position, so he waited for circumstances to determine whether and when he should change it. If he credited all he saw and heard, he could not doubt his election if nominated; but experience had taught him caution in believing even agreeable things. He was assured that he could carry New York by an immense majority since the Whigs in the legislature of that state had passed a caucus resolution indirectly designating him and excluding Taylor. He had reason to believe that the

21, 1848. Stephens, January 10, 1848, in R. M. Johnston and W. H. Brown, *Life of Alexander H. Stephens,* p. 224.

[7] Letter of A. H. Stephens, January 11, 1848, Johnston & Brown, *op. cit.,* p. 225; *Observer and Reporter,* January 5, 1848, quoting New York *Herald,* December 25, 1847; New York *Tribune,* January 19, February 7, 1848; Frankfort *Kentucky Yeoman,* February 3, 1848. Gen. Z. Taylor to Col. J. P. Taylor, March 10, 1848, Taylor Papers.

Virginia convention would express no preference for anyone.[8]

It was with these ideas that Clay departed for Philadelphia, where, as usual, he had legal business. Two days before he left Washington, John Quincy Adams had been stricken, dying the day of Clay's departure. Thus it happened that Clay's departure from Philadelphia and arrival at New York, both previously arranged, conflicted with the progress of the funeral cortege of the "Old Man Eloquent." This gave Clay's opponents a chance to carp which they did not neglect, their comments not always showing either good temper or good taste. The feeling between Clay's and Taylor's supporters in New York was growing embittered, for this eastern visit marks the climax of the Clay campaign. In both Philadelphia and New York he was entertained as the guest of the city. It was said that probably no private citizen had ever been given such a reception.[9]

Informed opinion at this time clearly was that Clay had definitely checkmated Taylor, but whether he could win the nomination for himself was another matter. In anticipation of a deadlocked convention, the opponents of both began to make plans for a compromise candidate. Judge McLean made friendly approaches to Clay, who appeared to be the heir of Corwin in Ohio, and whose entrance had destroyed the plans of the judge's adherents in Illinois. The McLean and Webster men in New York felt it necessary, much to the disgust of those distinguished gentlemen, to unite with the Taylor men in launching a Taylor meeting in that city—which thus became in effect merely an anti-Clay meeting. A great Clay meeting at Castle Garden, February 17, however, drew twelve thousand people. A Taylor meeting in Cincinnati was a failure, and it was reported to McLean that in the talk on the steamboats in the West and on the trains but little was said in favor of

---

[8] Clay to Jas. B. Clay, January 16, February 1, 1848; Clay to H. T. Duncan, February 15, 1848; Clay to Leslie Combs, February 18, 1848; Colton, *Private Correspondence,* pp. 553-56. D. Ullman to Clay, February 18, 1848, Clay Papers. A. H. Stephens to Linton Stephens, January 11, March, 1848, Johnston and Brown, *op. cit.,* pp. 225, 227.

[9] *Observer and Reporter,* March 4, March 15, 1848. Dowling to McLean, February 28, 1848, McLean Papers.

Taylor, and "all the cry was Clay, Clay, Clay!"[10]

Already, however, the Clay candidacy had received a well-nigh fatal blow, and that in his own state. The Whig state convention met on Washington's Birthday, and failed to nominate the "Old Chief"!

The Kentucky Whigs were paying the penalty of a long tenure of power. The party was torn by factional animosities and the personal ambitions of its leaders. The chief factions were headed by Governor Owsley and his predecessor, "Black Bob" Letcher, Crittenden's most intimate friend. Men like the Wickliffes, Ben Hardin and John L. Helm played their own games. It is evident that almost everywhere smouldered elements of disaffection. This factionalism led to a bitter contest for the gubernatorial nomination between Archibald Dixon, of the Letcher faction, and William Jordan Graves, of the Owsley faction. Their antagonism threatened to extend beyond the convention and endanger the state in the presidential election. In view of this, the convention which was to have met in December was postponed, the Whig members of the legislature to set the exact date. Dixon and Graves, meanwhile, each developed a state of mind in which he preferred the nomination of a third candidate rather than risk the triumph of his rival. Each in turn saw in the nomination of Crittenden an honorable exit from the tense situation, with the result that the senator was nominated by acclamation and felt constrained to accept, notwithstanding the personal sacrifices involved.[11]

---

[10] James S. Wendell to Clay, March 11, 1848, Clay Papers. Calhoun to Mrs. Clemson, February 20, 1848; same to Clemson, February 4, March 7, 1848, Jameson, *op. cit.*, pp. 743, 746. Mowrer to McLean, February 7, February 25, March 20, 1848; David B. Ogden to McLean, January 15, January 25, 1848; M. C. Vaughn to McLean, February 11, 1848; S. P. Chase to McLean, February 12, 1848; Wm. Burnet to McLean, February 23, 1848; H. E. Spencer to McLean, February 24, 1848, McLean Papers. Webster to Blatchford, January 30, 1848, G. T. Curtis, *Life of Daniel Webster*, II, 336. New York *Tribune*, January 17, 19, February 23, 1848. *Observer and Reporter*, February 26, 1848.

[11] John L. Helm to Crittenden, January 11, February 21, 1848; Letcher to Crittenden, January 1, January —, January 29, February 16, February 21, 1848; Graves to Crittenden, January 21, 1848; Addison White to Crittenden, February 3, 1848; Leslie Combs to Crittenden, February 27, 1848;

Beyond the formal action taken, it is difficult to ascertain just what occurred in connection with the presidential aspirations of Clay and Taylor. The Taylor convention met simultaneously with, and many of its delegates were also members of, the state convention, the sessions being arranged for their convenience. In consequence, in the subsequent discussions it is not always possible to distinguish which meeting was the scene of the incident referred to. Only forty-four out of ninety-nine counties were represented in the Taylor meeting, which adopted the Whig electoral ticket and declared that Taylor had the "entire confidence of the people" recommending him "to the consideration of the Whig National Convention and to the people of the United States as a candidate for the Presidency." The state convention, without a nomination or instructions, chose two delegates-at-large to the National Convention, and directed the county delegations of the respective districts to choose the other delegates.

Both sides claimed a majority in the state convention. The Taylor men declared that the Clay men dared not attempt a nomination, and that they were prevailed upon to refrain from nominating Taylor by the reading of letters from Crittenden, Morehead, and Gaines, saying that Clay would retire from the race on his return home, and urging that he should not be pushed from the track by the convention. Such letters, indeed, had been urgently requested by Letcher for that very purpose. The official record, however, shows that Clay's friends, on being questioned, declared that no one was authorized to state Clay's position. Since one of the delegates-at-large was supposedly a Clay man, it may well be doubted that the Taylor men had control. However, their superior leadership revealed itself in the choice of the district delegates. Also, by confusing the two conventions, it could be made to

A. W. Andrews to Crittenden, February 14, 1848; Thos. Metcalfe to Crittenden, February 17, February 20, March 3, 1848; Harry I. Todd to Crittenden, February 23, 1848; Orlando Brown to Crittenden, February 23, 1848; Philip Swigert to Crittenden, February 24, 1848; John W. Russel to Crittenden, March 1, 1848; R. Hawes to Maria K. Crittenden, February 23, 1848; James Harlan to Crittenden, March 4, 1848; Crittenden Papers. In the last two of these letters are the earliest mentions of Clay's return to the Senate.

appear in other states that Kentucky had repudiated Clay and nominated Taylor.[12]

That day, at once Washington's Birthday and the anniversary of Buena Vista, was everywhere marked by Taylor demonstrations. Its selection for the meeting of the Kentucky, Virginia, and North Carolina Whig state conventions indicates the strength of the Taylor forces in all three states. John Minor Botts asserted, however, that the Virginia Convention was about to yield to the Clay men and send an uninstructed delegation, when William Ballard Preston stampeded it to Taylor by claiming to have received telegrams saying that Kentucky and North Carolina had gone for the General.[13]

Clay's proponents had been consistently handicapped by the asseverations of the Taylor men that he would not allow his name to go before the convention. They now became clamorous for assurances on this point as essential for the pushing of his candidacy. Governor Bebb, of Ohio, failing in a desperate attempt to secure the nomination of Corwin by a state convention, made approaches to Clay. At the same time, Stevenson of the Cincinnati *Atlas,* Clay's Ohio manager, urgently advised Clay to issue a definitive denial that he would forbid the consideration of his name by the National Convention, and also a positive pronouncement against the extension of slave territory.[14]

These approaches from Ohio came on the heels of the declaration of the New York legislative caucus that Clay was the first choice of the New York Whigs.[15] Accordingly, under date of April 10, 1848, Clay published a statement which was

---

[12] *Observer and Reporter,* February 26, March 1, March 4, 1848; *National Intelligencer,* February 29, 1848; Maysville *Eagle,* February 24, February 29, 1848; Maysville *Herald,* March 1, 1848. Toombs to Jas. Thomas, April 16, 1848, Phillips, *op. cit.,* pp. 103-4. C. M. Clay to H. Clay, April 13, 1848, *Observer and Reporter,* April 22, 1848, from *Courier and Enquirer.* A. H. Stephens to Linton Stephens, March, 1848, Johnston and Brown, *op. cit.,* p. 227.

[13] *Observer and Reporter,* April 8, 1848.

[14] D. Ullman to Clay, February 18, 1848; A. Pricer to Clay, March 24, 1848; T. B. Stevenson to Clay, April 8, 1848; L. J. Gartrell to Clay, April 15, 1848; Clay Papers. Teesdale to McLean, January 20, 1848, McLean Papers. *Observer and Reporter,* April 4, 1848.

[15] *Observer and Reporter,* February 26, 1848,

in effect an announcement of his candidacy. He had left Ashland in December determined to announce his withdrawal. He had frequently expressed this determination, but no one was authorized to publish anything in regard to his intentions. Reflection had led him to consult his friends before taking a decisive step. During the past eight months he had fully and freely done so and had received many appeals not to execute his purpose, which he was told would lead to failure and perhaps to the dissolution of the Whig party, especially in the free states. His availability was based on his strength in New York, Ohio, and Pennsylvania, whose concurrence would secure the party against defeat, and two of which were essential to its success. Ohio would give her vote to no other candidate from the Slave States. The foreign-born citizens desired an opportunity to vote for him because they had been deceived into opposing him in the last election, while the "great body of the Whig party" entertained "a strong and decided preference" for him. Therefore, he had finally decided to leave his name to the consideration of the National Convention, in whose decision he would promptly and cheerfully acquiesce. Owing to the doubt as to his intentions, many of his friends had expressed preferences for other candidates; for these he had "no regrets to express, no complaints, no reproaches to make."[16]

The technique of politics was but slowly adjusting itself to the democratization of the ballot which characterized the Jacksonian epoch. In theory, still, the presidency might not openly be sought, although candidates no longer were required to disguise their aspirations for other offices. In practise, of course, it merely compelled resort to all sorts of subterfuges to mask the inevitable manoeuvres of the candidates for president. Clay's announcement was, therefore, a distinct break from precedent, a daring appeal from the old methods of internal manipulation by leaders to the mass of the party. A universal chorus of criticism and abuse rose from the Taylor politicians whose webs were thus rudely demolished, and even from those who were hoping for the nomination of a compro-

---

[16] New York *Tribune*, April 13, 1848; *Observer and Reporter*, April 12. Sent in full by telegraph, it appeared in eastern metropolitan papers the next day.

mise candidate. Clay's own undoubted supporters, however, welcomed it as clearing the air and giving them a definite basis for a fight, and a number of newspapers hauled down the Taylor flag and hoisted that of Clay. But, on the whole, the announcement seems to have been a grave tactical error.[17]

The growth of the Clay candidacy had meanwhile determined the Taylor managers to take desperate means to force his nomination. With the cotton states solidly behind him, they could hold over the Whig Party the threat of an independent candidacy and consequent election of the Democratic candidate, either at the polls or by the House of Representatives. This idea was not Taylor's own, but plainly was conceived by Burnley, Peyton, and other hotheads who had grouped themselves around him at Baton Rouge.

From Monterey, he had written to Clay in November stating that he was ready to stand aside if Clay or any other Whig should be the choice of the party. He wrote to Crittenden to the same effect, fully authorizing him, at his discretion, to withdraw his name at any time before the election. But on January 3, from Baton Rouge, he explicitly withdrew this authorization—he would let those who had brought him forward drop him at the proper time. At the same time, he complained of the determination of the Whigs to make a convention nomination. By February 13, he doubted if he could accept a convention nomination because of the pledge that would be imposed, but regardless of its action he would now withdraw from the canvass, the time for doing so having passed.

During the winter, however, rumors of his willingness to withdraw became current. Therefore, he anxiously wrote to Crittenden on March 25, reiterating his position and inquiring about his letter of November 15, which he professed not to remember. He clearly suspected Crittenden of having shown

<hr />

[17] W. C. C. Claiborne to Clay, April 26, 1848, Clay Papers. Wm. Minor to McLean, April 19, 1848; Teesdale to McLean, April 15, 1848; J. D. Defree to McLean, April 16, 1848; Harvey to McLean, April 27, 1848; Dowling to McLean, May 4; Hugh White to McLean, May 6, 1848; McLean Papers. Calhoun to A. P. Calhoun, April 16, 1848, Jameson, *op. cit.*, p. 75. Toombs to Jas. Thomas, May 1, 1848, Phillips, *op. cit.*, pp. 104-5. *Observer and Reporter*, May 8, 1848.

it, but the reports were finally traced back to Clay's exhibition of the similar letter which Taylor had written to him. It was this determination, to be an independent candidate if denied the Whig nomination, which was now published. On April 30, Taylor addressed a letter to Clay giving him formal notice of his new intention.[18]

In a letter addressed to the editors of the Richmond *Whig*, dated April 20, 1848, Taylor stated that he would not refuse a nomination by the Whig National Convention if left free of pledges and allowed to remain in the independent position in which he had been placed by the people and his own sense of duty. However, he intended, and had always intended, to be a candidate regardless of the Democratic and Whig nominations. This letter created an extremely bad impression among partisan Whigs, and if it had been left unmodified might well have been the death-knell of the Taylor candidacy.[19]

However, a group of Taylor members of Congress had previously decided that the situation called for an authoritative and well-considered statement of the General's position. Accordingly, Crittenden, in conference with Stephens and Toombs, prepared an answer to a letter written by Truman Smith, who was flirting with all the candidates with an eye on the vice-presidency. This was dispatched to Baton Rouge by Major Bliss, the General's son-in-law and aide, who evidently arrived just too late to head off the letter of April 20. Therefore, two days later, under address to a Captain Allison, the Crittenden-Toombs-Stephens concoction was given to the world, thus appearing practically simultaneously with the Richmond letter and counteracting its bad effects.

This "First Allison Letter" stated that he was a Whig, but could not be a party president. The veto power was to be used only in cases of clear violation of the Constitution, or

---

[18] Taylor to Crittenden, November 15, 1847; January 3, February 13, March 25, 1848; Burnley to Crittenden, April 4, 1848; Crittenden to Burnley, May 17, 1848; Crittenden Papers. Greeley to Clay, April 28, 1848; Taylor to Clay, April 30, 1848; C. S. Morehead to Clay, May 3, 1848; Clay Papers. Harvey to McLean, May 16, 1848, McLean Papers. Taylor to Clay, November 4, 1847, Colton, *Private Correspondence*, pp. 548-49. *Observer and Reporter*, February 26, 1848, quoting Philadelphia *North American*.

[19] Maysville *Herald*, May 8, 1848.

manifest haste and want of consideration by Congress. The personal opinion of the president ought not to control the action of Congress on questions of domestic politics. He would accept Congressional action on the tariff, currency, and internal improvements. As to the war, he rejoiced at peace. The principle of our government was opposed to the subjugation and dismemberment of other nations. The national honor being vindicated, we could be magnanimous.[20]

The Allison letter mitigated the bad effects of its predecessor, but at the moment the Richmond letter and Clay's announcement appear merely to have increased the trend toward a compromise candidate, with Scott most frequently favored.[21] Throughout the spring attempts were also being made to draw strength to the various candidates through combinations with vice-presidential aspirants. At the beginning of February the Washington correspondents claimed that the Taylor men were favoring Abbott Lawrence for vice-president. As the candidate had to be a Northern man, Lawrence being a cotton manufacturer, was obviously satisfactory to Taylor's Southern managers, and at that date Taylor's was almost entirely a Southern candidacy.

Indeed, the sectional aspect of the campaign had become

---

[20] Maysville *Herald*, May 5, 1848. It was evidently this "First Allison Letter" of April 22 and not the "Second Allison Letter" of September 4, that A. H. Stephens referred to in his letter to Mrs. Coleman, October 13, 1870. (Coleman, *op. cit.*, I, 294.) Crittenden, Toombs and Stephens were all in Washington in the spring and messing together. (Johnston and Brown, *op. cit.*, p. 226; Toombs to Thomas, April 16, May 1, 1848, Phillips, *op. cit.*, pp. 103-5.) From June 20 to August 5, Crittenden was in Kentucky speaking in his gubernatorial campaign and on August 30 addressed a letter from Frankfort. Stephens was seriously wounded by Judge Cone on September 3; while he and Toombs wrote to Crittenden from Georgia on September 26 and September 27 (Crittenden Papers). T. W. Barnes (*Memoirs of Thurlow Weed*, p. 169) states that the "Second Allison Letter" was to counteract Taylor's acceptance of a Charleston Democratic nomination, published August 22. Thus Thurlow Weed's claim to authorship of the "Second Allison Letter" is confirmed (Weed, *op. cit.*, pp. 578-82). On the other hand, the circumstances of the "First Allison Letter" were known at Washington in advance of its publication; cf. Harvey to McLean, April 27, 1848, McLean Papers; New York *Tribune*, April 15, 1848.

[21] Whittlesey to McLean, May 11, 1848; Dowling to McLean, May 4, 1848; McLean Papers. Greeley to Clay, April 28, 1848, Clay Papers. New York *Tribune*, May 2, 1848.

alarming. The radical Taylor men were even threatening to refuse to send delegations to the Whig National Convention. Clay's Lexington speech had set them irrevocably against his candidacy. These "Hotspurs" little knew of Taylor's willingness to come out for the rejection of all territory south of the old Missouri Compromise line, a proposal abandoned by Crittenden's advice. Yet Clay had not gone far enough to satisfy the followers of Corwin and Seward. He was advised that short of complete acceptance of the Wilmot Proviso he could not carry Ohio, while Seward had decided that he would jeopardize his own position by accepting a place on the ticket with Clay.[22] The Clay men thereupon turned to Scott, and so, on his arrival from Mexico, sounded him as to his willingness to take the place designed for Seward. He expressed his willingness to run for vice-president on the ticket with Clay to a member of Congress, supposedly a friend of Clay's, whom he authorized to make it known on his return to Washington. Thereafter until after the convention, Scott unfortunately was either out of Washington, or ill, and so in no condition to exercise any influence.[23]

Clay was defeated, however, before the delegates reached Philadelphia. The effective organization which had captured or divided delegation after delegation knew no relaxation. As the divided or doubtful delegations from the Upper South and the West arrived in Washington on their way to the convention, they were met at the train by committees from the Palo Alto Club and indoctrinated with the belief that Clay was unavailable, and that Taylor was the only man who could be elected. It was conceded that Taylor could not carry Ohio, but his friends insisted that he would make it up in Louisiana, Mississippi, and Georgia. The fact that with two exceptions

---

[22] Taylor to Crittenden, January 3, 1848; Balie Peyton to Crittenden, February 25, 1848; Burnley to Crittenden, April 4, 1848; Crittenden Papers. Gen. Z. Taylor to Col. J. P. Taylor, January 19, 1848, Taylor Papers. T. B. Stevenson to Clay, April 8, 1848; Corwin to Clay, May 3, 1848; Clay Papers. Toombs to Jas. Thomas, May 1, 1848, Phillips, *op. cit.,* pp. 104-5. Chase to Sumner, December 2, 1847, Bourne, *op. cit.,* pp. 125-27. Seward to Weed, December 14, 1847, Seward, *op. cit.,* II, 59. *Observer and Reporter,* October 9, 1847.

[23] Scott to Clay, July 19, 1848, Colton, *Private Correspondence,* pp. 570-71.

the Kentucky delegation in Congress was known to be adverse to Clay's nomination laid the foundation for his defeat in the convention, and he had only one "true-up-and-down-friend" among the convention delegates from his own state.[24]

The Clay men controlled the temporary organization of the convention; but they were consistently defeated on every crucial vote, although Morehead of North Carolina, who voted for Clay to the last, was made permanent chairman. The first test came on the appointment of the credentials committee, which would pass on the right of the single Taylor delegate from Arkansas to cast the three votes of that state, and of the Taylor-controlled Louisiana delegation to cast the four votes of Texas as proxies for its absent delegation. This committee reported and permanent organization was effected in secret session. When the public was admitted, discussion was in progress on the unit rule and a proposal of the Ohio delegation to require a pledge from all candidates to support the nominee of the convention. Both were rejected. The Taylor men, however, made a statement to the effect that they were authorized to withdraw his name from the canvass if he were not nominated.

On the first ballot Taylor received a hundred and eleven votes to Clay's ninety-seven, the difference representing the seven Kentucky delegates who "tomahawked" the "Sage of Ashland." Scott received forty-three, twenty of whom came from Ohio, five from New York, and six from Pennsylvania. Webster had twenty-two, all from New England, eighteen from Massachusetts and New Hampshire. Six votes went to McLean and the two Claytons. Twenty-eight of the thirty-six votes of New York, with the solid delegations of Connecticut, Rhode Island, and Maryland, formed the nucleus of Clay's strength; from the South he had only fourteen votes. With the exception of two votes for Clay, Taylor held a solid block extending from Georgia to Missouri, with majorities in the delegations from North Carolina, Virginia, and Kentucky. He received eighty-six votes from the slave states to twenty-two for Clay, and twenty-five from the free states to Clay's seventy-five.

[24] James Harlan to Clay, June 2, 1848; Leslie Combs to Clay, June 10, 1848; Clay Papers.

Clay's votes came from Whig states and Whig districts in Democratic states; three-fourths of Taylor's came from Democratic states and Democratic districts in Whig states.

The second ballot showed a slight shift of lukewarm Clay votes to Taylor and Scott, whereupon the convention adjourned. The caucussing that ensued effected no combination of Webster, Scott, and Clay to defeat Taylor, and on the following day the nomination was consummated. On the third ballot, Taylor lacked only eight votes of a majority and by the time New York was passed on the fourth ballot, these were secured and it remained only for the later delegations to climb on the band-wagon. On the final ballot, Clay had only six votes from the slave states, while Taylor received a hundred and five. Only sixty-six of the one hundred and sixty-nine free state delegates voted for Taylor.

Greeley asserted in the *Tribune* that

it was at no moment possible for the opponents of Gen. Taylor to have changed the result. If the vote of every delegate at heart adverse to Taylor could have been concentrated on one candidate at first, it would simply have nominated General Taylor a little earlier. The first three ballots were simply so many acts of a farce, played off to enable tenderfooted delegates to break through the instructions of their constituents gradually. . . . If it had been necessary to General Taylor's nomination to give him 140 votes on the first ballot, he would have got them.

Leslie Combs, however, reported to Clay that the Clay men, apparently out of pique at the obstinacy of the Scott and Webster delegates, turned to Taylor and nominated him. This suggests that the Clay delegates from the slave states, realizing that Clay had been merely used by Bebb and Corwin and "Seward, Weed and Greeley" to break down Taylor, determined at all hazards to prevent a deadlock and the nomination of an "abolitionist" candidate. That night, at any rate, Combs left a sick bed to speak at a "ratification meeting," which of course was regarded as voicing the acquiescence of the Clay stalwarts in Taylor's nomination.[25]

---

[25] New York *Tribune,* June 10, June 12, 1848; *National Intelligencer,* June 10, 1848. Leslie Combs to Clay, June 10, 1848; T. B. Sherman to Clay, June 19, 1848; J. L. Lawrence to Clay, June 23, 1848; Clay Papers.

But Clay was infuriated by the action of the convention and remained for several weeks unreconciled. Combs and Morehead had some difficulty in appeasing his resentment at what he considered their too ready acceptance of the result.[26] Especially angered by the defection of the Kentucky delegates, he indited a scathing denunciation of their conduct, exposing in no measured terms the whole procedure of Crittenden and the "croakers." The publication of this Clay entrusted to his son James, who delayed it until his father's wrath had in some measure subsided and then secured his consent to its suppression.[27] This action of James B. Clay's had far-reaching effects. Had publication occurred, Crittenden probably would have been defeated for governor and Taylor's own election might well have been endangered, while Clay himself could hardly have been returned to the Senate—that is, the rest of this narrative would have been radically different.

The Democrats fully realized the significance of an open breach between Clay and Crittenden. Details of Crittenden's manoeuvres were brought to Clay's ears and it was reported that Linn Boyd had possession of a letter from Crittenden to an Ohio gentleman in which he characterized Clay as "a dead-weight on the Whig party for the last twenty years." Crittenden, however, unhesitatingly stigmatized this letter as "either a fabrication or a gross perversion"; the other charges were explained to Clay's apparent satisfaction; the two statesmen remained on terms of civility, and in August Clay reluctantly cast his vote for Crittenden.[28]

"Seward, Weed and Greeley" were also disappointed, though only Greeley was in a position to vent his chagrin. With the vice-presidential nomination of Seward's rival, Fillmore, they were completely hoisted by their own petard.

---

[26] J. M. Botts to Clay, August 23, 1848, Clay Papers.

[27] On agreeing to the suppression of his statement, Clay characteristically tore up the manuscript. Mrs. James B. Clay, however, gathered up and copied the fragments. This copy, which is no longer in existence, was in part read to me in August, 1920, by her son, Mr. George H. Clay, who at that time related the circumstances.

[28] Clayton to Crittenden, June 19, 1848; Metcalfe to Crittenden, July 15, 1848; James Erwin to Burnley, July 18, 1848; statement by Crittenden, July 27, 1848; Burnley to Crittenden, September 23, 1848; Crittenden Papers. Stevenson to Clay, July 19, 1848, Clay Papers.

Greeley undertook to organize the disaffected Whigs of New England and New York for a bolt, putting Clay forward as the candidate. As early as July 4, Clay notified George W. Curtis that he could not countenance the use of his name in that connection. By mid-September, Combs was campaigning New York for the Whig ticket, and by the end of the month the movement died down. For several weeks, however, the Taylor managers were considerably alarmed.[29] Clay remained quiescent at Lexington during the campaign, and an illness which confined him to his home for three weeks spared him the necessity of going to the polls.[30]

---

[29] Clay to Curtis, July 4, 1848, Clay Papers. Crittenden Papers, August-September, 1848, *passim.*

[30] *Observer and Reporter,* November 23, 1848.

CHAPTER XIII

THE YOUNG INDIANS

THE TRIUMPH of Taylor brought exultation to the "Young Indians," who naturally enough expected to dominate his administration. They, as well as most of the other Whig leaders, expected Crittenden to be the "premier" in a very full sense of the term. Taylor's own inclinations coincided with this sentiment, and he accordingly made the offer, but Crittenden resisted all solicitations to resign his governorship, even after he learned that his plan of making Letcher Postmaster General as his representative in the Cabinet was impossible of execution.[1]

In this matter Taylor gave an ominous foretaste of the disadvantages inherent in making president a mere soldier, devoid of political experience or aptitude. This danger had not been apparent in Jackson or Harrison, both of whom were really politicians by profession and only incidentally soldiers, whereas Taylor had never voted and had given no consideration to political matters until his military success made him a presidential candidate. Totally lacking in tact and finesse himself, utterly unable to grasp the delicate nuances of political procedure, his military career had habituated him to concentration of responsibility and made him averse to consultation. Flattered by campaign encomiums, he had discarded his early feeling of inexperience and timidity, and now he went to the other extreme. He became prone to adopt "principles" to which he thereafter clung with bulldog tenacity. The man's honesty and conscientiousness won all who came into intimate association with him; but his blundering directness, his ill-conceived ideas, and his unconquerable stubbornness strewed the path of his advisers with thorns.

It was one of these mistaken but unalterable principles which now upset Crittenden's plans for the cabinet. Before leaving Baton Rouge, the General evolved from his inner con-

---

[1] Crittenden Papers, November, 1848-February, 1850, *passim.*

sciousness a scheme for awarding cabinet places to specific states, the individuals to be determined later; and should the first-selected individual decline, the post was then to go to some other state. Now, although informed of Crittenden's inability to accept, General Taylor would neither forbear to offer him the State Department nor deviate from his resolve not to make a second tender to Kentucky, thus barring Letcher from the Cabinet.[2]

Taylor had allowed a bare twenty-four hours for his sojourn at Frankfort, where everyone expected the Cabinet to be constructed in consultation with Crittenden. He later showed a peculiar imperviousness to unofficial counsels which still further upset Crittenden's plans. It is not improbable that Crittenden, having declined the official headship of the Cabinet, encountered this impenetrability. At any rate, Taylor departed with nothing decided except that John M. Clayton was to be "premier." Crittenden also advised consultation with Toombs and Stephens, which seems to have been done. Yet so well-informed a politician as Seward thought that the Cabinet had been made at Frankfort by Crittenden.[3]

Although deeply chagrined at not being called into consultation, Seward did not sulk. With characteristic patience and tact he managed to insinuate himself into the negotiations. He was instrumental in bringing together Taylor, Truman Smith, and Corwin, and also Taylor and Reverdy Johnson. He also made himself useful to the President-elect, during the closing days of the Polk Administration, by making known his desires in regard to pending legislation and organizing the Whigs to effectuate them. Thus, when the inauguration was at hand, he could inform Weed that Clayton was becoming confidential and General Taylor improving in favor.[4]

Seward's first problem was to neutralize the influence of the

---

[2] Burnley to Crittenden, January 12, 1849, Crittenden Papers; Crittenden to Clayton, February 17, 1849, Clayton Papers.

[3] Crittenden to Clayton, February 17, 1849, Clayton Papers. Avary, *op. cit.*, pp. 24-25; Johnston and Browne, *op. cit.*, p. 252. Seward to Mrs. Seward, February 27, 1849; same to Weed, February 27, 1849, Seward, *op. cit.*, II, 100-101.

[4] Seward to Weed, March 1, March 4, 1849, Seward, *op. cit.*, II, 101, 103; Seward in *National Intelligencer*, March 29, 1849, quoted by *Observer and Reporter*, April 7, 1849.

Vice-President in the interest of New York factionalism. One of Taylor's notions was that Fillmore was a sort of partner in the administration, and even that he would sit in the Cabinet. After a brief period of coöperation, apparently directed against the influence of Crittenden and the Southerners in cabinet-making, the Senator came to an issue with the Vice-President over appointments. Weed had negotiated an agreement between them at Albany in February, but Fillmore, seeing his favored position with Taylor, disregarded it on his arrival at Washington, and put forward his own adherents for the New York patronage. When the time for action arrived, however, Seward had insinuated himself into the good graces of the Cabinet, to whom the President, faced with unexpected conflict, had "passed the buck." But the Cabinet was timid in the matter, and would not make a definite decision until the happy device was found of accepting the recommendations of Governor Fish, ostensibly to strengthen the state administration at Albany. "Let Governor Fish now write to me," wrote Seward to Weed, "when you have any advice to give the Cabinet."[5]

When Seward left Washington toward the end of March, he had good reason to be satisfied with his month's work. He had secured control of the New York patronage to the discomfiture of his rival, Fillmore. He had been influential in the appointment of part of the Cabinet and had established confidential relations with Clayton and Ewing, its most influential members at this time, and the only ones bringing to it personal prestige. Meredith, the Secretary of the Treasury, a "dark horse" in politics gradually emerging as a very strong minister, was to become his chief personal intimate. In time, Clayton was to become unpopular and be discredited, Ewing was to be weakened by the taint of scandal and extreme partisan antagonism, and Meredith was to stand as the leader of a Northern faction in the Cabinet. Preston, Secretary of the Navy, would then head the Southern group, and with him Seward had made at least the beginning of an entente.

Preston had won the full confidence of President Taylor, and

---

[5] Seward to Weed, March 10, March 24, 1849, Seward, *op. cit.*, II, 107; Weed, *op. cit.*, pp. 584-87.

thus had strong personal as well as party reasons for being primarily concerned with securing his reëlection in 1852. He accordingly seized upon the idea of avoiding Northern competition through an alliance with Seward, who was to be built up as leader of the Whig party in the North through control of the patronage of that section, and who would accordingly throw this strength to General Taylor for renomination. Seward already controlled the New York appointments. The President allowed Ewing to control the patronage of the West, except Kentucky, while Meredith and Johnson held that of Pennsylvania and Maryland. This control extended not only to the offices within these localities, but also to candidates from them. These men were Seward's allies; so was Truman Smith, who largely controlled the New England patronage. Collamer, the Postmaster General, was friendly, but chiefly concerned with holding his job and drawing his salary. Thus, with the consent of all the Cabinet except Crawford, Secretary of War and spokesman for Toombs and Stephens, Seward was able to make himself the master of the Whig party in the North. A year later he admitted his control of the Wisconsin patronage through a Milwaukee editor, a son of Rufus King, and even boasted that his endorsement had been potent in Southern appointments, specifically in South Carolina.[6] Therefore, Seward left Washington in a highly complacent mood. "The beginning has been successful beyond anticipation," he wrote to Weed on March 24, 1849. "Things have ripened until suspicion has given place to confidence and weakness to strength. . . . The Cabinet are sound, the Senators wise, and there is yet no ascertained way upstairs through the kitchen of the White House."[7]

But the elements of a would-be "Kitchen Cabinet" were gathering. General Taylor had been accompanied to Washington by Alexander C. Bullitt, a member of the distinguished Kentucky family of that name, editor of the New Orleans

    [6] Toombs to Crittenden, April 15, 1850, Johnston and Browne, op. cit., pp. 252-53 (the elided names are readily supplied from Avary, op. cit., pp. 24-25). Washington Union, May 5, 1850, quoting an alleged "leak" from an executive session of the Senate from the New York Evening Post. New York Express, May 21, July 23, 1850.
    [7] Seward, op. cit., II, 107.

Picayune, and a personal friend. By mid-June Bullitt was installed with John N. Sargent, formerly an editorial writer on the New York *Courier and Enquirer,* as editors of *The Republic,* which was intended to be the organ of the administration. The financial "angel" of the enterprise was Albert T. Burnley of Kentucky, Louisiana and Texas, one of Crittenden's intimate correspondents. This group was intensely devoted to "Old Zach" personally, and felt that the great party organ, the *National Intelligencer,* had been only lukewarm, and was too conservative, even old-fashioned. Burnley, at least, was one of those Southerners, nominally Whigs, who had no enthusiasm for the orthodox Whig principles represented by Clay's "American System." To them, the non-partisan phase of the Taylor candidacy had been more than a political stratagem; it was a portent of the dissolution of the national parties as then constituted. Burnley's idea of party reconstruction was the repudiation of exclusive "Whiggery" and a return to the comprehensive Republican party of James Monroe.[8]

About the time *The Republic* made its debut, Bullitt and Burnley were reinforced by Orlando Brown, the new head of the Indian Bureau in Ewing's newly-created Interior Department. He had a familiar acquaintance with Taylor, and shared with Letcher Crittenden's closest personal and political intimacy. He had been editor of the Frankfort *Commonwealth,* Crittenden's personal organ, and had just resigned as Crittenden's Secretary of State. By every politician in Washington, Brown was at once recognized as the personal representative of the great Kentucky kingmaker, the supposed *deus ex machina* of the administration. Ewing had seen the portent and had sought to interpose an objection when Taylor broached the appointment in the Cabinet, but was peremptorily silenced by the General. Crittenden asserted that the appointment had been made without solicitation, and informed Clayton in unambiguous phrases not only of Brown's relation to himself, but

---

[8] Burnley to Crittenden, January 12, July 22, 1849, Crittenden Papers. T. M. Green, *Historic Families of Kentucky,* p. 150. Martha A. Burnley, "Albert Triplett Burnley," *Texas State Historical Association Quarterly,* XIV (October, 1910), 150-54, is an interesting biographical note.

of the part he expected him to play toward the Cabinet and the President.[9]

Brown worked in close collaboration with Bullitt and with Letcher, who was in Washington during the autumn, but his mission was a total failure. With his own chief, Ewing, he came to an all but open rupture by January, 1850. Ewing had kept in his own hands the patronage of Brown's office and in other ways made his position so unsatisfactory that by April, 1850, he had yielded to his homesickness for his Frankfort cronies and determined to resign at the end of his year. Most of the ministers he found very "stately" and unapproachable both politically and socially. Clayton had received him with over-effusive cordiality, but seems to have disregarded Crittenden's injunction to rely on his advice in regard to Kentucky patronage as on Crittenden's own. Brown was decidedly "cold-shouldered" by the other ministers except Crawford, who was an old friend, and, oddly enough, Meredith. One suspects that Meredith realized how innocuous politically Brown was, for in his unbelievable political obtuseness, "Old Zach" was utterly oblivious of the function for which Brown had really come to Washington. Brown could call at the White House immediately after breakfast and before the Cabinet met and have a private interview; the General could spend hours of an evening at Brown's house, pouring out his woes into a sympathetic ear for transmission to Crittenden; but in his strange dependence on official advisers, it never seemed to occur to the President that his Commissioner of Indian Affairs was trying to give advice. Orlando Brown was merely a confidant, not a counsellor. He was indeed the "favorite" Crittenden warned Clayton he would be, but it profited Crittenden nothing.

Yet during the early days of the administration, Crittenden's position was not far from what the politicians supposed it would be. His correspondence with Clayton reveals a remarkable situation. The Secretary clung to the Governor as the vine clings to the oak. Repeatedly he offered to resign that his friend might take his place. On every question he sought encouragement and advice, for every act he craved his

---

[9] Crittenden to Clayton, June 1, June 8, June 9, June 24, 1849, Clayton Papers. Brown to Crittenden, January 11, 1850, Crittenden Papers.

approval. He urged Crittenden to come to Washington to advise them. He longed for a conference if only for a single hour. They could meet at some intermediate point such as Cumberland, if Crittenden thought it inadvisable for him to come to Washington. Crittenden handled the delicate situation with characteristic tact. He was lavish with advice of a tentative suggestiveness and in a humorous tone of playful supererogation that avoided any tinge of offensive dictation. But in its scope, his advice included everything from foreign affairs to the distribution of patronage and even Clayton's demeanor toward individuals.[10]

In the meantime, the "Young Indians" had been much disturbed by the reëlection of Henry Clay to the Senate. The factional contest, which Crittenden had accepted the governorship to prevent, was about to be renewed over the Senatorship he had resigned. The fences of the younger aspirants were still so insecure, however, that they were not sorry to see the contest postponed. Governor Owsley at once offered the post to Clay; and on his declining, appointed another aged statesman, former Governor Metcalfe, to serve until the meeting of the legislature in January, 1849. The suggestion of Clay's election meanwhile bore fruit both in the gradual formation of a strong public opinion in its favor, and in the creation of a keen, but scarcely recognized, desire in the mind of Clay himself.[11]

With health and finances improved by six years of private life, he doubtless craved the excitement of Washington politics. His friends beyond question wished to give the world a demonstration of his unshaken hold on the Whig party in Kentucky, and openly defied the "bushwhackers" to manipulate the legislature as they had the convention. Since the settlement of the territorial question had not yet developed into a crisis, the oft-

[10] Clayton to Crittenden, March 16, April 8, April 18, May 7, May 31, August 23, 1849; Crittenden Papers. Crittenden to Clayton, March 13, April 6, April 11, April 16, April 17, April 23, May 12, June 1, June 8, June 9, June 24, June 28, June 29, July 8, July 20, July 23, August 3, August 4, September 1, September 3, September 29, October 6, 1849; Clayton Papers.

[11] Jas. Harlan to Crittenden, March 4, 1848; Crittenden Papers. Frankfort *Kentucky Yeoman,* June 29, 1848.

repeated tale of his purpose to enact another compromise is decidedly apocryphal. Perhaps Clay wanted to display his mastery over the party which had refused him its formal leadership, and his superiority to the crude soldier it had preferred. Since he has left no evidence of his motives, he may even have felt all the malignity toward Taylor which the "Young Indians" feared.[12]

Balie Peyton, who, as a Tennesseean, knew Kentucky politics, took it for granted that Clay would be elected, and he feared that "with his energy, and vigor of character, impelled by a morbid state of feeling, he will play hell, and break things . . . and unless the old general obeyed his orders in all things, he would make war upon him too." Every Whig at Washington expected him "to kick up a row as sure as he comes." The Democrats were delighted at the prospect, "the old Hunkers of the Whig party who have been accustomed to the crack of his whip" were "scared to death," but the "Young Indians" would "fight him like wild-cats." For the "Young Indians" felt that their position toward "Old Master" was like that of "Mad Anthony" Wayne at Yorktown, when he said to his men, "Boys, there they are; if you don't kill them, they will kill you." Toombs thought he meant to "make a party of his own and perhaps join the free soilers." To all of which Crittenden replied that he was "surrounded and enthralled by such circumstances" as scarcely to give him any control of himself. Many would regret that, under existing circumstances, Clay should desire to return to the Senate, "but," wrote the governor, "Kentucky can hardly refuse it to him if he makes it known that he desires it."[13]

Clay's friends asserted that Clay and Taylor maintained a "cordial and friendly correspondence," and in the Whig legislative caucus a letter from Letcher was read declaring that Clay had no intention of opposition, but rather a wish to give General Taylor's administration a cordial support. Even Crittenden decided that there was "nothing to be dreaded in the

---

[12] *Observer and Reporter*, December 27, 1848; January 3, 1849.

[13] Peyton to Crittenden, August 29, 1848; Gaims to Crittenden, January 18, 1849; Pendleton to Crittenden, September 14, 1848; Toombs to Crittenden, December 3, 1848; Crittenden Papers. Crittenden to Clayton, January 7, 1849, Clayton Papers.

result," and there was a general concurrence of the Whigs in his support. The Democrats made no caucus nomination, but cast forty-nine votes for Richard Mentor Johnson to the Whigs' ninety-three for Clay.[14]

Indeed, at this time Clay gave every indication of a strong desire to maintain amicable relations with Taylor, if not something closer. Before leaving for New Orleans, according to the press, he had invited Taylor to visit Ashland on his way to Washington and had received in return an invitation to spend a week at Baton Rouge. However, he there encountered the General, who was seeing Burnley and Peyton off on the same boat, and no invitation to stop was extended. Some of the men who immediately surrounded General Taylor both hated and feared Clay, and lost no opportunity to impress it upon him that Clay was inspired by inveterate personal rivalry. Taylor, indeed, seems to have been only too prone to view everything in a merely personal connection. This may have been a result of lack of experience with politicians, but he sometimes appeared to lack magnanimity. Thus, when Clay, in May, 1849, solicited for his son James a foreign mission which he said Harrison had promised to Henry, who fell at Buena Vista, and which Tyler had refused, Taylor at once agreed to send the young man to Lisbon. But Taylor and Clayton gloatingly told all and sundry of the request, and when the appointment drew criticism from the "original Taylor men," actually contemplated making an official explanation. This drew from Crittenden a really peremptory letter.[15] He wrote:

Anything like an official or authoritative explanation to show that it was *solicited*, would take off all the good & grace of the act, &, perhaps, make things worse. . . . Mr. Clay, I am persuaded, is disposed to be Genl. Taylor's friend, & will duly appreciate any mark of favor & confidence—& from my heart I desire as a matter of policy & feeling, to see a cordial reconciliation between them. Let no more be said about Mr. Clay's *letter* requesting office for his

[14] *Observer and Reporter,* December 10, December 20, December 27, 1848; January 24, February 3, 1849; Frankfort *Kentucky Yeoman,* January 25, 1849.

[15] Burnley to Crittenden, January 12, 1849; Clayton to Crittenden, May 31, 1849; Brown to Crittenden, June 23, 1849; Crittenden Papers.

son—not a word—it is not *necessary*—it will be in bad *taste,* & will do *mischief.* These little things must not be allowed to have such consequence. I pray you, talk with the General about it.[16]

But Crittenden was either ineffectual or too late, for the conduct of the President and the Secretary of State came to Clay's ears and aroused intense resentment.

Clay was too old a hand not to appreciate the coldness of General Taylor's demeanor that January day at Baton Rouge. So when the Kentucky papers reached New Orleans with the news of his election to the Senate, it was at once denied that he "had written a letter pledging his warm support" to Taylor's administration, with the further statement that he stood "Wholly uncommitted to the course he intends to pursue in the next Congress." When his attention was called to a feeler which Clayton had put out through the press as to his going into honorable exile, "he replied in his usual bland style, that the office of Minister to France was offered to him by Mr. Madison thirty years ago, and it was hardly possible that he would accept the post at his present advanced age, and in his present circumstances."[17]

While these events were transpiring in the West, the Taylor men at Washington were making a final effort to save the incoming administration from the embarrassment of the territorial question. From the time when David Wilmot moved his "Proviso" as an amendment to the "Three Million Bill" and "Honest John" Davis stupidly talked it to death in the final moments of the Twenty-ninth Congress, the situation had grown increasingly difficult. Clayton had tried his hand at a compromise in the summer of 1848, only to fail. Now the issue was to be forced upon the country in a manner which brooked no further delay. News of the discovery of gold in January, 1848, reached the East by the beginning of the following winter, and by spring the epic rush of the "Forty-niners" was under way. The rapid influx of population and the peculiar problems of maintaining law and order inherent

---

[16] Crittenden to Clayton, June 27, 1849, Clayton Papers.
[17] *Observer and Reporter,* February 17, February 24, March 17, 1849.

in the situation made imperative the early establishment of a government resting on a popular basis and functioning through familiar channels, rather than the provisional government with its vague authority.

But when Congress met in December, 1848, the leaders little conceived the political significance of the gold discovery. Stephens hoped the South would "let the question rest until the time comes for the territories to be formed into States and admitted just as they like." Six weeks later, the Southern Whigs were trying to put through Preston's scheme "to erect all of California and that portion of New Mexico lying west of the Sierra into a *State* as soon as she forms a constitution and asks it," which they anticipated existing conditions would soon drive her to do. That would leave "but a very narrow strip, not averaging more than fifteen or twenty miles, between this California line and the Rio Grande line of Texas," to which the Democrats and some of the Northern Whigs were committed, who would then vote this strip to Texas. This in effect was a nominal division by a north and south line, for everyone was quite certain that California would prohibit slavery by her own action, and the Southern Whigs were equally convinced, as Crittenden wrote, "that no sensible man would carry his slaves there if he could."[18]

To Crittenden at that time, "For the North or the South to talk of dissolving the Union for such a question, decided one way or the other, sounds to my ears like nonsense or something worse." He therefore thought a project of Clayton's for settling the slavery question quite practicable. It was simply to give a hint to the people of both California and New Mexico to follow the Michigan and Arkansas precedents to organize as states, and present themselves for admission at the next session of Congress. The failure of the Preston scheme left this plan as the next alternative of the administration. In April, Crittenden reminded Clayton of the importance of the matter, hoped that he had had no reason to change his opinion as to

[18] Stephens to Crittenden, December 6, 1848; Clayton to Crittenden, December 13, 1848; Toombs to Crittenden, January 9, January 22, 1849; Crittenden Papers. Crittenden to Clayton, December 19, 1848, Clayton Papers.

its feasibility, and suggested "that no proper means" should be "left unemployed to effect the object."

"It seems to me," he continued,

that it ought to be regarded as the *great object* of the Administration and its accomplishment sought with all its policy and energy. Not only the safety of the Administration, but the safety of the country, may depend upon it. Your constant attention will, I have no doubt, be directed to this subject. All the government agents & officers there ought to have sense & discretion enough to see the importance of the object, & to act upon it, *without any formal instructions*. . . . My anxiety has made me notice with more than ordinary attention the appointments . . . to California.

To this Clayton responded, "As to California & New Mexico, I have been *wide awake*. Everything is done as you would wish it. The plan I proposed to you last winter will be carried out fully. The States will be admitted—free and Whig!" But the Secretary of State failed to add that T. Butler King had been dispatched on his mission by the advice of the junior Senator from New York.[19]

Before they left Washington that spring, the Georgia inseparables had begun to suspect the designs of Seward. The character of the New York appointments and other incidents increased their suspicions. The fear excited by the growing influence of the wily New Yorker was a definite factor in the rapprochement of the Southern Whigs and Democrats, which was effected in the fall by the correspondence between Senator Foote of Mississippi and Clingman, a North Carolina Representative who wrote with the full concurrence of Senator Mangum. By the opening of Congress, the people of the South were united in demanding that Congress should not pass the Wilmot Proviso or abolish slavery in the District of Columbia. Ten months before, Alexander H. Stephens had recognized that the passage of these "together would produce revolution, dissolution & civil war."[20] So far as the Cotton States were concerned, the only divisions were as to just what step of Northern

---

[19] Clayton to Crittenden, December 13, 1848, April 18, 1849, Crittenden Papers. Crittenden to Clayton, December 19, 1848, April 11, 1849, Clayton Papers. Seward, *op. cit.*, II, 114.

[20] G. Duncan to Crittenden, January 15, 1849, Crittenden Papers.

aggression should be regarded as necessitating secession, and as to the tactics to be used in the conflict. Recent detailed studies of public opinion in the South make it impossible longer to doubt that by March, 1850, the South was ripe for secession should the Wilmot Proviso be enacted, slavery abolished in the District of Columbia, or the inter-state slave trade prohibited. One state, Georgia, included the admission of California as then proposed.[21]

It was indeed, the demand of California for statehood which precipitated the crisis. The people of California had needed no prompting from Thomas Butler King, President Taylor's special agent, to assemble in convention, adopt a constitution, and apply for admission as a state. With frontier directness, quite reasonable under the circumstances of pressing necessity and delayed communication, they dispatched the application by the Senators and Representatives whom its grant would seat in Congress, and immediately set in operation the new State Constitution. Their action was irregular in form, and went beyond the precedents set in the cases of Michigan and Arkansas in omitting altogether the territorial stage, in fixing boundaries not previously drawn by Congress, and in organizing the State Government without waiting for congressional approval of their actions.

The highly-suspicious Stephens got wind of the understanding between Seward and Preston about as soon as it was arrived at, doubtless through Crawford. Keeping a keen eye on developments through the summer of 1849, he was confirmed in his suspicions. As he appraised the situation, the Wilmot Proviso was to be made an administration measure with the double object of destroying the Northern Democrats, who were bound as partisans to oppose it in favor of "Popular Sovereignty," and of absorbing the Free Soilers by making the Northern Whig party a free soil party. He and Toombs therefore came to the meeting of Congress determined to block this "nefarious transaction" at all costs, clearly perceiving that its consummation would destroy the Whig party in the South.

---

[21] C. C. Hearon, *Mississippi and the Compromise of 1850,* pp. 16-90, gives an admirable account of the "Southern movement." For other similar studies see footnote, p. 208.

Negotiations with the Northern leaders proving fruitless, they organized the Southern remnant of the "Young Indians," and, after first seeking to put the Whig caucus on record against the Wilmot Proviso, "seceded" from the caucus.

It is unnecessary to rehearse the story of the long deadlock over the organization of the House and the final election of Howell Cobb by plurality vote. The "seceders" opposed to the last the change in the rules, their purpose being to prevent any organization on party lines. The sensational Brown episode has obscured a similar effort on the Whig side which is especially significant as foreshadowing the future alignment on the compromise measures. The "seceders" were willing to support Morehead of Kentucky for Speaker, who was also more acceptable to the Northwestern Democrats than Cobb, whom they were inclined to regard as a Southern "ultra." Morehead, had declined being a candidate before the caucus, partly at least, because as representative from Clay's old district he was not cordially regarded by Taylor, but now he consented, Winthrop having withdrawn. But although enough Democratic votes to elect him were pledged, he was unable to command the full Whig strength, a number of Northern Whigs refusing to support anyone acceptable to the "seceders."[22]

Thus, the immediate effect of Seward's attempt to form a coalition of Northern Whigs, Free Soilers and Wilmot Proviso Democrats was to provoke a secession of the Southern Whigs and their alliance with the more moderate Southern Democrats and the Democracy of the Northwest led by Douglas and his lieutenants. It was also their suspicion of Seward's influence over the Taylor administration which led Toombs and Stephens and their associates to make the combination of the compromise measure into an "omnibus" bill a *sine qua non* so long as Taylor lived, while they acquiesced in their separate enactment after the accession of Fillmore.

[22] Avary, *op. cit.*, p. 26; Morehead to Crittenden, December 25, 1849, Crittenden Papers.

CHAPTER XIV

THE GREAT PACIFICATOR

THE ORGANIZATION of the House permitted the President's Message to be received. It informed Congress of the action of the California convention with a recommendation of favorable action on her application for statehood; and also that it was believed that New Mexico would shortly take similar action. The President advised that by leaving the settlement of the territorial question to these spontaneous movements, the introduction of exciting sectional topics could be avoided. But this advice was disregarded, a multiplicity of measures dealing with the dangerous subject being submitted. Among them were to be found practically all the elements of the future compromise. Not less significant, moreover, were the calls for information in regard to the proceedings in California and New Mexico which eventually passed both Houses.[1]

On January 21, after several days' delay, the President's reply to this call was at last read in the House. It revealed not only the details of what came to be known as "the President's plan," but also the movements of the administration to effectuate it. The real mission of T. Butler King was officially avowed, as well as the President's advice to California and New Mexico to frame state constitutions and apply for admission to the Union. The organization of New Mexico as a state, it added, would enable the Supreme Court to take jurisdiction in the matter of the disputed boundary of Texas. Otherwise, Congress in settling the territorial limits of New Mexico would practically settle the question either adversely to Texas or in her favor. The remainder of the territory eastward of California, the President understood from unofficial information, would also shortly present itself for statehood. Meanwhile, it would suffer no practical inconvenience from the absence of a government established by Congress, the Mormon organization being sufficient for its needs.[2]

---

[1] *Congressional Globe,* 31st Cong., 1st Sess., pp. 69, 87, 90, 103, 110, 150, 185.

[2] *Ibid.,* pp 195-96, 200-209.

This message drew a speech on the following day from Clingman of North Carolina which was sufficient to alarm all conservative men. He took the ground that concession on any one point of the anti-slavery program would not check but merely accelerate the movement. The long and systematic propaganda of the abolitionists had produced a state of public opinion that even fair and moderate Northern representatives were unable to resist. Rehearsing all the grievances of the South, the speaker asserted that concession now would produce within five years a Northern majority in both Houses, by which, under certain circumstances, they could abolish slavery in the states. Within twenty years, they would have enough states to amend the Constitution to that effect. Many Southerners had already begun to weigh the alternative of separation. Meanwhile, he was for resistance by the same constitutional means that the North had contemplated using to defeat the Walker amendment. A majority was necessary to pass a measure, but one-fifth of the members could demand the yeas and nays, and if they stood firm and were supported by the people at home, they could stop the wheels of the government. He was prepared to see all the appropriations fail unless they could get, in advance, a fair settlement. The South would thus secure time to take concerted action through a convention, to prevent its being deprived of its right to share in the territories. As for the threat of expelling those who obstructed the majority, such a collision there might electrify the country as Lexington did the colonies.[3]

The South had been so much in the habit of vaporing about trifles, that the North was inclined to regard Clingman's speech as mere bluster and to assimilate the present excitement to the past. But the correspondents of conservative newspapers gave warning that the secession talk was not mockery, but a solemn earnest, and that the facts should be understood. One of the oldest Northern Senators told a correspondent "that he never witnessed anything like it in the history of the country before, and that the excitement preceding the Missouri Compromise was a mere bubble compared to it."[4]

---

[3] *Ibid.*, pp. 200-205.
[4] New York *Express*, January 10, January 19, 1850.

The month which had elapsed since the reading of the Annual Message had not increased the disposition to regard the President's recommendation as final. To his disgust, men insisted upon waiting to hear what Clay and Webster would have to say. Before long it was known that Clay intended at the proper time to make a move for adjustment. Even before the meeting of Congress, he had given much thought to the subject, and from the beginning of the session, cutting himself off from all the usual social enjoyments, he had confined himself almost exclusively to his own lodgings. The excitement which the President's California message produced in the House seemed to call for action, and so he that night sought to enlist the coöperation of Webster.[5]

Although the inclemency of the weather comported ill with his feeble health, without any previous intimation of his visit, he called on Webster at his house. He "seemed very feeble, had a bad cough, and became quite exhausted in the interview," which lasted about an hour. Clay explained his plan, stating that it would suit some Democratic Senators and most of the Southern Whigs except those from Georgia. Webster agreed to the principle of the plan, though not prepared to concur in all its details, and promised to give it the utmost attention. After his visitor had gone, however, he confided to a friend, who had been present during part of the interview, that his first impression was that they could adopt the whole of it, and that he felt that perhaps Clay's return to the Senate had been designed by Providence to avert a great evil from the country.[6]

Evidence is lacking as to Clay's further negotiations, though it is impossible to doubt the fact. Cass was known to be meditating a conservative plan of settlement, and all indications point to Benton as one of the elderly gentlemen whom Seward said were emulous for "the honors and rewards of compromise." At the time, Clay's compromise effort was not regarded as indicating any intention other than "to play fair with the

---

[5] *Congressional Globe*, 31st Cong., 1st Sess., p. 116; *Observer and Reporter*, November 23, 1850; Brown to Crittenden, January 11, April 19, 1850, Crittenden Papers.

[6] Curtis, *op. cit.*, II, 397-98.

Administration and give it his support."[7] Such were the conditions under which Clay, on January 29, introduced his compromise resolutions in the Senate.

The preamble declared their purpose to be "to settle and adjust amicably all the existing questions of controversy . . . arising out of the institution of slavery, upon a fair, equitable, and just basis." First, then, California, with suitable boundaries, ought to be admitted as a state upon application, Congress imposing no restriction positive or negative in regard to slavery. Secondly, since slavery did not exist by law in any territory acquired from Mexico, and was unlikely to be introduced, it was inexpedient for Congress to pass any law either introducing or excluding it from that territory, and territorial governments ought to be established without any such restriction. Thirdly, the boundary between Texas and New Mexico ought to be established on a stated line, and fourthly, in consideration of the acceptance of this line, the United States should assume a fixed amount of the public debt of Texas, contracted prior to annexation, for payment of which the import duties had been pledged. Fifthly, it was inexpedient to abolish slavery in the District of Columbia, so long as it continued to exist in Maryland, without the consent of the people of the District, and without compensation to the owners. Sixthly, it was expedient to prohibit within the District trade in slaves brought from without for the purpose of sale, or for transportation. Seventhly, more effective provision ought to be made by law, according to the constitutional requirement, for the recovery of fugitive slaves. Eightly, Congress had no power to interfere with the interstate slave trade.

Having presented and briefly explained his resolutions, Clay concluded with a plea for concession. The North, as the more powerful section, should be magnanimous. In addition, concession by the North involved only sentiment, without sacrifice, danger, hazard or loss. As for the South, a vast amount of property was involved, but also, in addition, "the social fabric, life, and all that makes life desirable and happy." In delivering this speech, Clay was said to be equal in manner to

---

[7] Brown to Crittenden, January 11, 1850, Crittenden Papers; Seward to Weed, December 3, 1849, Seward, *op. cit.*, II, 113.

his best days. Toombs was in perfect ecstasy at his splendid display of oratory, nerve, and power.[8]

Clay's speech was talked of everywhere, but Orlando Brown thought its effect greater upon the North than upon the South, since the inhabitants of the latter region seemed "to be incapable of being made satisfied by anything short of the North getting down on its knees and begging pardon." Conservative Northern Whig papers at once gave his plan support, even pointing out that the effect of settling the slavery question entirely to Northern satisfaction might result in a "continuous factious and bitter opposition to every measure . . . that might incidentally benefit the North," such as river and harbor improvements for the West, a tariff for the middle and eastern states, and commercial protection for the Atlantic cities. Both the President's Message and Clay's resolution showed that no Wilmot Proviso could or should be passed; both took ground against it as "unnecessary, if not uncalled for." The *Observer and Reporter* seems to have well represented Kentucky sentiment in endorsing the resolutions. Though it might not approve all of the proposals, concessions must be made in a compromise. Even Ritchie's *Union*, representing the conservative Democracy, decidedly approved at least one thing in them —the proposal to settle the whole question at once and forever. They also might prompt additional discussions and excite other minds to devise other and better modes of adjustment.[9]

Although, despite Clay's deprecation of hasty commitments, various spokesmen for the South immediately took ground against his resolutions, the formal debate began only on February 5, when Clay took two hours and a quarter to deliver less than half of a great speech which he concluded on the following day. The news that he was to speak brought numbers, both men and women, from Baltimore, New York, Boston and even more distant places to hear him. The galleries, the cloak rooms and even the corridors were packed. Winthrop, speaking

---

[8] *Congressional Globe*, 31st Cong., 1st Sess., pp. 244, 247; Brown to Crittenden, February 1, 1850, Crittenden Papers.

[9] Brown to Crittenden, February 1, 1850, Crittenden Papers; New York *Express*, January 30, 31, February 5, February 6, February 7, 11, 20, 1850; *Observer and Reporter*, February 2, February 6, 1850; Washington *Union* February 2, February 3, 1850.

in the House, could not hold his audience. Like Alexander H. Stephens, they had crossed over to the Senate Chamber to hear Henry Clay.

When the order of the day was called, Clay folded the papers on which he had been writing, put them in his desk, and rose gracefully and majestically. Instantly there was a burst of applause, of which he took no notice; but it was heard without, and the great crowd raised such a shout that Clay perforce paused until the officers could clear the entrances. He was "apparently no more excited than if he were quietly endeavoring to calm the heated passion of a friend at his own fireside, by words of sage advice." "His voice is good," wrote Stephens, "his enunciation clear and distinct, his action firm, his strength far surpassing expectation. He held the riveted gaze of the multitude the whole time. When he concluded, an immense throng of friends, both men and women, came up to congratulate him and to *kiss* him."[10]

On the following day, the galleries and lobbies were again filled exclusively by ladies, and in every nook and corner of the space behind the Vice President's chair were members of the other house and distinguished persons. Amid the throng and the attendant excitement, Clay quietly resumed his speech where he had left off, as if the occasion were but one of the most ordinary character. To the surprise of an auditor who had thought Clay's "enthusiasm" of character sprang from egotism, "his manner and address was the personification of modest greatness."

To attempt to give an adequate summary of such a speech, embracing all the features of the compromise resolutions, presenting elaborate legal and historical arguments in support of each, and reinforcing those arguments by every device in the repertory of the finished orator, is hopeless. According to one auditor,

Mr. Clay's peroration . . . was in all his ancient and unclouded splendor,—patriotism of the highest order, uttered in tones and emphasis that made the blood of every man, every woman in that

---

[10] Johnston and Browne, *op. cit.*, p. 249, letter of February 20, 1850; New York *Express*, February 6, 1850.

vast crowd run and thrill through their veins, and that drew tears in many an eye. There seemed to be a solemnity, and a grandeur in his appeal that lifted him as it were from the earth, and seemed as a voice speaking from Heaven.[11]

The debate on Clay's resolutions got under way February 11, and ended March 27, although they were formally disposed of only on April 18, when they were referred to the Committee of Thirteen. The climax of the debate came early in March, when within eight days Calhoun, Webster and Seward made the classic presentation of the case for their respective parties. But the first week of the debate saw a sensational encounter between Clay and Foote of Mississippi which raised Clay to the very pinnacle of his influence.

Foote, who was then acting with the Southern ultras, reminded Clay in the course of debate that he came from a Slave State. Says a contemporary account;

No report can lift itself up to the towering grandeur, the flaming eye, the outstretched arm, the extended muscle, the radiant air, the sublime manner in which he thundered forth in all the sweetness of his organ tone, "I know no South, no North, no East, no West to which I owe any allegiance. I owe allegiance to two sovereignties, and only two; one is to the sovereignty of the Union, and the other is to the sovereignty of the State of Kentucky." It withered all the plotters of a Southern Confederacy that heard him. It actually made them tremble.[12]

Even Webster was reported to have paid him the compliment, "You improve in eloquence, Sir; you are a younger man than ever." That evening his outburst was the theme of every tongue in the city.[13]

"The very presence of the man is an influence," wrote one correspondent.

His patriotism, his self-sacrifice, arouse the patriotic and the selfish to imitate his glorious example. His rebukes hush and over-

---

[11] *Congressional Globe,* 31st Cong., 1st Sess., pp. 115-27; New York *Express,* February 7, 1850.

[12] *Congressional Globe,* 31st Cong., 1st Sess.; New York *Express,* February 18, 1850.

[13] New York *Express,* February 18, 1850.

awe the fanatical in both extremes of the Union. . . . He alienates both the North and the South. But no man in Washington has the adoration he now has. He is the first asked for, the most thought of, the last forgotten. The fair sex, of both parties, and of all sections, vie in expressing their admiration, their friendship, their devotion,—and his winning manners, and wonderful conversational tact bewitch all who come within his fascination. Beyond all doubt, . . . if he were a candidate for a high public office, old ambitions and almost forgotten wounds would be reopened,—but as he is, all parties pay him compliments and bear tributes to his service.[14]

But this was gall and wormwood to the President, who, with all his honesty and courage, was strangely lacking in magnanimity. His suspicions of Clay's intentions were continually fed by the men who surrounded him, and he was firmly convinced that Clay had come to Washington for the express purpose of usurping his leadership of the Whig party. He believed that Clay had announced his intention of proposing a compromise in order to divert attention from the recommendations of the message, and that but for his meddling the "President's plan" would have been enacted without serious opposition. As he saw the public voice giving to Clay the primacy to which he thought himself entitled, he developed a morbid jealousy. When Clay, toward the end of April, at last criticized his plan, he felt that it reflected the same attitude as Webster's, when he declared his nomination one "not fit to be made." For Webster, also, though in less degree, was the object of his jealousy. At length Taylor was ready to believe that Clay had deliberately "cut" him on the Avenue, though he had spoken first. Clay hastened to call at the White House. "General Taylor, I am incapable of such a discourtesy," he said. "I hold you in too much respect to think of such a thing, much less to indulge in it. I walk for air and exercise. To be able to walk, and to escape the kindness of my friends, I look straight ahead to see nobody. I never knew I passed you till told that

---

[14] New York *Express,* February 18, 1850. "But let it always be said of old Hal that he fought a glorious and a patriotic battle. No man was ever governed by higher & finer motives. The same remark is true of Gen'l. Cass." Douglas to Lanphier & Walker. August 3, 1850, Lanphier Papers, a copy of which I owe to the kindness of Professor F. H. Hodder, of the University of Kansas. Cf. note 26 below.

you were told I intended a slight upon you." To such a pass had their relations come by the end of April.[15]

During those weeks when threats, tumults, and demonstrations were the order of the day and apprehensions of "the most disastrous conclusion" were on the increase, a well-placed and intelligent observer found the President "as calm, collected and determined as a great and good man alone can be on the eve of momentous events in which he may be called upon to be the most conspicuous actor." The antagonism of the Southern Whigs was as yet confined to the Cabinet, for they were not yet aware that General Taylor himself had succumbed to the charm of the New York Senator. In January, they still cherished the hope that in spite of his campaign declarations against the use of the veto, he could be brought to exercise it against the Wilmot Proviso. They argued that since the practical effect of the Proviso would be to destroy the Constitution by precipitating the dissolution of the Union, he could consistently veto it as not only inexpedient but "practically unconstitutional." But they needed assurance. These arguments were therefore transmitted to Crittenden by Brown, and, in a forceful letter of February 18, Crittenden presented them to Clayton, but they could hardly have reached Washington before the Southern Whigs had come to an open rupture with the President for whose nomination they were mainly responsible.[16]

On Wednesday, February 13, President Taylor had transmitted the California constitution to Congress, and at once a debate arose in the House on the question of printing. On the following Monday, it being "resolution day," Doty of Wisconsin, a Democrat, offered a resolution instructing the Committee on Territories to report a bill for the admission of California under her constitution, and called the previous question upon it. Although a large majority of the House favored the admission of California, the Southern Whigs were determined that the territorial question should be settled first. They therefore resisted Doty's resolution in the only way open to them under

<hr>

[15] Brown to Crittenden, April 19, 1850, Crittenden Papers; New York *Express*, April 29, 1850. Douglass to Lanphier & Walker, August 3, 1850, Lanphier Papers.

[16] Brown to Crittenden, January 11, 1850, Crittenden Papers; Crittenden to Clayton, February 18, 1850, Clayton Papers.

the rules, as indicated by Clingman a month before, by dilatory motions, on all of which the yeas and nays were demanded. Southern members generally joined zealously in this game. The movement was rapidly organized even while the struggle was in progress. Alexander H. Stephens made a list, saw the members and secured the pledges of more than the requisite one-fifth to resist the question and prevent its ever coming to a vote under such circumstances. The contest consumed the whole day and the early hours of the night, the roll-calls revealing at length a completely sectional division. Party lines were so disrupted that little intercourse occurred between Northern and Southern members of either party. The struggle continued until midnight, when the Speaker ruled that the legislative day had ended, and that Doty's resolution, which could be considered only on Mondays, was no longer in order. The exhausted House acquiesced in the decision and adjourned.[17]

While the filibuster was in progress, McClernand of Illinois, Douglas's chief aide in the House, conferred with Stephens and Toombs as to the possibility of some arrangement. The Georgians stated their position with great frankness, and set forth their propositions in writing. The territorial question was to be settled in advance of the admission of California. Not only should there be no Congressional exclusion of slavery from the public domain, but in organizing territorial governments, "the people under each should be distinctly empowered so to legislate as to allow the introduction of slaves, and to frame their Constitution in respect to African slavery, as they pleased, and when admitted as States into the Union, should be received without Congressional restriction upon the subject." On reading them, McClernand stated that he thought they might form the basis of a compromise.

Before adjournment, McClernand arranged with the Georgians a conference for the following night at Cobb's house. Cobb and Linn Boyd, Toombs and Stephens, McClernand and Richardson of Illinois, Miller of Ohio and one or two others were present. McClernand stated that he had conferred with Douglas, who had agreed to coöperate in any course Mc-

---

[17] *Congressional Globe,* 31st Cong., 1st Sess., pp. 375-85; A. H. Stephens, *A Constitutional View of the Late War Between the States,* II, 201-2.

Clernand might agree to on the subject. Douglas did not attend the meeting merely because it was a conference of members of the House. It was agreed that California should be admitted and the territorial governments organized as stated, the whole group working for that result. They also pledged themselves to resist any attempt to abolish slavery in the District of Columbia. The actual phrasing of the crucial provisions of the territorial bills was agreed upon and reduced to writing, and in due time embodied in bills prepared by Douglas and McClernand for their respective committees. The House committee reported them in "omnibus" form, but the Senate committee, after considering their union, decided to report them separately. In this, Douglas acted in accordance with advice he sought and received from Clay and Cass.[18]

As a sequel to the negotiations with McClernand, Toombs and Stephens sought an interview with the President. Their specific object cannot be determined, but certainly involved a use of the veto power—possibly to prevent the enactment of the Wilmot Proviso in any form. Whatever their question, the President replied that he would approve any constitutional bill that Congress might pass. To this they naturally objected that the Wilmot Proviso was "practically unconstitutional." In presenting their arguments, they of course referred to the probability of secession, should the contingency arise which they were seeking to prevent. To them such an argument was merely a statement of accepted fact, but to General Taylor it was a threat. In great excitement, he informed them that if it became necessary in executing the laws, he would take command of the army himself, and that if they attempted to carry out any such designs they should be dealt with by law as traitors. Thus the rupture between the President and the "seceders" was violently accomplished, though it was to be another two months before he similarly alienated the more moderate Whigs of the upper South.[19]

---

[18] Stephens, *op. cit.*, II, 202-14; New York *Express,* February 20, February 21, 1850; *Congressional Globe,* 31st Cong., 1st Sess., p. 1830. Douglass to Lanphier & Walker, August 3, 1850, Lanphier Papers.

[19] Barnes, *op. cit.*, pp. 176-79. This account must be interpreted in the light of Stephens' letters of January 21 and February 11, 1850, Johnston and Browne, *op. cit.*, pp. 243-45, 248, and of December 6, 1848, Crittenden

While this crucial situation was developing in the House of Representatives, and in the Senate, spokesmen for the South in rapid succession gave utterance to the grave discontent and resentment of the section, even more alarming conditions appeared outside of Congress. A growing body of newly exploited materials has brought conviction to historical scholars that there really was grave danger of secession in 1850, a danger only averted by the compromise, and that this danger was most acute during the latter half of February and the first week of March. Thirteen Southern States took some sort of action in support of the radical position, and nine appointed delegates to the Southern Convention which was to meet at Nashville in June. It was during this crucial four weeks from February 6 to March 6 that Georgia, Texas, Tennessee, Virginia, Alabama, and Mississippi appointed their delegates to the Nashville Convention. During this same period several other state legislative bodies expressed their sympathy with their brethren of the lower South. "Before the assembling of the Southern Convention in June," wrote a distinguished Northern scholar, "every one of the Southern States save Kentucky had given some encouragement to the Southern movement, and Kentucky had given warning and proposed a compromise through Clay."[20]

Papers. Also Toombs to Crittenden, January 9, January 22, 1850; Brown to Crittenden, January 11, 1850, *ibid.* Also Stephens, *op. cit.*, II, 199-201. Cf. Cole, *op. cit.*, p. 166.

[20] H. D. Foster, "Webster's Seventh of March Speech," *American Historical Review*, XXVII (January, 1922), 251, 254. This article is an admirable synthesis of much of the material alluded to above, with much additional matter. Other valuable studies bearing on this general problem are: Cole, *op. cit.*, and "The South and the Right of Secession in the Early Fifties," *Mississippi Valley Historical Review*, I (December, 1914), 376-99; R. P. Brooks, "Howell Cobb and the Crisis of 1850," *Mississippi Valley Historical Review*, IV (December, 1917), 279-98; St. George L. Sioussat, "Tennessee, the Compromise of 1850, and the Nashville Convention," *Mississippi Valley Historical Review*, II (December, 1915), 313-47 and by the same author, "Tennessee and National Political Parties," *American Historical Association, Annual Report, 1914*, I, 243-58; U. B. Phillips, *Georgia and State Rights (American Historical Association, Annual Report, 1901*, vol. II); M. J. White, *The Secession Movement in the United States*, and by the same author "Louisiana and the Secession Movement of the Early Fifties," *Proceedings of the Mississippi Valley Historical Association*, VIII (1914-15), 278-88; Philip M. Hamer, *The Secession Movement in South Carolina, 1847-1852;* Hearon, *op. cit.;* C. S. Boucher, "The

This, then, was the delicate situation when Doty made his ill-advised attempt at "a nigh cut to get California in" without any settlement of the other questions, and the Southern Whigs discovered that they could expect nothing from the President. The practical result was the consolidation of a Southern bloc in the House under the active leadership of Stephens and Toombs, who, vigorous as they might be in upholding Southern rights according to their conception of policy, were so far from being "Calhoun secessionists" as actually to represent "union" sentiment in Georgia. Indeed, their determined opposition was in part due to the realization that the failure of compromise would destroy their own leadership and throw their state into the arms of their radical rivals. Unless the North would consent to certain concessions, even they would be constrained, both by policy and sentiment, to go for secession.[21]

The best-informed Northern newspapers about this time began to recognize the real danger of secession unless concessions were made, and Webster, who had believed, a week before, that "if on our side, we keep cool, things will come to no dangerous pass," now felt that the extremists on both sides might well destroy the Union. For, as the likelihood of Southern secession was driven home to the consciousness of the North, only too many were sufficiently tinged with abolitionism to agree with the Springfield *Republican* that "if the Union cannot be preserved without the extension of slavery, allow the tie of the Union to be severed." More conservative persons who condemned Clay's resolutions now put their trust in some vague idea that Webster could do something better. On February 22, however, a great meeting at Castle Garden, New York, endorsed Clay's resolutions as a basis of compromise.[22]

The same day, Saturday, that the Southern representatives had their stormy interview with the President, several South-

Secession and Coöperative Movements in South Carolina, 1848 to 1852," *Washington University Studies, Humanistic Series,* vol. II, pt. 2. Cf. also Crittenden to Clayton, April 6, 1850, Clayton Papers.

[21] Phillips, *Toombs, Stephens and Cobb Correspondence, passim;* Johnston and Browne, *op. cit.,* pp. 243-55.

[22] Foster, "Webster's Seventh of March Speech," *American Historical Review,* XXVII, 257-59; New York *Express,* February 12, February 26, 1850.

ern members of Congress, among whom were Mangum, Badger, and Dawson, had a long conference with Webster. "The whole subject was discussed, and . . . the limitations of a compromise . . . explained," satisfactorily to the South. The next day, Webster wrote to his son in great discouragement and doubt as to how to meet the crisis, but his mind seems to have been made up to take a definite stand for compromise. When Clay resumed his place on the twenty-eighth, after a week's absence at Philadelphia, Webster both surprised and pleased the moderates by walking around to his seat, where the two statesmen shook hands and conversed for a moment or two with great apparent cordiality.[23]

The receipt of the California constitution by the Senate precipitated no such violent scene as that in the House, but had an equally profound effect. It presented the admission of California as a concrete political object for the attainment of which a majority existed in each House. The ultras had declared its admission a cause for secession, while Southern moderates were unwilling to go so far unless the Wilmot Proviso were also applied to the territories. To permit action on California alone would force them to oppose a secession movement at home, with the possibility of having to reverse their position whenever the territories should be organized. Thus, even before Toombs and Stephens had outlined the Southern *sine qua non* to McClernand, plans were being made for the joining of the various compromise measures. These plans involved the reference of all questions concerned with slavery to a specially constituted committee and Foote of Mississippi seized the question of the reference of the California constitution to broach the proposition.[24]

Clay expressed the opinion that California should be kept separate from the other questions, which might well be referred

[23] New York *Express,* February 22 and 23, March 1, 1850; Foster, "Webster's Seventh of March Speech," *American Historical Review,* XXVII, 259-60. Johnston and Browne, *op. cit.,* pp. 249-50. New York *Herald,* April 13, 1852, quoted by Cole, *The Whig Party in the South,* p. 165, footnote.

[24] H. S. Foote's account of the inception of the committee scheme (*Casket of Reminiscences,* pp. 25-26), is hardly consonant with Clay's first reception of the proposition.

to such a committee, though the time for that had not yet arrived. Foote, professing to think this position inconsistent with Clay's compromise resolutions, accused Clay of an alliance with Benton to force the admission of California, thereby enabling Benton's son-in-law, Frémont, to take his seat in the Senate. Clay denied any change of attitude. He thought the organization of the two territories and the Texas boundary settlement might well be embraced in one bill, though he did not think it necessary. He had expected the Senate to express its sense on his resolutions in order. They could then be referred to the appropriate committees for shaping into bills, and would be ready for action about the same time. Since the Senate had decided affirmatively on all, he supposed they could trust one another to play fair in the passage of all the measures regardless of their order. In this, of course, Clay either failed correctly to gauge the excited feelings of the time or else deliberately ignored them, for the absence of such confidence was the main cause of the excessive prolongation of the contest.[25]

The matter was dropped for the time, but Foote brought it up again on February 25, during Clay's absence in Philadelphia. On the following Monday, Doty's resolution would be in order again, and Foote expressed his fear of a violent collision in the House which might put the whole question beyond the control of Congress. Having consulted a number of leaders of both Houses, he now moved the reference of "all pending questions growing out of the institution of slavery" to a select committee of fifteen. The resolution was allowed to go over, but its prospects seemed so good that, on the twenty-seventh, Toombs himself moved the substitution of the California message for the Annual Message, and yielded the floor for Doty to introduce a California bill into the committee of the whole on the state of the Union, under a pledge that the previous question would not be invoked. Thus the anticipated clash was averted and time given for the compromise to be shaped in the Senate. The radicals found that they had gained a barren victory, however, for the facilities for obstruction in the committee were sufficient to prevent the bill ever getting out.[26]

---

[25] *Congressional Globe*, 31st Cong., 1st Sess., pp. 365-69.
[26] *Ibid.*, pp. 416-21, 424; New York *Express*, February 26, 1850.

These discussions and manoeuvres made patent to everyone by the end of February the issue which was to hold the Senate helpless for five months—in what order should the measures under discussion be enacted? Should California be considered alone, or only in conjunction with the other questions at issue? These alternatives soon became the respective *sine qua non* of Northern radicals and Southern ultras, while Clay and the moderates were for the enactment of the measures in whatever form could most readily secure a majority.

But these thorough-going compromisers numbered scarcely a quarter of the Senate. Clay was consistently followed by six or seven Whigs from the border Slave States, and Cass by four or five Northern Democrats. Foote—if he belongs here at all— was the lone Southern Democrat. Douglas gave his support at crucial moments, though ostensibly unfriendly to "omnibus" legislation. As the situation developed, it appeared that the irreconcilable opposition was composed of two groups, at first bitterly antagonistic but finally coöperating to defeat any compromise. From the North came nine of the twelve New England Senators, with Seward and the Senators from New Jersey, Ohio, and Wisconsin—two Free Soilers, three Democrats and eleven Whigs, sixteen in all. From the South came the Senators from Virginia and South Carolina, with one each from Florida, Mississippi, Louisiana and Tennessee—eight Democrats. The Northern group was unwilling to join California to any other measure. They would either apply the Wilmot Proviso to the territories or leave them unorganized, and they were against every other feature of the compromise except the prohibition of slave trade in the District of Columbia. Their Southern allies were opposed to the admission of California under her irregular constitution and wished to cut off her Southern half by an approximate extension of the Missouri Compromise line to the Pacific; for the rest, they favored what their Northern associates opposed. They all agreed, therefore, only in opposition to concession. But stranger still, they all followed the leadership of Benton, who favored—and eventually voted for—every feature of the compromise separately, but whose opposition to Foote's compromise committee and to "omnibus" legislation was implacable.

Thus of fifty-nine Senators who voted on the various compromise propositions, twenty-five were unalterably opposed to all concession, or, counting Winthrop who replaced Webster in time to participate in the final upset of the "omnibus," twenty-six. Of the other thirty-four, Clay could count with confidence on scarcely fifteen. The doubtful remainder from whom he must gather a slender majority consisted of four from the East, Webster and Cooper of Pennsylvania being the only Northern Whigs not counted with the opposition; four or five Democrats from the Northwest; three or four Southern Whigs, his own colleague being especially skittish; a bloc of five Democrats from the Southwest who were mainly interested in the Texas boundary and debt proposition; and three other Southern Democrats. The Southern Whigs were made unreliable by the crotchety notions of individual Senators, and also by administration influence, first in Delaware and later in Maryland. With such materials to work with, it is amazing that the "omnibus" was steered so nearly to success. The debacle was precipitated by the lack of a single vote. How this score of doubtful votes would have been cast on a final vote on the Omnibus Bill it is impossible even to conjecture.[27]

Neither section had received Clay's compromise resolutions with marked favor, but the South had been vociferous in its disapproval, especially after Clay had avowed his opposition to including California in an "omnibus" bill. On the last day of February, therefore, John Bell presented another scheme of compromise more acceptable to the South. It adopted the

---

[27] This summary of the alignment of the Senate is based on an analysis of a hundred and ten votes, the standard of zeal for compromise being consistency in voting with Clay. But that compass, Webster was a veritable weathercock. Cf. Coie, *Whig Party in the South*, pp. 165 ff. "The Compromise Bill was defeated by a union between the Free Soilers & disunionists & the administration of Gen'l. Taylor. All the resources and patronage of the Gov't. was brought to bear against us & at last the allied forces were able to beat us. . . . Col. Benton has done much to delay action & to defeat all the measures. In my opinion no justification—no reason can be made for his conduct. On the other hand I must say that if Mr. Clay's name had not been associated with the Bills they would have passed long ago. The Administration were jealous of him & hated him & some democrats were weak enough to fear that the success of his Bill would make him a President." Douglas to Lanphier & Walker, August 3, 1850, Lanphier Papers.

"omnibus" principle, but proposed to deal only with the Texas boundary and the territory acquired from Mexico. A somewhat more favorable financial consideration was offered to Texas for the cession of all her territory west of the Colorado and north of the thirty-fourth parallel, which was to be incorporated with New Mexico, organized as a territory with nothing said about slavery, and admitted as a state when its inhabitants should adopt a constitution with the consent of Congress—a procedure to be strictly required hereafter. Veiling a concession of Texas ownership in a maze of complicated phrasing, a future state, slave or free as the inhabitants desired, was blocked out between the Colorado and the Rio Grande and south of the thirty-fourth parallel. The remnant of Texas, east of the Colorado and south of the thirty-fourth parallel was to be immediately divided into two states, one on either side of the Trinity. California with her adopted constitution and boundaries was to receive immediate admission. Bell believed slavery would never gain a foothold in New Mexico, because it was unsuited to slave agriculture, and in the mines free immigrants and Indian labor, cheaper than slave labor, would be used. The future state between the Colorado and the Rio Grande would probably be a slave state, "the last of its race." The proposed bill was to be framed by the Committee on Territories, of which Douglas was chairman.[28]

Bell's resolutions apparently were a counter-project from those Southerners who were not ready to go so far in concession as Clay or the group who had negotiated with McClernand. They constituted primarily a rival plan of settlement to Clay's, for they were enthusiastically supported by the *Republic*, which represented the Southern revolt against Clay's leadership. This had the effect of making even well-informed politicians in Washington, to say nothing of the press, believe that Bell's plan had the support of the administration. That widespread impression strikingly reveals contemporary ignorance or incredulity of Seward's dominance over the preponderantly Southern Taylor Administration. This insistence that a comprehensive scheme of territorial settlement differed from the "President's plan" only in detail marks the beginning of the breach between the *Republic* and the administration. That breach became evident to all a fortnight later, when the *Republic* made a vehement editorial attack on Seward's "higher law" doctrine. At once the political world grasped its significance; had the administration broken with Seward, or had it broken with the *Republic?* Within a few days the answer came in an authoritative disavowal of the *Republic's* editorials, for Seward's speech, though too radical for Clayton, had been read and approved by Ewing. Thus, before the end of March, Seward was clearly revealed as the guiding genius of the administration.[29]

By that time even the Northern radicals had abandoned the Wilmot Proviso, though they from time to time made the empty gesture of moving its adoption. As Cass said, neither the Wilmot Proviso nor the Missouri Compromise line could pass Congress, and, whatever the extremists continued to say, it was quite generally conceded that natural causes would bar slavery from New Mexico.[30] Either the organization of New Mexico with explicit recognition in the law that the Mexican statute barring slavery was in force, or the President's laissez faire plan would satisfy all of them but the most fanatical. They were also willing to concede the enforcement of the "runaway slave compact" and the acknowledgment of the "guarantee" to make more slave states out of Texas, together with a settlement of the boundary. This was tentatively suggested as a Northern "compromise" plan, the inclusion of California in "omnibus" legislation being definitely rejected. The striking thing about all these plans is, however, the median position in which they leave Clay's plan, revealing the scanty favor it at first received as a tribute to its fairness and the wisdom of its author.[31]

---

[29] Washington *Republic* (hereafter cited as *Republic*), March 15, March 20, March 22, March 27, 1850; Washington *Union* (hereafter cited as *Union*), March 16, March 22, 1850; New York *Express,* March 1, March 6, March 8, March 16, March 17, March 21, March 22, March 25, 1850; Seward, *op. cit.*, II, 124.

[30] The correctness of this attitude is conclusively demonstrated by Prof. C. W. Ramsdell's brilliant article, "The Natural Limits of Slavery Expansion," *Mississippi Valley Historical Review*, XVI, 151-71.

[31] New York *Express,* March 13, March 18, 1850; *Republic,* March 22, 1850; *Congressional Globe,* 31st Cong., 1st Sess., pp. 517-18.

Before the Northern radicals were brought to this position, the oratorical climax of the whole long debate had packed the Senate chamber and thrilled the attentive country. Historians have agreed in accepting the great speeches of Calhoun on March 4, of Webster on March 7, and of Seward on March 11, as representing, together with Clay's speeches on proposing his resolutions and on presenting the report of the Committee of Thirteen, the various sections of opinion. When this mighty cannonade had ceased and the rattling musketry of editorial comment had subsided, a new stage of the struggle had arrived.

All those who resented Clay's leadership were concentrating on other plans, especially Bell's, which on March 12 was taken from the table and made the vehicle for the creation of the select committee. Clay, ever ready to adopt the plan which promised the most results, had receded from his position of a month before so far as to agree to the immediate creation of the committee. In forming this alliance with Foote, Clay broke with Benton, who steadily advanced to the leadership of the opponents of the committee and "omnibus" legislation; for, although not necessarily equivalent, from Foote's first suggestion the whole situation made the creation of the committee virtually a decision in favor of joining at least the California and the territorial bills. Since the administration stubbornly adhered to the "President's plan" of "non-action," which had become the practical alternative to the committee, its orthodox Whig supporters found themselves, to their disgust and the ribald mirth of the *Union,* following the leadership of the "Knight of the Stuffed Cravat;" for the "higher law" speech made Seward impossible as leader, while Truman Smith had amply proved his incapacity.[32]

The situation was further complicated by certain obscure manoeuvres of Buchanan's, who was present in Washington in an unofficial capacity. He was believed to have offered the Southern Ultras the support of Pennsylvania in return for a tariff on iron and coal and his own nomination for the presidency. In pursuance of these designs, the Pennsylvania legisla-

[32] *Ibid.,* pp. 508-10; *Union,* March 16, 1850; New York *Express,* March 1, March 6, March 8, 1850; *Observer and Reporter,* March 16, 1850.

ture was said to have tabled an anti-slavery resolution and a meeting was held at Philadelphia. Tammany followed suit in New York. It was partly to head off these projects that Webster took his stand for the compromise. It was charged that by these activities Buchanan had "strangled" the Wilmot Proviso.[33]

So the debate dragged its weary length along. Whether Senators elected to speak on the California message, on Clay's resolutions, or Bell's, or on Foote's committee proposition, they surveyed the whole field of the slavery question. The first week in April marked another stage. Clay at last was converted to the "omnibus" plan and Webster reluctantly gave his approval to the committee. Crittenden advised Clayton that the situation demanded the abandonment of the laissez-faire policy, and that the administration should take the lead in effecting a comprehensive settlement of the slavery question; otherwise they might be held responsible for the failure of any settlement. Truman Smith, the still recognized spokesman of the administration, however, tactlessly revealed the real purpose of the supporters of the laissez-faire policy—they would secure the admission of California while holding off on the organization of New Mexico so long as there was a majority against the Wilmot Proviso. In the House, McClernand introduced his compromise bill, a clear indication of the lengths to which the Douglas crowd were prepared to go, though their leader as yet kept himself uncommitted to the "omnibus." Clay, however, late in March, had had an interview with Ritchie; and the *Union*, which had been standing out for a compromise of Democratic authorship, now applauded the "conciliatory and patriotic spirit" Clay had displayed in "rising above all selfish pride" to accept Foote's plan.[34]

To all these conservative elements which had accepted Clay's

<hr>

[33] New York *Express*, March 11, 1850, "Many of our friends talk hard of Buchanan," wrote Douglas to Lanphier & Walker, August 3, 1850. "It is supposed that he encouraged the nullifiers and disunionists out of jealousy of Gen'l. Cass. I hope this will turn out not to be true." Lanphier Papers.

[34] *Congressional Globe*, 31st Cong., 1st Sess., pp. 652, 656-64; Morehead to Crittenden, March 30, 1850, Crittenden Papers; New York *Express*, April 8; *Union*, April 7, 1850; Crittenden to Clayton, April 6, 1850, Clayton Papers.

leadership, was now added the following of the Vice President. James Brooks, a prominent member of Congress, was one of the editors of the *Express*, Fillmore's organ in New York City. It had been vigorous in support of Bell's plan, but on April 10 came out for the committee. It was more important, declared the *Express*, to stop the slavery agitation than to stand out for an impracticable organization of New Mexico, for after all, the North was only yielding a point of etiquette in dropping the Proviso. The North must either consent to join the measures or let California go over to the next session or the next Congress, for the "Clingmanizing" of Doty's resolution had shown the South's power to block California and stop the whole business of the government. Clay said, "connect them, with the curtailment of the claims of Texas, and give us peace"—and Clay, Webster, and Cass united were an irresistible combination.

Thus, by early April there had been drawn together a powerful compromise party under Clay's leadership. In addition to his own Border State following of Whigs, the Southern Whigs had one and all accepted the principle of a comprehensive settlement, though divided as to details, and with them came the *Republic*. To these had been added the conservative Democrats of Cass's following, with the *Union*, while the more aggressive Douglas group could be counted on when need arose. At this stage, even most of the Southern ultras were supporting Foote. Some of the Northwestern Senators still held out, who later voted for the Omnibus Bill, but only Benton had been lost. All this Clay had gained by conceding a point of form and procedure—the union of the measures by a select committee. It was only a matter of time until the opposition would be overcome and the committee created.

The administration was the less able to cope with this legislative situation because of inopportune developments in the House. The patronage policies of the administration had continued to give offence to the Whigs in Congress. The President and his advisers took no practical measures to secure their coöperation on any question, not even the all-important one of territorial organization. When Clay inquired if the President had consulted his friends in Congress as to the formulation of his policy on that question, he coolly replied, "No, but I have consulted my Cabinet, and my mind is made up." So when, on the same day that McClernand introduced his compromise, Humphrey Marshall of Kentucky, who was no friend of Clay's and who had fought at Buena Vista, launched a virulent attack on the Cabinet, it was regarded as merely the first rumble of the long pent-up thunder of Whig discontent. The same day Secretary Crawford demanded a Congressional investigation of the Galphin Claim, to which the *Union* had been giving scandalous publicity.[35]

While Congress was thus consuming time in seemingly fruitless debate, public opinion also was crystallizing in favor of moderate measures. One house of the Ohio legislature refused to pass a more stringent law "for the escape of fugitive slaves." The Connecticut legislature by a strong vote postponed finally a set of Wilmot Proviso resolutions, and the House voted fifty to twenty-nine to repeal the objectionable section of the Act of 1847 to prevent the recovery of fugitive slaves. In Massachusetts, where a year before the Wilmot Proviso had passed with only a single dissenting vote, the Senate, on April 9, tabled by fifteen to eleven a resolution instructing Webster to vote for the insertion of the Wilmot Proviso in the territorial bills and against Mason's Fugitive Slave Bill. In Rhode Island, the Free Soil candidate for governor received only two hundred votes.[36]

The opportune incidence of Clay's seventy-third birthday also afforded occasion for demonstrations in favor of compromise. In New York, flags were flown by the hotels and public buildings and by much of the shipping in port. A brilliant celebration was held at Niblo's Saloon, at which Senator Cooper and James Brooks were the speakers. Brooks in particular took a laudatory tone toward Clay's recent efforts. At Washington, the venerable statesman was honored by a serenade. Of the New York newspapers, the *Courier* was against the "omnibus," declaring it could not be passed. The *Tribune*, while against mixing up California with the other

---

[35] New York *Express,* April 5, April 6, 1850; *Union,* April 3, April 4, 1850; *Republic,* April 3, April 4, 1850. *Congressional Globe,* 31st Cong., 1st Sess., pp. 628-29; App., pp. 406-10.

[36] New York *Express,* April 12, 1850.

questions, accepted the saving of New Mexico from Texas as the equivalent of the Wilmot Proviso. That, Greeley thought, would be a Northern victory; but it might be neutralized by the formation of a slave state from Texas. The *Express* was editorially favorable to compromise, though one of its Washington correspondents continued to report the views of the "non-action" forces. In Illinois, the *State Register*, Douglas's organ, quoted with approval from the *Union*'s editorial supporting McClernand's compromise bill.[37]

After a postponement to allow the return of eight absent Senators who favored the select committee, the debate was resumed for two days, when it once more gave way, this time to the Deficiency Appropriation Bill. With Webster protesting against the delay, Benton had initiated his policy of proposing an endless list of instructions to the committee, all devised to withhold California from its consideration; and the final phase of the contest over the committee became a two day struggle to break through Benton's entanglement of instruction. Before that stage was reached, however, Clay and Webster gave the weak-kneed to understand that they could not avoid a vote on the union of the bills by defeating the committee. In that contingency, Douglas would call up the California Bill, to which Clay pledged himself to move as amendments the territorial bills and the Texas Boundary. As Webster pointed out, these would have to be disposed of in reverse order, so that California would be reached last of all.[38]

As it became manifest that Benton, in defiance of a clear majority of the Senate, was trying to embarrass action and create delay, Clay finally hit upon "a sort of Previous Question" to shut Benton off. Webster, however, refused to support Clay's closure device and now wavered away from support of the committee, preferring to have the "omnibus" put together by the Senate itself through amendments. Benton agreed to support such an "omnibus" if constructed, but no one could doubt that he would oppose it desperately. Hamlin of Maine,

---

[37] New York *Express,* April 10, April 12, April 13, April 15, 1850; *Illinois State Register,* April 15, 1850.

[38] *Congressional Globe,* 31st Cong., 1st Sess., pp. 704-14, 721-22.

however, contrived to get in an amendment, and the Benton tacked his long string of amendments on to that, thus checkmating Clay. It was at this juncture, late in the afternoon of April 17, that the disgraceful encounter between Benton and Foote occurred. When the final day of the struggle opened, the compromise forces had fallen back upon that last resort of majorities, the "steam-roller." Mangum, Clay, and King urged their followers to a policy of silence and, one after another, Benton's amendments were voted down. Thus sweeping all parliamentary obstacles aside, Bell's resolutions were at last referred to a select committee of thirteen to be chosen on the morrow. The final vote on reference was thirty to twenty-two, Webster in the negative. Every slave state Senator save Benton voted aye. With them went Cass, Dickinson of New York and Sturgeon of Pennsylvania, Bright and Whitcomb of Indiana, and Dodge and Jones of Iowa. As a sort of afterthought, by grace of the Vice President and in violation of strict procedure, Clay's resolutions were also referred to the committee.[39]

The next day, the committee slate which Foote and his coadjutors had constructed was duly elected by ballot, although by varying votes. The Senators opposed to the committee for the most part refrained from voting. On the count of the vote for chairman, no quorum appeared, but Webster, arriving late, was permitted to cast his vote for Clay, who thus received twenty-eight votes. As constituted, the committee consisted of Cass, Bright and Dickinson, Northern Democrats; Webster, Phelps and Cooper, Northern Whigs; King, Mason and Downs, Southern Democrats; and Mangum, Bell and Berrien, Southern Whigs. Five of the thirteen members were consistent compromise men; only two, Phelps and Mason, were irreconcilables. The radicals in the House signalized the event, and revealed the purpose of Benton's campaign of delay, by making a third abortive attempt to close the debate on Doty's California Bill, which had been in progress for a month. The Senate rested from its labors while the committee deliberated

---

[39] *Ibid.*, pp. 722, 747-48, 751-64, 769-74; New York *Express,* April 17. April 19, 1850,

and another committee accompanied the remains of Calhoun to their last resting place in South Carolina.[40]

---

[40] *Congressional Globe,* 31st Cong., 1st Sess., pp. 775, 780.

CHAPTER XV

NON-ACTION OR ADJUSTMENT

THE PROGRESS of the debate had revealed but little interest in those resolutions of Clay's which were merely declaratory; the crisis had focussed attention exclusively upon practical measures. Thus, it was a foregone conclusion that the committee must deal with the admission of California, the organization of the territories, the settlement of the Texas-New Mexico boundary, and a new fugitive slave law. Both Northern and Southern opinion was agreed on the imminence of these subjects, far apart as might be their respective views as to treatment.

From a practical standpoint, however, the question of form almost overshadowed the content of the measures. The Northern radicals insisted that the admission of California had no relation to the other measures, and even moderate men from the North found the idea of an "omnibus" bill repugnant. Here again, however, they opposed "sentiment" to the material interests of the South. The fear that once California was admitted the other measures would fail of passage, or be vetoed if passed, was well-founded and caused the Southerners to insist on the inclusion of all the territorial measures in one bill. The appointment of the committee was in itself a concession of this point to the stubborn insistence of the South, but the last passenger to be admitted to the "omnibus," to adopt the contemporary metaphor, was the Texas boundary proposition. Its inclusion was doubtless due to the practical difficulty of separating it from the New Mexico bill, which necessarily specified the limits of the new territory.

While the measures reported as a whole were those specified in Clay's resolutions as constituting a comprehensive plan of compromise on a basis of mutual concession, both in the exclusion of other measures and in the details of those included the spirit of compromise prevailed. The Northern demand for abolition of slavery in the District of Columbia and the Southern proposal for the immediate subdivision of Texas were left out as not immediately pressing, but formal recognition, conceded by the North, was given to the "compact" with Texas for her eventual division. The Southern demand for the limitation of California by a southern boundary which essentially applied the Missouri Compromise was denied; just as was the Northern demand for the application of the slavery prohibition of the Ordinance of 1787—otherwise the Wilmot Proviso—to the new territories. The division of the latter into northern and southern segments again conceded to the South a shadowy Missouri Compromise line, though, with the existing nuclei of settlement on the upper Rio Grande and in the valley of the Great Salt Lake, it was the only feasible division.

Clay's own opinion, expressed in his resolutions, that pending enactment of new legislation the Mexican laws, including that prohibiting slavery, remained in force, was not incorporated in the bill as the North desired, any more than the Southern demand that the Constitution of the United States be specifically extended to the territories; but the territorial legislatures were specifically forbidden to enact any legislation dealing with the institution of slavery. The courts, if necessary, could pass on the validity of the Mexican law. Meanwhile, if the "law of nature" were not sufficient to bar slaves from New Mexico by economic discouragement, the absence of local police regulations for their control would constitute a practical legal obstacle to their introduction. Back of the whole New Mexican settlement, indeed, including the carelessness as to the exact boundary line of Texas, was the realization by all candid persons that, no matter what the legal status of slavery in New Mexico and the plains region of Texas, the economic opportunity it offered in competition with the cotton lands of eastern and central Texas was insufficient to draw slaves to that remote region. Therefore, in view of this practical certainty, the purely sentimental demands of both sections for formal action on the subject were wisely disregarded.

Whatever the legality of the Texan claim to the Rio Grande boundary from mouth to source, it had at least sufficient basis, in view of the technical impossibility of securing a judicial decision and the political impracticability of settling it otherwise without provoking civil war, to justify, even to demand, the offer of compensation for its renunciation. Then, too, equity demanded some provision for the payment of that part of the Texan debt for which the import duties, now payable to the United States instead of Texas, had been pledged. To this proposal all the members of the committee assented. As an offset to the more stringent Fugitive Slave Law which rational Northern opinion recognized as a reasonable demand, Clay, apparently with no particular support from anyone else, threw in the prohibition of the sale in the District of Columbia of slaves imported into it for that purpose.

The committee was very conservative in its action. It constructed the "omnibus" by simply tacking together Douglas's California and Territorial Bills, and, with a modification in details, the boundary settlement included in the latter. The Fugitive Slave Bill was that introduced by Mason and already reported, in amended form, from the Judiciary Committee by Butler. The District of Columbia Slave-trade Bill was alone original, the work of Clay, and it merely extended the law of Maryland over the District. By April 22, all this had been decided, except the inclusion of the boundary bill in the "omnibus." Even that must have been decided by the twenty-fifth, when Clay, entrusted with the preparation of the report, retired with an amanuensis to the country home of Mr. Calvert in Maryland. The decision was made on each item by a formal vote of the committee, ten members being present. The "omnibus" plan was adopted by a decisive majority.[1]

The atmosphere of the Senate was already thunderous when Clay arose on May 8 to present the report of the Committee

---

[1] New York *Express,* March 18, April 25, April 26, April 30, May 1, May 4, 1850; See also the *Union,* March 20, March 28, April 18, 1850; *Republic,* March 22, May 1, May 4, 1850; *Illinois State Register,* April 15, 1850; *Congressional Globe,* 31st Cong., 1st Sess., pp. 944-49. "The Committee . . . took my two printed Bills & put a wafer between & Reported them back without changing or writing a single word, except one line. The one line inserted prohibited the Territorial Legislatures from legislating upon the subject of slavery. This amendment was voted in by the Com. in opposition to the wishes of Gen'l. Cass & Mr. Clay, and they gave notice that they would move to strike it out in the Senate & it was stricken out." Douglas to Lanphier & Walker, August 3, 1850, Lanphier Papers.

of Thirteen. Jefferson Davis, under instruction, had just submitted the report and resolutions of a select committee of the
Mississippi legislature on Federal and State Relations. The
seventh of those resolutions was the call of the Nashville Convention. Davis improved the occasion by reading selections
from the resolves of public meetings North and South and by
exposing the organized petition machinery of the Abolitionists.
"It is my opinion," he concluded,

> that justice will not be done to the South, unless from other prompt-
> ings than are about us here—that we shall have no substantial
> consideration offered to us for the surrender of an equal claim to
> California. No security against future harassment by Congress will
> probably be given. The rainbow which some have seen, I fear was
> set before the termination of the storm.[2]

Aside from the actual bills it embodied, the report was
comparatively brief. The "Hotspurs" lost no time in repudiating the work of the committee their votes had created, while
the dissidents on the committee and half a dozen others seized
upon the formal motion to print to express their disapproval.
Hale claimed that the bill turned the whole of the territories
into a "slave pasture" while the North got nothing. Yulee, at
the other extreme, declared that it gave the North the kernel
and the South only the shell. The objections of such extremists
may be disregarded, but those of more moderate Senators
whose support might be won, and whose votes in the end were
essential to its passage, are significant.

Downs objected to the admission of California with her
present boundaries, though he agreed with most of the provisions of the report. Berrien also could not acquiesce in the
proposed boundaries of California, and he considered it clearly
unconstitutional to allow her two representatives in advance
of the census. He would accept the proposed boundary of
Texas, if it would leave within her limits certain settlements
near El Paso. Houston withheld judgment, but was for the
Union and all honorable efforts to preserve it. Clay merely
spoke of the spirit of kindness, conciliation and consideration
which had characterized the work of the committee, leaving the

---

[2] *Congressional Globe*, 31st Cong., 1st Sess., pp. 941-44.

vigorous defense of the report to the capable hands of Mangum, Cass, and Dickinson.

When Jefferson Davis expressed his gratification at the evident dissatisfaction of a considerable proportion of the committee, he brought Jesse Bright of Indiana to his feet with a significant pronouncement. There were Senators on the committee, Bright said, who objected to many or several provisions of the different bills, and who differed as to the conclusions of the report, but on the whole the work, as summed up by Clay that morning, met with very general acceptance. He regretted the haste of some Senators to condemn it. It looked as if there were some who intended to be satisfied with no measure having the appearance of compromise. If the extremes took this course, Bright hoped there would be enough to take the conservative middle ground to settle the pending controversies. In spite of the feeling in the free states for a direct inhibition of slavery in the territories by Congress, he personally was opposed to it in the case of these territories. He was instructed by his legislature to vote for the Wilmot Proviso. He regretted it, but the right of instruction was part of his political creed and he had ever observed it. There were features of the report in which he did not entirely concur in committee, but he would not pettily indulge in reservations on special points. He personally now endorsed it broadly, distinctly and emphatically, and pledged to Clay his aid and support throughout the struggle. But if the Southern friends of reference did not support the joint measures, and the ultimate admission of California should be jeopardized by the union of the measures, then he would fall back on the separate bill for that purpose. He would support the compromise only to the point where hope of success failed.[3]

This brief preliminary debate revealed that the five-fold division of the Senate still prevailed, but that the alignment of the groups had shifted. The Hotspurs, who had made Southern support of the select committee unanimous, chagrined at the formulation of a real compromise, had swung into violent opposition. Clay must reconstruct his majority; the wavering Southern moderates must be confirmed in the

[3] *Ibid.*, pp. 949-56.

faith, while the less irreconcilable opponents of slavery were
to be won. Hampered by Northern instructions for the Wilmot
Proviso, and by Southern instructions against the admission
of California, by Democratic insistence on this and Whig insistence on that, by the crochety notions of individual Senators,
and by the determination of Benton to oppose every detail
that differed from his own propositions, anyone but Henry
Clay would have despaired. Experienced observers already saw
an effective coalition of Southern Ultras and Free Soilers
against the compromise. They also foresaw that if the Southern
Ultras held their bloc together, the "omnibus" would be upset;
but, as one correspondent put it, "such an overset will induce a
great many national people to jump in, and take in, his
measures singly, in a 'cab'." It was of this that Bright had
warned Davis, and most Northern moderates distinctly preferred it. It was probably with an eye to leadership in that
contingency that Douglas maintained his attitude of aloofness
to the "omnibus." Some thought it was what Clay really expected, but if so, he made no sign, and apparently used every
exertion to drive the "omnibus" to its destination with all its
passengers inside.[4]

Meanwhile, ominous developments marked the course of the
administration. Alarmed by a letter from Morehead, Crittenden had written to Clayton early in April advising that the
administration should effect a more cordial coöperation with
the Whigs in Congress. It should also take cognizance of the
changed circumstances and the temper and excitement of the
times, and itself take the lead in enacting a positive settlement
of the whole slavery controversy. So far as the extant correspondence shows, Clayton never replied to this letter and
Crittenden wrote no more to the Secretary of State. About
the same time, Orlando Brown, realizing the futility of his position, determined to resign, despite his reluctance—oddly
enough, urged on him by Meredith—to deprive "Old Zach"
of the solace of his society. Probably this attitude of Seward's
chief friend in the Cabinet was due as much to a sense of
security as to a recognition of Orlando's political nullity,

---

[4] New York *Express*, May 9, May 10, 1850.

for by that time the *Republic* also had been reduced to sub-jection.[5]

The rapport between the editors of the *Republic* and the Cabinet had always been imperfect, but the first definite con-flict had arisen in mid-March over the *Republic's* bitter attacks on Seward's "higher law" speech. This episode had finally culminated in a formal disavowal of the *Republic's* sentiments by the administration. In the ensuing weeks Bullitt kept off the slavery question and occupied himself with defending the Cabinet against the Galphin scandal. He could do this whole-heartedly, since Crawford was the one minister on cordial terms with this group; but that did not help the editor with Ewing and Seward, who had already determined to eject Crawford from the Cabinet.

Meanwhile, Taylor's jealousy of Clay, fed by the men who surrounded him, was fast becoming an obsession. He was con-vinced that the activity of Clay and Webster was solely moti-vated by hostility to him, by a determination to disregard his victory over them in the presidential campaign and to assert their leadership in opposition to him in order to degrade him. It would be almost incredible that General Taylor was so unable to rise above mere petty personalities in his concep-tion of the motives of such men, had he not poured out all his grievances into the sympathetic ear of Orlando Brown on the night of April 19. That very night, in obedience to the General's desire, Orlando embodied them, with his own com-ments, in twelve large pages to Crittenden. So sensitive was the President, that he resented as personal disloyalty even the perfunctory compliments which the *Republic*, while sup-porting the "President's plan," had found it necessary to pay to Clay and Webster.[6]

Now, however, the President and his organ had come to a parting of the ways. Bullitt was a Southern publicist and un-

[5] Morehead to Crittenden, March 30, 1850; Brown to Crittenden, April 19, May 9, 1850; Crittenden Papers, Crittenden to Clayton, April 6, 1850, Clayton Papers.

[6] Brown to Crittenden, April 19, 1850, Crittenden Papers. New York *Express,* March 16, March 19, April 29, 1850; *Union,* March 16, March 22, 1850; *Republic,* February 23, March 15, March 20, March 27, 1850.

doubtedly perceived the full tendency of the administration policy, much of which may not have been understood by the inexperienced President. Bullitt, like Crittenden and all the Southern Whigs, recognized the necessity of compromise; and, since all who really wanted compromise were substantially agreed as to the measures requisite to effect it, the *Republic* sought to save the prestige of the President by insisting that the various comprehensive plans differed not essentially but merely in detail from the "President's plan." With the appointment of the Committee of Thirteen, the *Republic* gave in its adhesion to the compromise in advance of the report, despite a long and kindly interview in which the President fully explained his feelings to Bullitt and frankly disclosed his grounds of complaint. This action of Bullitt's, therefore, brought things to the breaking-point. At a meeting held on April 20, President Taylor laid the whole situation before the Cabinet, and demanded the establishment of a new organ that would loyally support his policies and not lavish compliments on his opponents.[7]

Notified by Crittenden and Brown, Burnley hastened to the capital. He speedily ascertained that the breach between the administration and the editors of the *Republic* was beyond repair, and also that the Cabinet had given no consideration to the practical difficulties of setting up a new press. He was therefore able to arrange for the withdrawal of Bullitt and Sargent, Allan A. Hall, formerly editor of the Nashville *Banner*, then serving as assistant secretary of the Treasury, taking over the editorial management of the paper. Of course the affair created a sensation, and it was reported that Ewing had promised Hall the printing of the census, out of which Blair and Rives were said to have made a hundred thousand dollars. Burnley very reluctantly made the change, actuated by personal loyalty to the President, while disapproving the policy of the Cabinet. "I don't know how it is, Mr. Crittenden," he wrote, "but my *heart* is not in this matter. . . . The Cabinet are silly enough to take a position about the Compromise which if it fails will enable their opponents with reason, to take the

---

[7] *Republic,* April 3, 4, 6, 12, 16, 20, 23, 24, 25, 1850; Brown to Crittenden, April 19, 1850, Crittenden Papers.

ground that they defeated it, & if it passes, will deprive them of all credit. Sad infatuation!"[8]

Bullitt had made the most of his last days in the editorial chair of the *Republic*. The burden of his theme was still the essential similarity of the compromise to the "President's plan," in its entirety, which, he said, offered the North an escape from the false position into which its politicians had betrayed it. Now, however, he advanced to the denunciation of those who supported only the California part of the "President's plan" while repudiating the "non-action" part of it and purposing to try to interpolate the Wilmot Proviso. This was aimed at the Seward following, but the climax of Bullitt's offending, which made reconciliation impossible, was an editorial of May 6, replying to a declaration in the New York *Courier and Enquirer* that adherence to the "President's plan" was to be made a test of party orthodoxy. He vigorously defended Clay and Webster against the charge of impropriety in opposing the administration after seeking appointments for their sons. "We venture to say," he added, "that the New York Senator who goes scathless has received ten—no, a score of favors of this sort—to any other Whig's one." The reorganization of the *Republic* took some time, so that the debate on the Omnibus Bill was well under way before the President's organ was in position to attack it. Hall then kept up a continuous bombardment of the Compromise, except as he was compelled to turn the defense of the administration against charges of corruption.[9]

Just as Hall assumed the editorial chair, the report of the committee investigating the Galphin claim had been presented. The Fillmore forces, led by James Brooks, who was himself to close his Congressional career under the blight of the Crédit Mobilier scandal, joined in the hue and cry against the Cabinet which had accepted Seward as its master. By another ironical turn, Crawford, the minister under attack, had alone refused

---

[8] Burnley to Crittenden, May 8, May 15, 1850; Brown to Crittenden, May 9, May 15, May 18, 1850; New York *Express,* May 13, 1850; *Union,* May 14, May 15, May 17, 1850; *Republic,* May 15, 1850.

[9] *Republic,* March 27, April 22, April 25, May 1, May 4, May 6, May 9, May 10, May 11, May 20, May 27, May 29, June 11, June 15, June 17, June 18, June 19, June 21, June 22, June 26, June 28, July 3, 1850.

to bow to the yoke. Ewing had secretly incited the attack on his colleague, and all that kept him in the Cabinet was the impossibility of dismissing him without also dismissing Meredith and Johnson. At a meeting on April 13, the day after the House had ordered a sweeping investigation, the Cabinet had voted to hold together. On the eve of the report, May 12, the action was repeated; and on May 14 the President issued a formal denial that he countenanced any attempt from any quarter whatever to "unsettle his Administration." But developments of the next month brought Taylor to the point of planning a reorganization which was prevented only by his death.[10]

Meanwhile, on May 13, Clay opened the debate on the Omnibus Bill with a great set speech of two and a half hours. Two days later a motion by Douglas to table the Omnibus Bill and take up the California Bill was defeated twenty-four to twenty-eight, Webster voting to table. Only Yulee among the "Hotspurs" went so far as to vote for this drastic step to defeat compromise, though the caucuses of "the Mountain" had already begun. Consideration in committee of the whole then began, to continue until abruptly interrupted on July 9 by Webster's announcement of the impending death of President Taylor. The debate revolved around some thirty-two amendments and amendments to amendments. These were proposed only to be rejected with the exception of four, two of which involved only slight changes of phraseology. One, by Soulé, provided for "popular sovereignty" on slavery at the admission as states of New Mexico and Utah. Another, originating with Hale, was finally modified to give the United States Supreme Court appellate jurisdiction in habeas corpus and slavery cases.[11] The Wilmot Proviso, presented in half a dozen different forms was rejected decisively as often as it came to a vote. The alternative of the Southern ultras, practically the extension of the Missouri Compromise line, met the same fate.

The opening of the debate on the Omnibus Bill also brought

---

[10] *Congressional Globe,* 31st Cong., 1st Sess., pp. 717-19, 1019; New York *Express,* April 17, May 14, 1850.

[11] *Congressional Globe,* 31st Cong., 1st Sess., App., pp. 902-11.

relations between Clay and Taylor to an open rupture. Clay afterwards professed that he had accepted the editorials of the *Republic* in support of the compromise as representing the position of the President, and that he had accordingly taken a conciliatory tone in his speech, carefully avoiding criticism of the "President's plan." On that very day, however, came the news of Bullitt's dismissal, and on May 20, the new editor, in announcing his policies, authoritatively stated that the President had "never for a moment changed or modified" the opinion expressed in his message of January 21. Clay accepted this as a declaration of war, and on the following day minced no words in drawing a contrast between the "President's plan" and the compromise. His speech was terrific in its excitement. Stamping his foot upon the floor with the most violent emphasis, he dared any friend of the President to meet him face to face in combat against the compromise. His face was turned towards Webster, who sat not far from him and who had just been defending Taylor against Yulee, as if he expected him to accept the challenge.[12]

The President was bitterly indignant at Clay's denunciation, and a week later the *Republic* vigorously replied in an editorial of four and a half columns. After elaborately expounding the "President's plan" and charging that Clay had misrepresented it, the editor launched a personal attack on Clay, ascribing his course to "the natural and laudable ambition of appropriating to himself the glory of a third compromise." "He came to lead, not to follow," declared the editor. "He came to originate measures of compromise and pacification, not to adopt such as others might recommend." In due time the *Observer* retorted that,

although the President and Mr. Clay may not be at daggers' points, yet a state of things had grown up by which the singular spectacle is exhibited of *Thomas H. Benton* leading the forces of a Whig Administration upon a particular subject, and HENRY CLAY placed in an attitude of hostility to that Administration.[13]

---

[12] *Republic,* May 10, May 11, May 14, May 20, 1850; *Congressional Globe,* 31st Cong., 1st Sess., App. pp. 614-15, 1091-93; New York *Express,* May 22, 1850.

[13] New York *Express,* May 27, 1850; *Republic,* May 27, 1850; *Observer and Reporter,* May 29, 1850.

The significance of the breach was at once apparent. The *Union* asserted that the *Republic* editorial meant that Clay and all who acted with him were to be expelled from "the Whig church under the Galphin dispensation." The *Republic* continued its attacks and throughout the country the Whig press aligned itself on one side or the other. The declaration of the Albany *Evening Journal* that the "experiment successfully practiced upon John Tyler will signally fail with General Taylor" was accepted as proving a coalition of Free Soilers and Seward men with the administration, and the Fillmore press gradually came to the support of the compromise, though still endeavoring to distinguish between the President and his Cabinet.[14]

While the Whig administration was declaring war on the compromise, leaders of the Democracy were rallying to its support, among them Robert J. Walker of Mississippi, George M. Dallas and James Buchanan of Pennsylvania, Cave Johnson of Tennessee, Levi Woodbury of New Hampshire, P. P. Barbour of Virginia, James Guthrie of Kentucky, and Louis McLane of Delaware. Judge Sharkey of Mississippi, the Whig president of the Nashville Convention, also pronounced in its favor. Great non-partisan meetings were held in all parts of Kentucky, all unanimously adopting resolutions in favor of the compromise and assuring Clay of the solid support of his own state. At the end of June a monster memorial from New York was brought to Washington. It requested the New York Senators to go for the Compromise Bill. Signed by over thirty thousand, six or seven thousand names were subtracted, leaving twenty-five thousand, of which a large number were mercantile firms counted as a single name. The very night before General Taylor expired, a great meeting was held at Philadelphia in favor of Clay and the compromise.[15]

Out of all the hubbub, calm observers were predicting, during the first week of June, that the bill would pass the Senate. The correctness of their forecast was attested by threats of a

---

[14] *Republic*, May 28-July 3, 1850, *passim; Union,* May 28, May 29, 1850; New York *Express*, May 27, May 28, May 30, May 31, 1850.

[15] New York *Express*, May 16, June 4, June 6, June 8, June 28, July 10, 1850; *Observer and Reporter,* May 27, June 5, June 8, June 12, 1850.

veto from Taylor supporters, and by the formation of a radical bloc in the House to "Clingmanize" against the Omnibus. But these were desperate measures of last resort. The immediate strategy of the administration forces was revealed on June 5, when Hale declared that it was Clay's purpose to force the Omnibus Bill through the Senate before the House could send them a California bill. On that occasion Jefferson Davis joined Hale in vainly opposing an earlier meeting of the Senate.[16]

In the House, Doty's California Bill was still under discussion in the committee of the whole on the state of the Union. Simultaneously with the opening of the debate on the Omnibus Bill in the Senate, Doty again attempted to close the debate on his bill, only to raise a storm from the South, whose representatives resorted to "every sort of Parliamentary and other resistance." A motion by Stanly of North Carolina to close the debate on June 11 was finally carried, but when that time arrived, the Southerners started a filibuster to prevent a vote to report the bill to the House. Their obstruction continued until June 18, when Doty's bill gave place to other legislation, which occupied the House until the end of the month. In spite of the efforts of the radicals, the Galphin case was then taken up and disposed of only on July 15, when it was already manifest that the "Galphin Cabinet" had fallen. Thus the dilatory tactics of "the Mountain" in the Senate were over-trumped by the Toombs-Stephens bloc in the House, where it became evident that a majority were determined to wait on the action of the Senate.[17]

Although the plan for delaying action until a separate California bill could come up from the House had for the time being failed, the administration still had a trump to play—a demand from New Mexico for admission as a state. The Polk Administration had in effect recognized the claim of Texas to the Rio Grande from mouth to source as her western boundary, according to her Act to Limits of 1836; and Secretary

---

[16] New York *Express*, May 29, June 7, June 8, 1850; *Congressional Globe*, 31st Cong., 1st Sess., pp. 1129, 1139-41.

[17] *Congressional Globe*, 31st Cong., 1st Sess., pp. 986-88, 1173-1226, 1317-72, *passim;* New York *Express*, May 15, June 12, June 13, June 14, June 15, June 17, 1850.

Marcy had instructed the commander of the United States troops on the upper Rio Grande not to interfere in local affairs unless it was necessary to support the Texan authorities. A few weeks after President Taylor's inauguration, Secretary Crawford confirmed the order of his predecessor. The President at that time apparently held the same view of the subject as in January, 1848, when, in a letter to Crittenden, he had proposed to take nothing south of 36° 30', west of the Rio Grande, which he considered the boundary of Texas.[18]

By November, 1849, however, Taylor had changed his views, for Crawford then instructed the commandant not to thwart a movement for statehood in New Mexico. Two months later still, the President informed Congress that he had urged New Mexico to pursue the same course as California, with the idea that as a state she could invoke the jurisdiction of the Supreme Court to settle the Texan boundary. Early in 1850, Texas established her authority at El Paso and took steps to do so at Santa Fé. But here her agents encountered popular opposition and the federal commander, Colonel Munroe, called a convention to frame a state constitution. The convention sat from May 15 to May 25, and within a month its work had been approved by the people. Before that time, however, on June 17, President Taylor exploded a bomb in the ranks of the compromisers by sending to Congress a special message on New Mexico. While denying that orders had been issued for forcible resistance to an assertion of the Texan claim, he informed Congress of the Texan move at Santa Fé, and asserted his belief that the United States ought to maintain possession until the boundary dispute was settled.[19]

In the meantime, news of the developments at Santa Fé had reached the centers of population in Texas, producing intense

---

[18] The question of the Texan claim to El Paso and Santa Fé is exhaustively and admirably presented, with the exception of its part in the compromise, by Professor W. C. Binkley, "The Question of Texan Jurisdiction in New Mexico under the United States, 1848-1850," *Southwestern Historical Quarterly,* XXIV (July, 1920), 1-38. Taylor to Crittenden, January 3, 1848, Crittenden Papers.

[19] Binkley, "The Question of Texan Jurisdiction in New Mexico under the United States," *Southwestern Historical Quarterly,* XXIV, 1-38; *Congressional Globe,* 31st Cong., 1st Sess., pp. 195, 1235. New York *Express,* May 8, June 27, 1850,

excitement which expressed itself in militant mass-meetings. By the middle of June, Governor Bell was writing to inform the Texan delegation in Congress of the situation and of his intention to act. He also wrote the President demanding an explanation and disavowal of Colonel Munroe's action. This letter reached Washington after President Taylor was stricken with his fatal illness and was opened only after his death. Governor Bell also called a special session of the Texas legislature to meet August 12. On receipt of the news of the movement in New Mexico, other Southern States, especially Mississippi, hastened to encourage Texas by offers of assistance, while it was reported in Washington that Sam Houston was about to resign his senatorship in order to assume command of the Texan forces.[20]

The telegraph on June 25 brought from St. Louis the news of the framing of a State Constitution for New Mexico, and this, together with the message of June 17, created an entirely new state of affairs at Washington and "knocked in the head all previous calculations." The Southern members of Congress began to hold caucuses, although the ultras and the moderates agreed only on New Mexico. The cause of Texas was at once made the cause of the whole South, and on July 4, Stephens published a card in the *National Intelligencer*, saying that in the event of a military collision in New Mexico, the whole South would rush to the aid of Texas and fight it out.[21]

The Southern caucus on the night of July 1 appointed C. M. Conrad of Louisiana, Humphrey Marshall of Kentucky and Robert Toombs of Georgia to remonstrate with the President about his New Mexican policy. All were "original Taylor men"; Conrad had played a prominent part in the Philadelphia convention; Marshall had served at Buena Vista. These gentlemen called separately and warned him that his Southern friends would be driven into opposition if he insisted on the admission of California and New Mexico as states and persisted in

[20] Binkley, "The Question of Texan Jurisdiction in New Mexico under the United States," *Southwestern Historical Quarterly*, XXIV, 1-38; New York *Express*, June 26, June 27, July 6, July 10, 1850; *Observer and Reporter*, July 3, 1859; *Union*, July 16, 1850.

[21] New York *Express*, June 23, 26, July 2, 6, 1850; *National Intelligencer*, July 4, 1850.

his hostile attitude towards Texas. Taylor insisted on California's right to come in at once and declared he would recommend the admission of New Mexico as soon as her constitution
arrived. He scouted the claim of Texas to the Santa Fé country. Since he must in any case offend one wing of his party,
he said that he could hardly be expected to sacrifice eighty-
four Northern men for twenty-nine from the South. In view
of the President's well-known obstinacy, it was evident that
further remonstrance was useless.[22]

Meanwhile the Cabinet had had the situation under consideration, and had voted by a majority of one to revoke
Crawford's order of March 23, 1849, repeating Marcy's injunction to the commandant at Santa Fé to avoid a collision
with the Texan authorities. Crawford, feeling that this action
would precipitate a civil war, refused to sign such an order,
but offered to resign and allow a Secretary of War to be appointed who was in sympathy with the policy of the administration. In view of the impending debate on the Galphin case, it
was not deemed prudent to make a change in the Cabinet; so
the President declared that he would himself, as commander-
in-chief, sign the order. Crawford of course communicated this
situation to his intimates and sponsors, Toombs and Stephens;
and the latter again attempted, on July 3, to alter the President's policy. Failing, he and Toombs sought to enlist the aid
of Preston, the leader of the Southern faction in the Cabinet
and personally the most influential with the President of all his
"constitutional advisers." Their discussion culminated in a
threat by Stephens to impeach the President if troops were
ordered to Santa Fé, and the next day Stephens published his
warning of the imminence of civil war.[23]

The President's answer to the threat of impeachment was
to order the drafting of a powerful and comprehensive message on the general state of the country. This would have
forced the resignation of Crawford and Johnson, who were both

---

[22] J. F. H. Claiborne, *Life and Correspondence of John A. Quitman*, II,
32-33.

[23] New York *Express*, July 6, July 9, July 18, 1850; Avary, *op. cit.*, pp.
26-27.

swinging toward compromise. The President had also come to a determination to free his administration of the Galphin scandal by sacrificing Meredith; and accordingly, on July 3, he conferred with Thurlow Weed as to the new ministers. Stanly of North Carolina was slated to succeed Crawford, and Bell (or possibly Crittenden) to succeed Johnson. By Weed's advice, the Treasury was assigned to Governor Hamilton Fish of New York, and Weed was authorized to prepare him for the offer. The message was to be sent to Congress after the national holiday, and the Cabinet reorganization would thereupon ensue. But all these plans were of course broken up by the sudden illness and death of the President.[24]

While the New Mexican crisis was thus developing, Clay was almost incapacitated by illness. Throughout the month of June his health had been precarious. He had suffered several severe attacks, but could not be kept away from the Senate long enough fully to recover. Finally, he retired to the country and appeared once more in the Senate on July 2 much improved in health and ready to carry the compromise to a vote. The events of the previous weeks had materially lessened the chances of the bill, though all calculations were different. A week before Clay had not been without hopes, though never at any time very sanguine of its passage. Two days later, things never looked worse, for only some nine or ten Senators could be rated as "moderate" by a friendly observer. It began to look as if the fate of the bill would turn on the casting vote of the Vice President, and there was keen speculation as to his position, his rivalry with Seward being by no means overlooked. At any rate, it could not pass the Senate by such a majority as would give it vantage ground in the House. On July 6, Clay laughingly said he hoped to get a vote by Christmas, and since Cooper of Pennsylvania was the only Northern Whig Senator who would touch the bill, Clay was said to feel at liberty to make concessions to gain Southern votes enough to pass it. The day before the death of the President, it was said to depend on the votes of Berrien and King, and Clay was determined to

[24] New York *Express*, July 13, July 18, 1850; *Union*, July 18, July 21, 1850; Weed, *op. cit.*, pp. 589-91.

push it to a vote before the end of the week, little as was its chance of passage.[25] This was the situation when the Senate adjourned upon the announcement of the impending decease of President Taylor.

[25] New York *Express,* June 10, July 8, July 10, 1850; *Observer and Reporter,* July 6, 1850.

CHAPTER XVI

OMNIBUS VERSUS CAB

THE ACCESSION of Millard Fillmore to the presidency was correctly regarded from the outset as effecting a political revolution at Washington. He had been very discreet in regard to the compromise, though the identification of Seward with its alternative, the "President's plan," justified the assumption that he would be friendly. The Fillmore press had been careful to treat the "President's plan" with respect, though supporting, on the whole, the compromise. They were conspicuously inclined to watch Webster's position and to hope that, in case the Omnibus Bill were defeated, he would present a scheme more acceptable to the North. So long as they could, even after the *Republic* editorial of May 27, they insisted that President Taylor was not irrevocably committed to the "non-action" policy which they identified with the Cabinet rather than with the President.

Indeed, antagonism to the Cabinet is the key to the policy of the Fillmore faction. Not until the very last, if then, did they realize that Seward's ascendancy over the President was quite as great as over the Cabinet. Thus they played up the Galphin scandal as remorselessly as the *Union* itself, quite oblivious of the fact that in destroying Crawford they were removing from the Cabinet the one consistent opponent of Seward's dominance. In nothing was this shown more clearly than in the matter of New Mexico. They interpreted the "non-action" policy to mean that, by Crawford's order of non-interference, Texas was to be permitted to conquer and absorb New Mexico. On the news of the statehood movement, they insisted that the President had not issued the order under which the convention had been called. They gave full credence to the unfavorable reports of the numbers and character of the population of New Mexico which became current, declaring it impossible that such a community should be admitted to statehood on a par with New York. They insisted that President Taylor had given no orders for forcible resistance to a Texan expedition, and stressed the danger of a collision should the compromise be defeated and a settlement of the disputed boundary postponed.[1]

In view of this attitude of the Fillmore press and with a full consciousness of their own proscription of his adherents, it is not surprising that on leaving President Taylor's death-bed the Cabinet agreed to resign, and, on announcing the event to Fillmore, tendered their resignations. The new President, embarrassed, requested them to hold on for the present, but the idea at once became current that he would appoint an entire new Cabinet with Webster as "premier." Seward hastened to advise the retention of the old Cabinet, all of whom, except Crawford, he thought wished to remain. Clayton was prostrated by the shock, Seward was too ill to see his friends, and John Bell, exhausted by a three-day speech, was also seriously ill, while the House's condemnatory vote on the Galphin case, on July 15, added Crawford to the casualties. July 11, Thursday, was taken up with conferences, Clay and Webster having an hour and a half between them, from which the knowing deduced that they and the new President were friends. By Sunday, Fillmore's New York friends had gathered around him, effectually blocking Seward's access, though opposing those who sought to bring about an open conflict between him and the President. Although there were three members of the Cabinet whom he would have been glad to retain, as it was understood, the new President was unwilling to make invidious distinctions, so probably would make a complete change. The division of the old Cabinet into Northern and Southern factions led by Meredith and Preston deprived it of the unity which Fillmore was said to consider essential to the conduct of the administration. Collamer cherished his hopes, the Pennsylvania delegation worked strenuously for the retention of Meredith—and Fillmore remained smilingly non-committal.[2]

On Sunday it was supposed that Webster was to head an entirely new Cabinet; on Monday, however, Fillmore requested

---

[1] New York *Express*, June 28, July 1, July 23, 1850.

[2] New York *Express*, July 11, July 12, July 13, July 15, July 16, July 17, July 18, 1850; Seward, *op. cit.*, pp. 143-47; Clayton to Crittenden, August 8, 1850, Crittenden Papers.

the old ministers to hold on for a month. On Tuesday, they replied that they would remain until the following Monday and no longer. Clayton and Crawford absented themselves from the Cabinet meeting that morning on account of illness, and on Thursday Crawford refused to do any more work. The great influence of Corwin and Pearce, the closest Congressional intimates of the new President, had by this time become apparent. At this stage, Winthrop replaced Webster as the probable "premier," but on Wednesday Webster made a great speech in the Senate which, it was thought, decided the question in his favor. A desperate effort was being made to retain Ewing, and by Thursday, July 18, only Webster, Crittenden, and Graham had been decided on, Corwin still declining the Post Office. Eventually Corwin was shifted to the Treasury, and Fillmore's law partner, N. K. Hall, took the Post Office. It was some time later, and only after several refusals, that A. H. H. Stuart and C. M. Conrad were found for the Interior and War Departments. As finally constituted, it was a much stronger Cabinet than that which it superseded.[3]

"The government is in the hands of Mr. Webster, and Mr. Clay is its organ in Congress," declared Seward; but Fillmore's friends thought Clay showed great magnanimity in urging Webster, whom some supposed his rival, for Secretary of State and in not objecting to Crittenden for Attorney General, even if he did not advise the appointment. Morehead, the particular candidate of the Clay men, was passed over, while Corwin had opposed Clay in 1848, and Conrad's part in the Philadelphia Convention made him especially odious to them. Despite Seward's assertion, in no sense could the change be said to have given Clay an ascendancy in the administration.[4]

Yet the chances of the compromise were much improved. This had been the general impression from the first; and the new President early let it be understood through his journalistic spokesmen, that while his administration would not use the patronage to pass the compromise, he would not oppose it,

---

[3] New York *Express*, July 12, July 13, July 16, July 17, July 18, July 20, July 24, 1850; Seward, *op. cit.; Union*, July 26, 1850.

[4] New York *Express*, July 15, July 17, July 19, 1850; Seward, *op. cit.;* Clay to Thomas H. Clay, August 6, 1850, Colton, *Private Correspondence*, p. 611.

and would approve the measure Congress might pass. It was also pointed out that both factions of the old Cabinet agreed in opposing the compromise and that their influence had been potent in maintaining the opposition of the Northern Whigs; with that pressure removed, these members would be free to act as they thought their constituents desired. Webster's appointment, following immediately upon his speech of July 17, in which he definitely took his stand for the Omnibus Bill, or, if it were defeated, for the separate passage of its details, made the compromise in effect an administration measure. His declaration that the Texas Boundary was now the most pressing of the measures, and one which he could not consent to leave unsettled, had been anticipated nearly a week before by a summary of the Santa Fé situation and the curt pronouncement, "A collision of arms was inevitable the way things were going on."[5]

On July 15, the debate on the Omnibus Bill was resumed, the committee stage brought to a close, and the amendments agreed to. Walker of Wisconsin then moved to strike out all but the California section, an indirect mode of killing the bill. Clay pointedly called the attention of the ultras to the alternatives they faced—either California with the compensation carried in the bill or California without compensation, for he was one of a clear majority on the bare question of California. Berrien, however, framed a point of order which induced Walker to withdraw his motion. Benton then proposed the hundred and second meridian from the Rio Grande to the thirty-fourth parallel and thence east to the Red River as the western boundary of Texas, which Foote countered on the seventeenth by proposing the thirty-fourth parallel from the Red River to the Rio Grande. These propositions represent the sectional extremes on this question, Clay's compromise line running from the Rio Grande twenty miles above El Paso, approximately thirty-two North by one hundred and seven West, to the thirty-fourth parallel at the Red River. At this stage, the

---

[5] New York *Express*, July 11-15, 1850; *Congressional Globe*, 31st Cong., 1st Sess., App., pp. 1260-70; Seward, *op. cit.*, I, 149; *Illinois State Register*, August 1, 1850.

other outstanding demand of the South was the restriction of California on the south by the mountain chain running to the Pacific about thirty-five thirty, practically an extension of the Missouri Compromise line.[6]

The change of administration which had advanced the cause of compromise, had paradoxically lessened the chances of the Omnibus Bill. There persisted a strong repulsion at the North to the admission of California as part of an avowed bargain, even among those who accepted the terms of the compromise as a practical necessity. Pride of consistency also kept many from supporting it after so vigorously opposing it. The close alliance and coöperation of the Free-Soilers and the nullifiers —"the Mountain"—was also hard to get over. A caucus or conference of Senators, with a few Representatives, met in Clay's room on the twelfth, but apparently was unable to reconcile the differences of the sections. Four days later it began to be reported that should the Omnibus Bill fail, a bill was to be offered establishing the territorial governments and settling the Texas boundary, and after this was disposed of, a separate California Bill would be brought forward. Authorship of this plan was even ascribed to President Fillmore himself.[7]

The next day, Webster drew from Douglas a definite statement, as chairman of the Committee on Territories, that should California be admitted by herself, he would at once move to take up the territorial and boundary bills and settle all the issues in detail if they were not settled in the aggregate. Douglas declared that this was the opinion and determination of a majority of his committee, and Webster approved the plan. The soon-to-be "premier" then explicitly pointed out that the "non-action" policy was thus no longer in the field of practical politics, affirming his own unalterable opposition to adjournment without the settlement of the Texas boundary.[8]

---

[6] *Congressional Globe,* 31st Cong., 1st Sess., pp. 1378-83, 1391-92, 1398, 1410-11.

[7] New York *Express,* July 13, July 15, July 17, 1850; *Union,* July 18, 1850.

[8] New York *Express,* July 20, 1850; *Congressional Globe,* 31st Cong., 1st Sess., App., p. 1266.

That night, July 16, James Brooks wrote to the *Express:*

The "Omnibus" jolts along in the Senate. The South have attacked it so bitterly, and the North lends it so little support, that even the celebrated "driver," Old Hal, thinks, it is said, of putting on new gearing, rearranging his horses, and changing his load a little. The South swears "all is lost," if the North gets into the Omnibus, and the North swears "all is (also) lost" if the South gets into the Omnibus. Old Hal thinks, it is said, under this state of facts, of re-arranging his team and his load.

The bill had, indeed, reached the point where amendment was all but impossible. Every possible Northern vote had been secured, but all would be lost by amendments that would satisfy the Southern ultras, while three or four would be lost even by what would satisfy such moderates as King and Berrien while scarcely gaining as many from the South. Even King, who had pretty consistently upheld Clay so far, and who had so far kept his hair-trigger colleague, Clemens, voting for compromise, on July 18 definitely took his stand for the limitation of California. "It is therefore proposed," wrote one well-informed correspondent,

to press the bill to a vote and let the agony be over. If the bill is defeated (it may barely be saved by one or two votes) then the Texas boundary question will be taken up by itself. It is the most urgent of all, and must be disposed of as soon as possible to prevent a collision of arms. Then will come California by herself, and then the territorial bills—the admission of New Mexico as a State is entirely out of the question.[9]

Such was the situation when Clay rose on July 22 to present his closing argument. "It was one of his peculiar efforts—a mixture of wit, satire, sarcasm, conciliation, and abounding with passages of thrilling eloquence," wrote an auditor.

No opportunity was lost of introducing those great effects of which he is master, and by turns his crowded auditory were convulsed with laughter, excited to noisy applause, . . . or stilled to profound and sometimes oppressive silence. . . . The most important feature of his speech was that he declared the willingness of the committee,

---

[9] New York *Express*, July 19, July 20, 1850. *Ibid.*, July 20, 1850, quoting Washington correspondence, July 18, Baltimore *Sun*.

including himself, to vote for separate measures should the Compromise fail.[10]

That very long speech is most difficult to summarize; for, essentially a rebuttal argument, it ranges over the whole field of the debate, countering the objections of opponents from both sections.[11] Clay began by indicating concretely the unprecedented tendencies toward disunion, not only Southern but Northern; indeed, he thought the obtuseness of the North to the realities of the situation one of the chief sources of danger. Then, after briefly sketching the history of the compromise, he undertook to answer the objections to its separate provisions. California, which had been expected to carry the other measures through, was proving the chief obstacle, for some Southern Senators were stubbornly objecting to her boundaries, although the alternative to the compromise was the separate passage of Douglas's California Bill. The territories must be organized in some way. The admission of New Mexico was impracticable, for the approaching census would confirm the opinion that she was immature. They were all agreed as to the necessity of settling the Texas boundary with its imminent danger of producing civil war. Clay then took up the objections to the compromise as such, and to its "omnibus" character. "It is not that the omnibus contains too much but too little," he declared, "but the weight of Mr. Wilmot would break it down, so it cannot contain him." Neither had it room for two or three new states from Texas.

The bill, however, had not half the incongruity of the elements of opposition to it. Referring to a charge made by Hale that Clay and Cass, Foote and Webster had been seen in close conference in a committee room, Clay readily avowed the fact. He only wished the conferences had been more numerous and longer, for there had been no differences of opinion between himself and the Democratic friends he had consulted. No subjects connected with party politics had been discussed, but only this measure, on which they had been perfectly agreed. But some of the opponents of the bill had been quite as frequent in consultation as its friends—"whose eyes have not

[10] New York *Express,* July 24, 1850.
[11] *Congressional Globe,* 31st Cong., 1st Sess., App., pp. 1405-15.

witnessed the consultations between the extremes of this
Chamber from day to day? The eyes of every discerning
Senator must have noticed it," he declared. Yet, "upon the very
subject under consideration there is among them no union of
sentiment, no coincidence of opinion, and yet a most cordial
and confidential coöperation." Butler, Hale, and Dayton here
disavowed participation in such conferences, but Clay elicited
from Mason the admission, "There certainly have been frequent
consultations between Senators from the southern States upon
questions involving the dignity, honor, and safety of the southern States, involved as they conceived in the provisions of this
bill." To which, amid loud applause from the gallery, Clay rejoined, "And so, undoubtedly, did our consultations relate to
the dignity, honor, and safety of the Union, and the Constitution of our country."

Clay then succinctly stated the necessity of compromise.

There is neither incongruity in the freight nor in the passengers
on board our omnibus. We are all heartily concurrent upon the
only topic which brought us together, and which constitutes the sole
subject of our consultation. . . . [How do these questions stand?]
One party wants the immediate admission of California, and wants
the imposition of the proviso in the territorial governments. The
other party wants the limits of California circumscribed, and the
Missouri Compromise line applied—some of them with the express
recognition of the right to carry slaves south of it, others without
such a recognition, trusting to an implied constitutional right, and
these other parties are strenuously opposed to the proviso. Some,
again, want the Texas boundary settled, and others want it to be
left open.

No one thought that Congress ought to adjourn without
settling these questions, and how could that be except by
compromise? He had heard that it was possible to carry these
measures separately if presented in succession, just as they
had been presented by the committee. The committee had
combined them because they thought that the most practical
way to procure their passage, but if the object could be better
obtained by a series of measures, not one of them would com-
plain. They cared not for the means, so long as the end was
attained.

"But . . . there is danger," he continued,

that in the presentation of those measures in detail, some of them would fail, and the result would be, that whilst one party got all that it immediately wanted, the other would obtain nothing which it desired. You know there was great cause to apprehend—I hope there may be none now—that, in the separate presentation of the measures, the consequence would be the attachment of the Wilmot Proviso in one or the other of the two Houses, and the utter failure to establish any territorial governments for Utah and New Mexico. It was thought then that . . . we would present a measure which would bind all, and that would lead both parties, as far as practicable, to unite upon it for the sake of harmony and tranquility. We thought then, as I think now, that Senators from the Northern States might go home to their constituents, after this measure shall have been passed, and say, "We have got California; she is secure; there is a prohibition of slavery in her constitution that will last perhaps forever, whereas the Wilmot Proviso would have had a limited and an evanescent duration, existing while the territorial form of government remained, but ending whenever the State should come to form herself a constitution. . . .

"Well, but why, then," they might reply, "have you not put in a restriction in the territorial bill, so as to secure that, at least until they come to be ripe enough to form State governments for themselves?" Would it not be a satisfactory reply to them to say, that in your opinion, and in the opinion of a large portion of this Senate, the law of Nature, and of Nature's God excluded slavery from these Territories, and, according to your opinion, also, the *lex loci* of the land also exclude slavery? And might you not further add, with propriety, that you endeavored to reconcile the distracted and disunited portions of this great empire, and you thought that no imposition or restriction was necessary to any object which you desired to attain, and in a spirit of conciliation, therefore, you forebore to vote against the final measure, because it secured so much of what the North wanted? Could you not say that you were not in danger of losing what you also wanted in respect to the residue of the country?

This subject has presented one of the most extraordinary political phenomena that I ever witnessed. Here is a united Senate almost in favor of all the measures in detail . . . , but opposed to them when they come to be presented unitedly to be acted on.

The Wilmot Proviso was unnecessary, Clay contended.

You have been told that the existence of African slavery depends upon the character of the climate and of the soil. The nature of the soil of New Mexico forbids the expectation that slavery will ever be planted there. Why, we all know that slave labor is applicable only to the great staples which constitute the subjects of our foreign commerce—cotton, sugar, hemp, tobacco, and rice. Slave labor has been found, according to American experience, to be utterly valueless, or at least to a great extent valueless, in those States where these staple articles are not cultivated. Does anybody pretend that the soil of New Mexico or Utah is adapted to the cultivation of these articles? Do we not all know that if it were adapted, and the climate and soil would allow of their being cultivated, the expense of transportation from New Mexico or Utah, either to the Pacific on one hand, or to the Gulf of Mexico or the Atlantic on the other, would be, perhaps, ten times the value at home of any of these articles? . . .

After deprecating Northern taunts against the South, Clay turned to the Southern opponents of the bill.

They interpret the Constitution according to their judgment; they ingraft their exposition upon it; and without listening to or giving due weight to the opposite interpretation, to the conflicting exposition which is as honestly believed by the opposite interpreters as they believe on their side, they proclaim their own exposition of the Constitution, and cry out, "All we want is the constitution!"

This is intolerance. "Any moderate, rational Northern wishes" should be satisfied by the admission of California, the probability that New Mexico and Utah would remain or become free territory, the avoidance of any introduction of slavery by authority of Congress, by seeing New Mexico detached from Texas with the probability of ultimately becoming a free state, and by the abolition of the slave trade in the District of Columbia.

The South avoids the assertion by Congress of the dangerous principle, as they regard it, of the Wilmot Proviso; places beyond controversy nine hundred miles of the territory of Texas on the Rio Grande, now in dispute; gains an efficient fugitive slave bill, and silences the agitation about the abolition of slavery in this District. . . . If she cannot get slave territory in California, New

Mexico, and Utah, whose fault is it? She cannot blame Congress, but must upbraid Nature's law and Nature's God! . . .

Now, it is inevitable, in my opinion, that southern slavery is excluded from the possession of any portion of California, Utah, and probably of New Mexico; and, if so, why contend for it? Now what is it that distracts the public mind? A mere abstraction. . . . Two hundred years hence, if not much sooner, our posterity will read the history of the present times, agitating and threatening the country as they do, with as much astonishment as we pore [sic] over the leaves of the historian in which he recounts the witchcraft, and the persecution and punishment of witches in former times. And why contend for carrying slaves to Utah and New Mexico, where is nothing upon which their labor can be employed —where nobody will take them? Let me remind gentlemen . . . who are desirous for the greatest extension of the theatre of slavery—of a . . . great and an imminent danger, which they are incurring. I venture a prediction . . . that if Texas includes all the territory now claimed by her . . . in some thirty, forty, or fifty years, there will be no slave State in the limits of Texas at all. I venture to predict that the northern population . . . will in process of time greatly outnumber the population holding slaves upon the Gulf and the lower waters of Texas; and a majority will be found to be adverse to the continuance of slavery, and it will either be abolished, or its limits effectually circumscribed.

This was no new opinion—Clay thought he had expressed it in his Raleigh letter.

Declaring that the South must face "facts as they exist" and reconcile themselves to the inevitable, Clay pointed out the divergent opinions as to the Texan claim to the Rio Grande boundary, which could be settled only by a compromise. He then took up the Southern demands for extension of the Missouri Compromise line, which he thought worthless to them without explicit authorization of slavery to the South of it; for he argued at some length against the view that the right existed in virtue of the Constitution. As for the explicit authorization, it could not command a majority—probably not a third of the votes—in either House. Thus the extreme claims of the South were impracticable, and the compromise was far better for the South than the previously considered measure, the "President's plan" of General Taylor.

If the compromise bill were defeated, there was danger of civil war on the Rio Grande. It was possible that the twenty-nine other states of the Union might repel an invasion of New Mexico by Texas, if other countries stood aloof and left the United States and Texas to fight it out. "But, sir," he declared,

Texas will not be alone; if war breaks out between her and the troops of the United States on the upper Rio Grande, there are ardent, enthusiastic spirits of Arkansas, Mississippi, Louisiana, and Alabama, that will flock to the standard of Texas, contending, as they believe they will be contending, for slave territory. And they will be drawn on, State by State, in all human probability, from the banks of the Rio Grande to the banks of the river which flows by the tomb of Washington. I do not say this will happen, but there is danger that it may happen. . . . I will not say which party would prevail in such a contest. . . . There are two descriptions of ties which bind this Union and this glorious people together. . . . I wish never to see the day when the ties of commerce and fraternity shall be destroyed, and the iron band afforded by political connections shall alone exist and keep us together. . . . Let blood ever be spilled . . . , and . . . thousands of gallant men will fly from the States which I have enumerated, if not from all the slave-holding States, to sustain and succor the power of Texas, and to preserve her in possession of that which they, as well as she, feel so deep an interest. Even from Missouri . . . herself a slave State, it is not at all unlikely that thousands would flock to the standard of the weaker party, and assist Texas in her struggles. . . .

Can you content yourselves with going home, and leaving it to be possibly realized before the termination of the current year? Are you not bound as men, as patriots, as enlightened statesmen, to provide for this contingency? And how can you provide for it better than by this bill, which separates a reluctant people . . . from Texas, and guards against the possibility of a sympathetic and contagious war springing up between the slave States and the General Government, which I regard as almost inevitable, if Congress adjourns with the admission of California alone, stopping there and doing nothing else. For, sir, the admission of California alone, under all the circumstances of the time, with the proviso still suspended over the heads of the South, with the abolition of slavery still threatened in the District of Columbia—the act of the admission of California, without provision for the settlement of the Texas boundary question, without the other portions of the bill, will aggravate, and embitter and enrage the South, and make them rush on furiously and blindly, animated, as they believe, by a patriotic zeal to defend themselves against northern aggression. I call upon you, then, and I call upon the Senate, in the name of the country, never to separate from the Capitol, without settling all these questions, leaving nothing to disturb the general peace and repose of the country.

The passage of the compromise, Clay insisted, would at once stop the slavery agitation, by leaving the agitators nothing to agitate about. After perturbing storms, a calm is sure to follow, as it did after the compromises of 1821 and 1833. Clay then appealed to the Senate to let patriotism triumph over selfish considerations. He made personal appeals to Mason as a descendant of George Mason and a Virginian, and to the Senators from Rhode Island and Delaware, "my little friends which have stood by me, and by which I have stood, in all the vicissitudes of my political life," and who would be in especial danger should the Union break up.

"If this Union shall become separated, new unions, new confederacies will arise," the orator declared.

And with respect to this—if there be any—I hope there is no one in the Senate—before whose imagination is flitting the idea of a great Southern Confederacy to take possession of the Balize and the mouth of the Mississippi, I say in my place never! *never! NEVER!* will we who occupy the broad waters [sic] of the Mississippi and its upper tributaries consent that any foreign flag shall float at the Balize or upon the turrets of the Crescent City —never—never! I call upon all the South. Sir, we have had hard words—bitter words, bitter thoughts, unpleasant feelings towards each other. . . . Let us forget them. . . . Let us go to the altar of our country and swear, as the oath was taken of old, that we will stand by her; we will support her; that we will uphold her Constitution; that we will preserve her Union, and that we will pass this great, comprehensive, and healing system of measures, which will hush all jarring elements, and bring peace and tranquility to our homes.

Let, me, Mr. President, in conclusion, say that the most disastrous consequences would occur in my opinion, were we to go home, doing nothing to satisfy and tranquilize the country upon these great questions. . . . Will not the monarchs of the Old World pronounce our Republic a disgraceful failure? What will be the

judgment of our constituents, when we return to them and they
ask us, How have you left your country? Is all quiet—all happy—
are all the seeds of distraction or division crushed and dissipated?
And sir, when you come into the bosom of your family, . . . [to
King], what response, Mr. President, can you make to that wife
of your choice and those children with whom you have been blessed
by God? Will you go home and leave all in disorder and confusion,
all unsettled, all open? . . . We shall stand condemned in our
own consciences, by our own constituents, by our own country.
The measure may be defeated. I have been aware that its passage
for many days has not been absolutely certain. From the first to
the last I hoped and believed it would pass, because from the first
to the last I believed it was founded on the principles of just and
righteous concession—of mutual conciliation. I believe that it deals
unjustly by no part of the Republic; that it saves their honor, and,
so far as it is dependent upon Congress, saves the interests of all
quarters of the country. But, sir, I have known that the decision
of its fate depended upon four or five votes in the Senate of the
United States, and upon whose ultimate judgment we could not
count upon the one side or the other with absolute certainty. Its
fate is now committed to the Senate, and to those five or six votes
to which I have referred. It may be defeated. It is possible that, for
the chastisement of our sins or transgressions, the rod of Providence
may be applied to us, may still be suspended over us. But, if defeated, it will be a triumph of ultraism and impracticability—a
triumph of the most extraordinary conjunction of extremes; a
victory won by abolitionism; a victory over peace and tranquility;
and I pray to Almighty God that it may not, in consequence of the
inauspicious result, lead to the most unhappy and disastrous consequences to our beloved country.

Before the meeting of the Senate the next morning, however,
a caucus was held which decided to adopt a substitute for
the boundary settlement of the bill. Proposed by Bradbury
of Maine, it provided merely for the appointment of commissioners by the United States to agree with Texan commissioners as to a line from the intersection of the one-hundredth
meridian and the Red River to the Rio Grande and the terms
upon which it should be established, subject to the approval
of Congress and the Texan legislature. It was understood that
this would bring over three or four Southern opponents of
the bill, and assure its passage by two votes. The "Mountain"

now resorted to all sorts of dilatory tactics in order to gain time for the successors of Corwin and Webster to take their places. Ewing presented his credentials on the twenty-seventh and Winthrop on the thirtieth. On the twenty-sixth, Bradbury's substitute apparently had been abandoned; it was unsatisfactory to the Texas Senators who wanted stipulations in regard to the present and future military course of the administration. Douglas prepared for eventualities on the twenty-seventh by presenting, on behalf of a majority of the Senate, a new rule providing for the previous question, which Atchison moved to postpone indefinitely. It was thought, however, that the Omnibus Bill would pass the Senate by a single vote.[12]

On Monday, July 29, the struggle continued to delay action until the opponents of compromise could have the benefit of Winthrop's vote. Eventually Bradbury's substitute was brought to a vote, only to be lost by a tie vote of 28-28, owing to the mischance of Douglas's momentary absence. Bradbury then introduced it again with a modification, but failed to secure a vote that day. That night a caucus including some new Northern men met, and agreed to a modification of Bradbury's substitute known as the Dawson Proviso. In effect, it prohibited the operation of the territorial government of New Mexico east of the Rio Grande until the commissioners' report should be agreed to by Congress and the Texas Legislature. After an all day struggle, the Dawson Proviso was accepted 30 to 28, Shields changing his vote to break a tie; and then the amended Bradbury substitute was passed, also 30 to 28, though no less than sixteen Senators shifted from one side to the other. Just before the vote on the Dawson Proviso, failure of which would have meant the loss of the bill, the Senate had refused, 25 to 32, to lay the bill on the table. Clay considered the battle won. Every sign was favorable, the Texas Senators satisfied, and even the opponents of the bill began to think for the first time that it would pass.[13]

---

[12] *Congressional Globe*, 31st Cong., 1st Sess., pp. 1448, 1466. New York *Express*, July 25, July 27, July 29, 1850. *Union*, July 27, July 28, 1850.

[13] *Congressional Globe*, 31st Cong., 1st Sess., pp. 1481-82. New York *Express*, July 30, July 31, August 1, 1850.

But, on the very eve of success, Clay had committed a fatal blunder. He had failed to give proper consideration to the views of James Alfred Pearce. Pearce was a quiet, scholarly man, whose chief interest as senator seems to have been the fostering of the Library of Congress. Clay, totally unable to comprehend a character so antithetical to his own, ignored Pearce at this crisis, though he was the closest intimate of the President among the Senators.[14] Pearce naturally felt some pique at not being included among the leaders summoned to confer on the Dawson Proviso. He voted against that amendment and abstained on the amended Bradbury substitute. The effect of the Dawson Proviso being to leave Texas free to assert her possession of the Santa Fé region, it was extremely offensive to the administration, which was taking a strong stand in maintaining the position of the United States in the disputed territory. Pearce was therefore delegated to secure the elimination of the Dawson Proviso.[15]

In anticipation of the final conflict over the Omnibus Bill, a great crowd assembled on July 31. Meredith, Preston, Judge Sharkey, were among the spectators who sweltered in the Senate Chamber, which "actually steamed with perspiration." The complicated parliamentary situation compelled Pearce to resort to heroic means to accomplish his purpose—nothing less than a motion to strike out the entire New Mexico section and then to reinsert all but the Dawson Proviso. The friends of the bill were filled with consternation. Foote, Mangum, Pratt, Dawson, hastened to remonstrate. Clay sent a substitute amendment from his desk which Pearce peremptorily rejected. Douglas brought one to which he had gained the assent of the Texas Senators, containing a reservation of the rights of both parties, the United States and Texas. Pearce agreed to this provided it should read "rights and possession," but to this the Texas Senators objected. Then Pearce, if he really did not desire to kill the bill, was guilty of the grossest stupidity. Yulee made the Machiavellian request that Pearce's motion be divided, and Pearce fell into the trap. The motion to strike

---

[14] B. C. Steiner, "James Alfred Pearce," *Maryland Historical Magazine,* XVI, 319.

[15] New York *Express,* August 1, August 2, 1850.

out was carried, 33 to 22, and to Pearce's motion to reinsert, Douglas moved the amendment he had submitted to Pearce, which was rejected 24 to 33. After further jockeying, the motion to reinsert was lost 25 to 28, and after repeated motions to adjourn or to postpone indefinitely had been defeated, the California sections were also stricken out 34 to 25, and finally the bill, now reduced to the organization of Utah, was ordered to engrossment, 32 to 18.[16]

During the long agony, no observer could help remarking "the concert between the Nullifiers and the Abolitionists in their combined efforts to put on any amendment, or take off any part, which would secure the destruction of the bill." Hale and Clemens, Benton and Ewing, worked together for this end. The amendments were so numerous that they baffled the reporters. During the discussion of Pearce's motion, Clay remained at his seat, apparently disheartened. He left at dark, worn out and exhausted by a session of more than seven hours, and so did not witness the triumph of "the Mountain." [17]

That triumph was quite vividly described by a spectator, obviously in imitation of Macaulay.

The old bitter enemies of the Omnibus were in the highest glee. Hale . . . could scarcely contain himself. Jefferson Davis's face grinned with smiles. Old Bullion's few hairs actually bristled with electrical delight. *He* had routed Clay! *He* had smashed his Omnibus to atoms! Seward was dancing about like a little top. Dayton shook his thick sides with sporadic spasms. Clemens reminded one of a New York *B'hoy* in an assembly of admiring G'hals,—Yulee looked solemn in solitary glory. Barnwell's spectacles twinkled, and Butler's gray hairs flourished more than ever. Chase was shaking hands with Soule the Frenchman. Bell was half-sorry, but two-thirds glad. Delaware was uneasy. Rhode Island felt she had not done her duty, and there sat Old Hal, as melancholy as Caius Marius over the ruins of Carthage. Cass too was unhappy. Winthrop seemed to say, "I've raised the d—l. If Webster had been here, in my seat, not I,—the Omnibus would

---

[16] New York *Express,* August 1, August 2, August 5, 1850; letter of Pearce, August 5, 1850, Steiner, "James Alfred Pearce," *Maryland Historical Magazine,* XVIII, 349-50. *Congressional Globe,* 31st Cong., 1st Sess., pp. 1490-91; App., pp. 1470-88.

[17] New York *Express,* August 1, August 2, 1850. *Congressional Globe,* 31st Cong., 1st Sess., App., p. 1482.

not have tumbled down this hill." But Foote, inspired Foote, now patriotic Foote, abandoned himself to absolute despair.[18]

The following day saw a painful dispute between Clay and Pearce as to the latter's responsibility for the evisceration of the bill, after which it was passed without a record vote. When the "Mormon mutilation" was brought into the House, it was greeted with "a loud, tremendous *yaw haw* from all quarters," and immediately a movement got under way to hitch on to it New Mexico and the Texas boundary. Meanwhile, with the Senate debating Douglas's California Bill, Clay left Washington for a much needed rest at Newport.[19]

Upon the upset of the Omnibus, Douglas assumed leadership to push through the separate measures which he had drawn and which the Committee of Thirteen had literally united by a wafer. It was with a view to giving the compromise measures this second chance that he had avoided close association with Clay's compromise, declining membership on the Committee of Thirteen and holding aloof from aggressive support of the Omnibus Bill, whose weakness he had perceived from the start. He now hastened to effect an alliance with the administration, and collaborated with its spokesman, Pearce, in framing the new Texas Boundary Bill which the latter introduced on August 5. This bill fixed the northern and western boundaries of Texas as they stand today, with the familiar $10,000,000 compensation. Pearce's bill, however, gave Texas 33,333 square miles more than the Omnibus. Rumor said that Webster participated in the concoction of the bill, and that the Texas Senators gave in to it reluctantly. The California Bill had progressed to debate on engrossment when Pearce, on August 6, undertook to secure precedence for his Texas Boundary Bill. On his failure, the Southerners began obstructive tactics, in the midst of which the Senate received an alarmist message from the President on the situation at Santa Fé, sanctioning the principles of Pearce's bill, and urging them upon Congress. The Southern resistance to California continued, finally developing into a regular filibuster led by Yulee,

---

[18] New York *Express*, August 2, 1850.

[19] *Congressional Globe*, 31st Cong., 1st Sess., App., pp. 1485-98. New York *Express*, August 1, August 5, 1850.

so at five o'clock Douglas gave up and moved an adjournment.[20]

The attempt to give precedence to the Boundary Bill, enforced by Yulee's filibuster against the California Bill, was at last successful on August 7, and two days later the bill was passed, all amendments being defeated. The vote shows that it was a triumph of the moderates over the extremists of both sections. On the tenth, California was once more taken up, and passed on the thirteenth, six senators from the Slave States voting in the majority. Douglas at once moved to take up the New Mexico Bill, and Foote stated significantly that nothing would be done by the House with regard to the measures already passed until this also was received. It was taken up on the fourteenth, ordered engrossed the same day, and passed the next, only ten Northern radicals voting in the negative. The Fugitive Slave Bill was then taken up on the nineteenth, and after six days of debate, passed without a record vote. The next day, Clay was once more in his place.[21]

Much prostrated by his arduous labors, Clay had arrived at Newport August 9. At Baltimore, at Philadelphia, at New York, and on his arrival at Newport, he was greeted by the usual cheering of crowds, apparently more enthusiastic than ever. He was said to look better than expected, though weak, and public appeals were made that his friends would refrain from their well-meant but fatiguing attentions. At New York arrangements were made to avoid the crowds, and finally Clay escaped after a few jocose sentences punning on the "Omnibus", which, flat as they read, were sufficient to evoke "tremendous laughter and cheers."[22]

[20] *Congressional Globe,* 31st Cong., 1st Sess., pp. 1520-21, 1531-33; App., pp. 1510-17. Seward, *op. cit.,* II, 151-53; New York *Express,* August 7, August 8, 1850. *Sketch of Texas prepared at the General Land Office U. S. from Disturnell's or the Treaty Map 5th September 1850.* Douglas to Lanphier and Walker, August 3, 1850, Lanphier Papers; J. W. Sheahan, *Life of Stephen A. Douglas,* pp. 132-34. George D. Harmon, "Douglas and the Compromise of 1850," *Journal of the Illinois State Historical Society,* XXI (January, 1929), 451-99, effectively summarizes Douglas's part in the framing and passage of the Compromise. I am constrained to dissent, however, from the view that any individual was the "author" of the Compromise.

[21] *Congressional Globe,* 31st Cong., 1st Sess., pp. 1543-1678, *passim.*

[22] New York *Express,* August 6, August 8, August 10, 1850; *Union,* August 6, August 9, August 10, 1850.

At Philadelphia, however, he spoke at some length, "for it was no use to say no." Though looking much harassed and fatigued, his voice rang out clear and distinct. The compromise, which would have restored peace to the country and good fellowship in Congress, had been destroyed by the two opposing elements of sectional contention. But it would never do to give up the ship at this crisis. When shadows, clouds and darkness were gathering, he was a recreant and a traitor who would not stand by her to the last. It needed, even now, but concert, unanimity, and courage among the good men of all parties to rescue the Republic from the rocks and shoals of fanaticism and disunion. He could find here no endorsement of Abolitionism and Disunion; he heard no reverberation of the threats and denunciations of which the Federal Capital had been and was at this moment the scene.

"A dissolution of the Union," he continued, "was a dream which could never be realized, if the Masons of the North and the Masons of the South would but stand by each other, shoulder to shoulder, determined to crush whatever faction set itself up to break asunder the bonds which have bound them in friendliness together." Nevertheless, he argued, the times were such as to demand of every true American, at the North and at the South, reciprocal kindness and forbearance. They must make concessions and receive concessions. Human life was a compromise. This government was made up of compromise, and with compromise only could it be held together.[23]

Clay passed his time at Newport as quietly as he was permitted. He was the lion of the town, though he often walked alone and escaped notice. He especially enjoyed bathing in the surf, and at the hour when he visited the beach, a crowd of visitors waited to catch a glimpse of him—the largest proportion being ladies. He visited his friends in and about Newport, and was formally received by the Rhode Island Legislature, but he declined any public demonstrations. On his return to Washington, he managed to avoid attention, and his reap-

---

[23] New York *Express,* August 6, 1850.

pearance in his seat on the twenty-seventh was the event of the morning.[24]

Clay at once started his bill prohibiting the interstate slave trade in the District of Columbia on its course through the Senate, but on September 4 had it postponed until the tenth. This was to permit the House to do its part in the enactment of the compromise by the "cab" method. Notice was duly received on the ninth that the various measures heretofore passed by the Senate, except the Fugitive Slave Bill, had also passed the House. After a five day debate, the bill was passed by the Senate on the sixteenth, and by the House on the following day. Since the House had passed the Fugitive Slave Bill on the twelfth, only the signature of the President remained for the full enactment of the compromise.[25]

The compromise measures had not had plain sailing in the House. Both extremes concurred and planned obstruction. The Southern Ultras, still fearful of the Wilmot Proviso, threatened to secede in a body if the Texas Boundary Bill were passed in advance of the New Mexico Territorial Bill, suspicious lest Fillmore, once free of the danger of civil war, should fall back on Taylor's "non-action" territorial policy. Northern men feared to vote for the territories lest California fail; Southern men, to vote for California lest the Wilmot Proviso be engrafted on the territories. The prospect was doubtful, though Webster, Graham and Crittenden were busy bringing to bear the support of the administration, for many members feared the effect on their constituents of affirmative compromise votes. The task of leadership was complicated by the inexperience of half the House and the absence so far of party discipline; yet a small group of leaders, by unsurpassed team work keeping control except for a single vote, were able to put through their program without alteration and with amazing celerity. They were fortunate in controlling the chair, the Cobb of course played

---

[24] New York *Express,* August 22, August 23, August 26, August 27, August 28, 1850; *Observer and Reporter,* August 21, 1850.

[25] *Congressional Globe,* 31st Cong., 1st Sess., pp. 1690, 1743-44, 1750, 1784, 1794-95, 1805, 1809-10, 1817, 1829-30, 1837; App., pp. 1630-74.

a leading part. The star of the performance, however, was Linn
Boyd. Political veterans must have rubbed their eyes in amaze-
ment, and then doubled up with ribald mirth, at the spectacle
of Linn Boyd, of all men, championing the great compromise
of Henry Clay. Boyd served as chairman of the Committee of
the Whole; and then, seizing the floor after reporting, he yielded
it only to whom he would, retaining it until his purpose was
accomplished. His chief assistants were Douglas's lieutenants,
Richardson and McClernand, and Webster's friend, George
Ashmun.[26]

This group skillfully manoeuvred the Utah Bill from its
position of priority, tacked the Utah and New Mexico bills on
to the Texas Boundary Bill—thus, with the exception of California, recreating the "Omnibus"—dropped off Utah, and
passed the other two as one—which the Senate accepted without a qualm. Never did the opposition succeed in placing the
bill in a position where it could be freely amended, though
once it was saved only by the vote of the Speaker, and again
by Cobb's ruling that seperate votes could not be taken on
commitment and instructions, thus disrupting the combination
of radicals and ultras for commitment, since they could not
agree on instructions. The decisive test came on engrossment,
which was defeated, reconsidered, again defeated, moved a
second time, ruled out of order, the decision appealed, the
appeal sustained, the reconsideration and engrossment voted,
and the bill finally passed, all by the most drastic application
of the previous question. The final vote was taken amid great
confusion, and all over the hall its announcement was greeted
with clapping of hands, stamping of feet, whistling and even
dancing. "The nullifiers put on long faces," wrote an observer,
"and the Fanatics looked stark mad." This contest lasted from
August 28 to September 6. Hectic as were the proceedings,
they were in amazing contrast to the long-drawn battle in the
Senate. The next day saw the passage of both the California
and the Utah Bills, and a single day was all either the Fugitive

---

[26] New York *Express*, August 15, August 17, August 19, August 20, 1850;
Union, August 18, August 20, 1850.

Slave Bill or the Slave Trade Bill required. By September 17 the compromise was complete.[27]

As clear-eyed observers had predicted four months before, the various measures had reached their destination by "cab," while the "omnibus" had been upset. Was Clay unwise in joining the bills and in pushing them so persistently? By so doing, he drew on them the powerful opposition of Benton, who actually was one of the seven Senators who voted for the passage of every one of them separately. (Clay would have made the eighth had he been present.) The plan of the committee was reluctantly adopted by Clay and the most potent advocates of compromise, Cass, Webster and Douglas; and the "omnibus" scheme was accepted by them even more reluctantly. Once adopted, both good management and good faith forbade its abandonment until all hope was gone. Were they justified, then, in yielding their own better judgment to the demands of the small group of Southern moderates?

At the time they made the concessions, Doty's California Bill, with all its explosive potentialities, was pending in the House; the Nashville Convention had not met, and the Upper South might even yet be provoked into participation in it. Perhaps most important of all, Zachary Taylor, constitutionally stubborn, committed to the laissez faire policy, unamenable to influence by Congressional leaders, intensely jealous of Clay and Webster, and dominated together with his Cabinet by Seward, was still President, and might use the veto to defeat separate measures. With that prospect, the South could not permit the California Bill to pass in advance of the territorial bills, to which the Texas Boundary Bill was then merely incidental. On the other hand, the North, with the Border State Whigs, would not consent to postpone California to the other measures. The accession of Fillmore, the rival of Seward, changed the whole situation, and the change was guaranteed by the inclusion of Webster and Crittenden in the Cabinet. Not only was the pressure which had necessitated

---

[27] New York *Express*, August 30, September 7; *Congressional Globe*, 31st Cong., 1st Sess., pp. 1502-1837, *passim*.

the "omnibus" removed, but the presence of Webster on the floor and Fillmore in the chair would actually have changed the result of several crucial votes. Pearce would almost certainly have pursued a different course, and King and Berrien might well have done so. Thus, the revolution at the White House at once facilitated compromise and reduced the chances of the Omnibus Bill.

After eighty years, no better judgment can be given than that of Senator Dickinson on September 16, 1850.[28] "It by no means follows," he said,

because these bills, at the end of a discussion, which has lasted about eight months, have most of them been passed separately, that it was not expedient under all the circumstances of the case, to have them united originally. . . . Neither the Committee of Thirteen, nor any other committee, nor Congress, have settled these questions. They were settled by the healthy influence of public opinion; and . . . have been settled more surely and satisfactorily because the whole questions [sic] were before the Senate and the country at one time, and under discussion and consideration together.

---

[28] *Ibid.,* p. 1829.

CHAPTER XVII

AFTERGLOW

CONGRESS took the rest of the month to wind up its business, but Clay left Washington several days earlier. He was unusually successful in evading public attentions and reached Lexington on October 3. He had chosen to arrive at night to avoid a public demonstration, but his neighbors, warned by telegraph, greeted him with the firing of cannon, the ascent of rockets and the blaze of bonfires. An immense crowd which had assembled in front of the Phoenix Hotel cheered him loudly as he descended from his carriage, and in a few moments he appeared upon the balcony and addressed them briefly on the momentous events of the past months. Then, pointing his finger toward Ashland "in a manner so irresistibly comic that for some time not a word could be heard from him," he said that glad as he was to see them, there was an old lady about a mile and a half off, with whom he had lived for more than fifty years, whom he would rather see than all of them.[1]

The next day Clay received another ovation on visiting the fair, and on the seventeenth a great union meeting and barbecue was given in his honor. Governor Metcalfe presided and John C. Breckinridge, the rising star of the Kentucky Democracy, presented the toast to Henry Clay. "It is enough to say," Breckinridge declared, "that Kentucky occupies no doubtful position in reference to the late adjustment. She considers it just and honorable to all sections of the confederacy—she feels that it has preserved both the Constitution and the Union— she endorses the votes of her representatives and applauds their patriotism."[2]

On November 15, Clay was given a public reception by the Kentucky Legislature, both houses having unanimously approved his course and invited him to address them. Clay was ceremoniously introduced into the crowded hall and received

---

[1] *Observer and Reporter*, October 5, 1850.

[2] *Observer and Reporter*, October 5, October 16, 1850; Maysville *Eagle*, October 22, 1850.

by the Speaker with an address. Then, amid an oppressive silence, and evidently laboring under the greatest emotion, Clay rose to speak. After remarks appropriate to the occasion, he took up the compromise measures and discussed them consecutively, expressing the opinion that they were settled definitely and permanently, and, with the exception of the Fugitive Slave Law, acquiesced in by the whole country.[3]

"I may be asked," he said,

as I have been asked, when I would consent to a dissolution of the Union. I answer never—never—never, because I can conceive of no possible contingency that would make it for the happiness of the people to break up this glorious confederacy and to separate it into bleeding and belligerent parts. Show me, what I believe it will be impossible to show me, that there will be greater security for liberty, life, property, peace, and human happiness, in the midst of jarring, jealous, and warring North American powers, than under the eagle of the Union, and I will consent to its dissolution. I would yield to it, if Congress were to usurp a power, which I am sure it never will, to abolish slavery within the limits of the States; for in the contingency of such a usurpation, we should be in a better condition as to slavery, bad as it would be, out of the union than in the union.

After paying an enthusiastically applauded compliment to President Fillmore, he alluded to the formation of a new party, saying that when the union was at stake, all such measures of policy as a distribution of the proceeds of the public lands or an Independent Treasury sank into insignificance. " 'And if it should be necessary to form such a party, and it should be accordingly formed,' he exclaimed, elevating his head, erecting his form and, with beaming eye, rushing toward the Speaker's Chair, 'I announce myself, in this place, a member of that union party, whatever may be its component element.' "

Clay then denounced the attempt to merge the Whig Party into an abolition party; he would that moment renounce the Whig Party. Without mentioning his name, he definitely announced his opposition to Seward for the presidency. He could speak freely of such matters, for, he declared, "wrapping his garments around him and stepping proudly about, 'I want

---

[3] *Observer and Reporter*, November 16, November 23, 1850.

no office, no place—Ah yes!' he exclaimed, 'I *do* want a place, a place in your hearts'." Clay spoke "so movingly, so sweetly, so pathetically," that his bitterest opponents sitting immediately about, strong and cold men as they were, are said to have wept like children.

This was the supreme moment of Clay's career, when his state could hail him with unanimous acclaim her most distinguished citizen. Even a violent Democrat declared that Henry Clay was incomparably the greatest of men, and, while he was speaking, he involuntarily pulled off his hat and shouted for him with more enthusiasm than ever he had for Old Hickory. But even in this golden hour, shadows were gathering around the aged statesman. Only a few days before he had been constrained to sell his fine blooded stock to meet his financial necessities. Well as he seemed—for everyone remarked upon his appearance of health—high as were his spirits at the success of his compromise, the *memento mori* was there. The face of his lifelong associate and rival, Richard M. Johnson, was missing from the crowd who heard him speak. A few days before Johnson had broken down on the floor of the Assembly; four days later he was to rejoin Calhoun, Adams, and Jackson. But the grim reaper was striking even nearer, for the same newspaper that told of Johnson's death announced the death in far away California of Clay's favorite grandson.[4]

But Clay had little time for mournful thoughts. Early December saw him once more on his way to Washington, where he arrived on the thirteenth, enjoying his usual health. Congress had not recovered from the exhaustion of its strenuous labors in the summer, so the session was tame, a mere epilogue to the great work of compromise. The compromise received its final touch in the acceptance of the boundary settlement by the Texas Legislature with only a single dissenting vote. In the middle of January, Clay delivered a speech on colonization and the slave trade, for by that means he hoped to see the final elimination of the problem which threatened his beloved Union.[5]

---

[4] *Observer and Reporter*, November 6, November 13, November 16, November 20, 1850.

[5] *Observer and Reporter*, December 11, December 18, December 21, 1850; January 25, 1851.

Believing that its only safety for the time being lay in a sectional truce based on a strict adherence to the compromise settlement, he joined some forty other members of Congress in a manifesto designed to shut off any movement by ambitious politicians toward renewal of the controversy. Cobb, Foote, Stephens and Toombs were among the signers, but Cass and Douglas refused to sign it. The means adopted was a solemn public declaration of the intention of the signers "to maintain the said settlement inviolate, and to resist all attempts to repeal or alter the acts aforesaid, unless by the general consent of the friends of the measures, and to remedy such evils, if any, as time and experience may develop." They also pledged themselves not to support for any office "any man, of whatever party, who is not known to be opposed to the disturbance of the settlement aforesaid, and to the renewal, in any form, of agitation upon the subject of slavery." On January 22, Clay had a debate with Hale, and on February 25, replied to Hale and Rhett.[6]

Hardly waiting for the session to end, Clay betook himself to New York, whence he was to sail for Havana. While in the metropolis, he attended a great ball given in his honor at Niblo's and large crowds assembled to see him off. During his stay in Havana, Clay received marked attentions from the Captain-General and other authorities, and made an excursion into the country in company with his friend, Dr. Mercer of New Orleans, and several gentlemen of Havana. He arrived at New Orleans exactly a month after his departure from New York, so ill that he was confined to his room. He was supposed to be suffering from a slight cold from which early relief was anticipated. As he came up the river, Clay's health was represented as greatly improved, but in June his visitors feared that he might not be able to appear again in the Senate. In August, however, after a sojourn at Blue Lick Springs, his health was very much improved, and "he looked as well and talked with as much vivacity as of yore."[7]

Clay's return home in the spring was another great ovation.

[6] *Observer and Reporter,* January 29, March 5, 1851.

[7] *Observer and Reporter,* March 12, March 15, April 16, April 19, 1851; Maysville *Eagle,* August 16, 1851.

On his arrival at Louisville he was greeted by the shouts of a great crowd and a national salute of thirty-one guns. The Louisville Guards escorted him to the Galt House, where a large number of both parties assembled to give him a heartfelt greeting, all pressing around, anxious to take his hand or at least to see his face. He was said to look as healthy, as vigorous, and "even as young" as at any time in the last six or eight years. A stranger, seeing Clay for the first time, declared that venerable as he looked, no one would take him, from his appearance, manners, actions, or conversation, for more than sixty years old. He stepped "as quick as a man of fifty" and conversed as freely, fluently, and with as much animation as he ever did. He travelled from Louisville to Lexington by train, sitting wrapped up in his cloak and leaning on his cane, while all eyes were attentively fixed upon him. At every station he was triumphantly greeted, though none were expecting him. As the train stopped, "There's Mr. Clay!" was heard simultaneously from all parts of the crowd, followed by a general rush to crowd around him. He arrived at Lexington unexpectedly, on the Sabbath, but a stranger was impressed that from that moment the whole of Lexington seemed alive—from every street one could hear, "Mr. Clay's come home."[8]

Political events, that summer and autumn, however, were not calculated to soothe the spirit and relieve the mind of the aged leader. The August elections proved disastrous to the faction-torn Whigs of Kentucky. Lazarus W. Powell was elected governor over Archibald Dixon by something more than five hundred votes, while in the Ashland district itself, by a similar majority, John C. Breckinridge defeated Leslie Combs. The Whigs retained control of the legislature on joint ballot by a narrow majority of eight, and a successor to Underwood was to be elected. Crittenden was put forward as a candidate, while the antagonistic faction supported Dixon. Crittenden was now to be repaid for the "tomahawking" of Clay four years previously; for Clay spent nearly a week at Frankfort, lending his support to the pretensions of George Robertson, who had taken the lead against the "bushwhackers."

[8] *Observer and Reporter*, April 23, May 17, 1851.

The supporters of Dixon refused to enter a caucus, until finally it was agreed that neither his name nor Crittenden's should be presented. They managed, however, to stack the cards against Robertson also, with the result that in December the Lieutenant Governor, John B. Thompson, a genial politician without strong factional affiliations, was elected.[9]

Friends had not been lacking who felt that 1852 should redress the wrong done Henry Clay in 1848. Accordingly, a meeting was called at Frankfort on February 22, 1851, to launch Clay's candidacy. The movement made slow progress, however, though the usual enthusiastic banquet was held at New York on Clay's birthday and vociferous cheers greeted the toast, "Henry Clay: You are still to us all you have been throughout our lives — still great, honorable, just, pure, patriotic and wise—still 'first of living men' and 'first in our hearts,' still greater than President or Monarch, for you are still Henry Clay." In August, the *Observer* thought presidential movements premature. It was for Clay, but disavowed knowledge of his wishes. In October, Clay wrote a vigorous letter denouncing the temporary coalition of the New York factions on the "Albany Platform," which he thought too equivocal in its acceptance of the compromise. In commenting on this, the *Observer* remarked that the Clay candidacy depended on getting his consent, and that again on the state of his health.[10]

Clay's health thus became a matter of prime political importance, as was indicated by the varied and almost contradictory accounts of its condition. Horace Greeley took the lead in ringing the funeral knell, while the administration organs insisted that his state was by no means critical. Clay's vitality had been seriously depleted by his excessive exertions in the summer of 1850, and the following summer found him feeble. Yet he rode to town every day, transacted his business as usual, and by October he seemed to be steadily improving.

---

[9] Little, *op. cit.,* pp. 582-90; *Observer and Reporter,* August 9, August 16, September 6, November 1, November 8, November 12, December 17, 1851.

[10] *Observer and Reporter,* January 25, April 23, August 20, October 22, 1851; Cole, *Whig Party in the South,* p. 227.

When he left home, his health was decidedly better than it had been since his return. He arrived in Washington early in December considerably fatigued by the journey, but otherwise looking well and in good spirits. He was thinner and less elastic in his tread, but still he had the noble port of the olden time, and his mind was as quick and vigorous as ever. He did not rally from his fatigue, however, and by the middle of the month President Fillmore, in defiance of etiquette, visited him in his lodgings at the National Hotel. Dr. Jackson was summoned from Philadelphia, and after sounding his chest, pronounced Clay's right lung to be infected by deeply seated bronchitis, while the left lung was in a perfectly healthy condition. His appetite and digestion were good, but notwithstanding this he had been constantly losing strength for the last six months, a very unfavorable symptom. Dr. Jackson thought, however, that quiet and good nursing would soon restore him; and Clay only waited for favorable weather to go to Philadelphia and place himself under the doctor's personal attention. At this time, Clay thought his health no worse than when he left Kentucky, except that he was a little more feeble, and he proposed to return to Ashland in the spring. Clay also wrote with his own hand his letter of resignation, which showed not the least indication of weakness, "every word displaying unchanged his peculiar neat, uniform and elegant chirography."[11]

This resignation was drawn from Clay by the unusual contingency of Kentucky's having a Democratic governor, who would of course appoint a Democrat in the event of Clay's death. By resigning, however, Clay enabled the legislature then in session, with its slender Whig majority, to elect a successor. The crisis was so grave that Whig dissensions were healed and the whole party strength cast for the election of Dixon, Crittenden professing not to desire the fragmentary term. Thus, by that irony of events so often seen in history, Clay was directly responsible for the election of the Senator at whose suggestion the formal repeal of the Missouri Compromise

---

[11] *Observer and Reporter*, October 11, November 19, December 6, December 17, December 20, December 24, December 27, December 31, 1851; January 10, January 14, 1852.

was embodied in the Kansas-Nebraska Act. But Dixon could not yet take his seat, for Clay's resignation was to become effective only on September 1, 1852.[12]

It has been said that Clay thus deferred his actual retirement because he wished to die a Senator, but the contemporary evidence does not indicate that at the time Clay despaired of at least a temporary recovery. His condition in the closing days of 1851 was very serious, and with the opening of the new year a fatal termination at any moment would not have surprised those about him. But early in January a recovery began which continued to the end of the month, when he was able to drive out with his physician. It was generally recognized, however, that it could be but a temporary struggle, that the energies of the physical man were nearly exhausted, and that nothing but the proud spirit remained.[13]

Just before the change for the better, Fillmore again called upon the stricken leader. Clay took occasion to express his approval of the President's reply to Kossuth and his determination, if able, to address the Senate in the same strain; for the dying statesman was now seeking to devote his last energies to combating the popular enthusiasm for the Hungarian chieftain which threatened to sweep the United States from its traditional foreign policy of abstention from interference in European affairs. In an interview which Kossuth sought with him, on January 9, he declared his opposition to any policy of European interference in terms highly mortifying to his visitor, and an official version of the interview was in due time published to settle contradictory accounts. Kossuth took deep umbrage at this, and was so foolish as to attack Clay in his speech at Louisville, to which Clay replied in a letter stating that he did not consider the interview private or confidential. A month after the Kossuth interview, Clay made the presentation of a gold medal by his friends the occasion of a speech reiterating his warnings against European entanglements; and a few days later, to the committee on the Congressional banquet

---

[12] Little, *op. cit.; Observer and Reporter,* December 27, December 31, 1851.

[13] *Observer and Reporter,* December 31, 1851; January 10, January 14, January 31, 1852.

in honor of Washington's birthday, he again avowed his adherence to Washington's principles of non-intervention in Europe.[14]

Clay's reception of the New York committee was peculiarly affecting to those present, who feared that they were hearing the last public speech the great orator would ever make. Not one of the sad, silent group of affectionate and devoted friends who surrounded him in his sick chamber was more affected than President Fillmore, who left his public duties to add to the occasion the sanction of his position. Clay himself was pleased and exhilirated, but every spectator was impressed by the solemnity and grandeur of the spectacle. Clay was dressed in a suit of full black, and stood towering and erect as of old; but the feebler, though yet sweetly musical, voice indicated the prostration of his energy. Standing throughout, he read his reply with a clear, distinct enunciation, but it evidently required such a mustering of physical effort as to make the observers feel that the great field days of his eloquence were all over. "The music of his words, and the grace of his attitudes were there," wrote James Brooks, to whom we owe these details; "but the lightning-like flash of his eyes, and the organ peals of his mellow voice with its rich and pathetic intonations were gone. I felt sad, indeed, and by struggle alone could keep the tears within my eyes."[15]

Early in January, Clay had been considered a dead man inevitably. He could not carry a spoon to his mouth without aid and his cough was severe and constant. Three weeks later, his cough had much abated, he sat up and ate his meals at the table without effort, and frequently wrote letters with his own hand. He was constantly receiving quack medicines from all parts of the country, recommended for all sorts of diseases. At the beginning of February he was gradually improving, but suffered a relapse about the middle of the month. It was during this relapse in Clay's health that the *Observer and Reporter* declared that he was no longer to be mentioned in connection with the presidency because of his health, and that

[14] *Observer and Reporter*, January 14, February 7, February 11, February 14, March 13, April 21, 1852.

[15] *Observer and Reporter*, February 25, 1852, from New York *Express*.

the Whigs of Fayette were unanimous for Fillmore. Before leaving home, Clay had expressed his preference for Fillmore, and frequently repeated it in private conversation at Washington. He did not wish to make a formal statement in the press over his own signature, but did not care how generally the fact became known, and in due time an extract from a private letter found its way into print. The ground of his preference was that since Fillmore's administration had been successful, it would be imprudent and unwise to make an unnecessary change. In due time Kentucky followed the lead of Fayette and recommended Fillmore to the Whig National Convention as her choice. Resolutions highly complimentary to Crittenden were also adopted, intended to indicate him as the appropriate nominee for vice president.[16]

Throughout this period of temporary and fluctuating recovery, Clay was deeply desirous of appearing once more in the Senate to present his views on the compromise and on non-intervention. It was early in January, at the very beginning of his period of improvement that Clay began to cherish this hope. During the relapse in February he did not relinquish the purpose of once more reaching his seat, if only for an hour. With March, he had so far improved, that it was believed that before many days his voice would again be heard in the forum of his glory. On March 13 he would actually have gone to the Senate had it been in session, but by the fifteenth he was not so well and the prospect of his taking his place gradually receded.[17]

In mid-April he continued feeble and subject to frequent changes, generally produced by the varying weather. He passed most of the hours of the day in sitting up or in promenading his chamber, for only occasionally was he obliged to keep his bed in the daytime. When the weather continued favorable for any length of time, improvement was always manifest. So Clay passed his last birthday, which his New York admirers

---

[16] *Observer and Reporter,* February 4, February 14, February 18, February 25, February 28, March 24, 1852.

[17] *Observer and Reporter,* January 7, January 21, February 25, March 17, March 24, 1852.

observed in the manner they had followed since 1844, and which they were to continue for many years after the death of their idolized leader. Barely a week later, however, Clay's eldest son Thomas was peremptorily summoned to Washington by telegraph. By the beginning of May his most sanguine friends despaired of his recovery, and on the fourth it was thought he could survive only a few days. Telegraphic bulletins at intervals of only a few hours began to be sent from Washington. The next day his sons Thomas and John arrived to find him feebler and in an attitude of peaceful and cheerful resignation.[18]

By May 6, however, Clay's illness was so far modified that he was able to get some repose, though the crisis was not past until the tenth, the change resulting from the arrival of a period of balmy weather. On the seventh, he sat up and smoked a cigar. Although perfectly resigned, calm, and cheerful, he had been much annoyed by the publication of his approaching end. During the crisis, he had made frequent and calm inquiry as to the manner of dissolution and the sensations attending it. He expressed to his physicians the fear of death by suffocation, and was gratified on being assured that he would pass away without himself or his friends perceiving his dissolution. "I welcome death," said he, "but do not desire an exciting one." Several Senators and other devoted friends joined his sons in watching by his bedside at night. He lay on a rosewood bedstead, presented by citizens of Philadelphia, which had been received shortly before the crisis. It was said that his condition was due not so much to pulmonary disease as to "a manifest wearing out of the physical machine." By the middle of May, his cough was increasing, he was unable to sleep, and he complained of great weakness. For some days there was no perceptible change in his condition and Dr. Jackson returned to Philadelphia pronouncing his early death inevitable. Yet a few days later he was resting better, his appetite had increased, his cough was less harassing. It was even thought that if his

---

[18] *Observer and Reporter*, April 21, May 1, May 5, May 8, 1852. New York *Tribune*, April 14, 1865, April 13, 1869.

improvement continued, Clay might again reach Kentucky alive.[19]

While Clay was making his desperate fight for life, the Whig party also was going through the throes of dissolution. On the very eve of Clay's birthday, ten Southern Whigs seceded from the caucus which met to fix the date of the national convention. The chairman, Mangum, ruled out of order resolutions asserting the "finality" of the Compromise, and absolving members from supporting the nominee unless pledged to finality. Whereupon, led by Humphrey Marshall of Kentucky and Gentry of Tennessee, the Southerners withdrew. The *Union* pronounced this the dissolution of the Whig party. This action led to a violent discussion at the South, as a result of which their delegates came to the national convention prepared to insist on a satisfactory declaration on the finality of the compromise. Partly by threats, partly by able management, the Southerners, in alliance with the moderates, secured the adoption of the "Georgia Platform" asserting unequivocally the "finality" of the Compromise. But the moderates then abandoned them and brought about the nomination of General Scott on the fifty-third ballot. Scott was subjected to terrific pressure from each section in regard to his letter of acceptance which would define his platform. His escape from the dilemma was a mere acceptance of the nomination "with the resolutions annexed." Stephens had already, on the preceding day, written a letter for publication repudiating the nominee. Six days later nine Southern Whig representatives joined in a manifesto against him. The Whig Party was hopelessly divided.[20]

While the national convention was setting the stage for these movements, Clay's illness once more took a turn for the worse, and on the very day when Scott's letter of acceptance appeared, the great leader expired. On the twenty-eighth, his attendants saw that a change had taken place which indicated the breaking up of his system. At night he was calm, but his

---

[19] *Observer and Reporter,* May 12, May 15, May 22, May 26, May 29, June 2, 1852.

[20] Cole, *Whig Party in the South,* Chaps. VII-VIII; *Observer and Reporter,* May 8, 1852; Phillips, *Toombs, Stephens, and Cobb Correspondence,* pp. 304-6.

mind wandered. In a low and distinct voice he named his wife and son and other relatives, but in a disconnected manner. A clergyman offered to watch during the night, but it was deemed unnecessary, for at a previous interview with Clay, the dying man had expressed entire patience, resignation and confidence in his Redeemer.

The next morning, Clay continued perfectly tranquil, though exceedingly feeble and disposed to slumber. About ten o'clock he asked for some cool water which he was accustomed to take through a silver tube. He had more difficulty than previously in swallowing, and turned to his son, saying, "Don't leave me." Soon after he motioned to have his collar opened, and then added, "I am going soon." His son, Thomas Hart Clay, and Senator Jones of Tennessee were with him. He was calm and quiet, apparently suffering but little, and to the last his countenance indicated a full knowledge of his condition. And thus serenely he breathed his last.[21]

---

[21] *Observer and Reporter,* July 3, 1852.

BIBLIOGRAPHY

Primary Sources
Manuscripts

THE FOLLOWING collections of the papers of public men are all
in the Library of Congress: the papers of Henry Clay, John Mid-
dleton Clayton, John Jordan Crittenden, Thomas Ewing, Francis
Granger, John Pendleton Kennedy, Willie P. Mangum, John Mc-
Lean, James K. Polk, Thaddeus Stevens, Zachary Taylor, Waddy
Thompson, Martin Van Buren, Daniel Webster, and Thurlow Weed.

Published Correspondence, Diaries, Memoirs, Reminiscences, Debates and Records

Adams, John Quincy, *Memoirs, comprising parts of his Diary
from 1795 to 1848*, 12 vols., Philadelphia, 1874-1877.

Austin, Stephen F., *An Address delivered by S. F. Austin of Texas
to a very large audience of ladies and gentlemen in the Second
Presbyterian Church, Louisville, Kentucky, on the 7th of
March, 1836*, Lexington, 1836.

Avary, Myrta Lockett, ed., *Recollections of Alexander H. Stephens*,
New York, 1910.

Barnes, Thurlow Weed, *Memoirs of Thurlow Weed*, Boston, 1884.

Benton, Thomas Hart, *Thirty Years' View*, 2 vols., New York,
1854-1856.

Bourne, Edward Gaylord, ed., *Diary and Correspondence of Salmon
P. Chase* (*American Historical Review, Annual Report, 1902,*
vol. II), Washington, 1903.

Claiborne, J. F. H., *Life and Correspondence of John A. Quitman*,
2 vols., New York, 1860.

Clay, Cassius Marcellus, *Life, Memoirs, Writings, and Speeches*,
vol. I, Cincinnati, 1886.

Coleman, Mary Ann (Mrs. Chapman), *Life of John J. Crittenden*,
2 vols., Philadelphia, 1871.

Colton, Calvin, *The Last Seven Years of the Life of Henry Clay*,
New York, 1856.

. . . , *The Life and Times of Henry Clay*, 2 vols., New York,
1846.

. . . , ed., *The Private Correspondence of Henry Clay*, Cincinnati,
1856.

"The Diary of Thomas Ewing, August and September, 1841,"
American Historical Review, XVIII (October, 1912), 97-112.

Foote, Henry S., *Casket of Reminiscences*, Washington, 1874.

Garrison, George P., ed., *Diplomatic Correspondence of the Republic of Texas*, 3 vols. (*American Historical Association, Annual Report, 1907-1908:* 1907, vol. II, 1908, vol. II, pts., 1-2), Washington, 1907-1908.

Harvey, Peter, *Reminiscences and Anecdotes of Daniel Webster*, Boston, 1877.

Jameson, J. Franklin, ed., *Correspondence of John C. Calhoun* (*American Historical Association, Annual Report, 1899*, vol. II), Washington, 1900.

Johnston, Richard Malcolm, and Brown, William Hand, *Life of Alexander H. Stephens*, Philadelphia, 1883.

Journal of the Kentucky House of Representatives, 1843-1844, 1848-1849.

Mallory, Daniel, ed., *Life and Speeches of Henry Clay*, 2 vols., New York, 1843.

Phillips, Ulrich B., ed., *Toombs, Stephens and Cobb Correspondence (American Historical Association, Annual Report, 1911*, vol. II), Washington, 1912.

Richardson, James D., ed., *A Compilation of the Messages and Papers of the Presidents, 1789-1877*, 10 vols., Washington, 1896-1899.

Sargent, Nathan, *Public Men and Events (1817-1853)*, 2 vols., Philadelphia, 1875.

Seward, Frederick William, *Seward at Washington*, 3 vols., New York, 1891.

Sheahan, James W., *The Life of Stephen A. Douglas*, New York, 1860.

Sketch of Texas prepared at the General Land Office from Disturnell's or the Treaty Map 5th Septr., 1850.

Steiner, Bernard C., ed., "Some Letters from the Correspondence of James Alfred Pearce," *Maryland Historical Magazine*, XVI (June, 1921), 150-78.

Stephens, Alexander H., *A Constitutional View of the Late War between the States; Its Causes, Character, Conduct and Results*, 2 vols., Philadelphia, 1868-1870.

Tyler, Lyon Gardiner, *Letters and Times of the Tylers*, 3 vols., Richmond, 1884-1896.

Tuckerman, Bayard, ed., *The Diary of Philip Hone, 1828-1851*, New York, 1889.

Van Tyne, Claude H., ed., *Letters of Daniel Webster*, New York, 1902.

Webster, Daniel, *Private Correspondence,* 2 vols., Boston, 1857.
. . . , *Writings and Speeches,* National Edition, 18 vols., Boston, 1903.
Weed, Harriet A., ed., *Autobiography of Thurlow Weed,* Boston, 1883.
Wise, Henry A., *Seven Decades of the Union,* Philadelphia, 1876.

Contemporary Periodicals

Cincinnati *Gazette.*
Columbia (Missouri) *Patriot.*
Columbia *Missouri Statesman.*
Congressional Globe.
Frankfort *Kentucky Yeoman.*
Hickman (Kentucky) *Standard.*
Jefferson (Missouri) *Inquirer.*
Lexington (Kentucky) *Intelligencer.*
Lexington (Kentucky) *Observer and Reporter.*
Louisville *Public Advertiser.*
Maysville (Kentucky) *Eagle.*
Maysville (Kentucky) *Herald.*
New York *Courier and Enquirer.*
New York *Express.*
New York *Tribune.*
Niles' National Register.
St. Louis *Missouri Republican.*
Springfield *Illinois State Register.*
Washington *National Intelligencer.*
Washington *Republic.*
Washington *Union.*

SECONDARY WORKS

Ambler, Charles Henry, *Thomas Ritchie; A Study in Virginia Politics,* Richmond, 1913.
Ashe, Samuel a'Court, *Biographical History of North Carolina,* 7 vols., Greensboro, 1905-1911.
Binkley, William Campbell, "The Question of Texan Jurisdiction in New Mexico under the United States, 1848-1850," *Southwestern Historical Quarterly,* XXIV (July, 1920), 1-38.
Boucher, Chauncey S., "The Secession and Coöperative Movements in South Carolina, 1848 to 1853," *Washington University Studies, Humanistic Series,* vol. V, pt. 2, No. 2 (April, 1918).

Brooks, R. P., "Howell Cobb and the Crisis of 1850," *Mississippi Valley Historical Review,* IV (December, 1917), 279-98.

Burnley, Martha A., "Albert Triplett Burnley," *Texas State Historical Association Quarterly,* XIV (October, 1910), 150-54.

Carroll, Eber Malcolm, *Origins of the Whig Party,* Durham, 1925.

Channing, Edward, *A History of the United States,* 6 vols., New York, 1905-1925.

Clay, Thomas H., and Oberholtzer, E. P., *Henry Clay (American Crisis Biographies),* Philadelphia, 1910.

Cole, Arthur C., "The South and the Right of Secession in the Early Fifties," *Mississippi Valley Historical Review,* I (December, 1914), 376-99.

. . . , *The Whig Party in the South,* Washington, 1913.

Curtis, George Ticknor, *Life of Daniel Webster,* 2 vols., New York, 1870.

Foster, H. D., "Webster's Seventh of March Speech," *American Historical Review,* XXVII (January, 1922), 245-70.

Gammon, Samuel R., *Presidential Campaign of 1832,* Baltimore, 1922.

Garrison, George P., *Westward Expansion, 1841-1850,* New York, 1906.

Green, Thomas Marshall, *Historic Families of Kentucky,* Cincinnati, 1889.

Griffin, G. W., *Memoir of Col. Charles S. Todd,* Philadelphia, 1873.

Hamer, Philip May, *Secession Movement in South Carolina, 1847-1852,* Allentown, Pennsylvania, 1918.

Harmon, George D., "Douglas and the Compromise of 1850," *Journal of the Illinois State Historical Society,* XXI (January, 1929), 453-99.

Hearon, Cleo Carson, *Mississippi and the Compromise of 1850,* Oxford, Mississippi, 1913.

von Holst, Hermann E., *Constitutional and Political History of the United States,* tr. by John J. Lalor, Alfred P. Mason, and Paul Shorey, 8 vols., Chicago, 1876-1892.

Linn, E. A., and Sargent, N., *Life and Public Service of Dr. Lewis F. Linn,* New York, 1857.

Little, Lucius P., *Ben Hardin: His Times and Contemporaries,* Louisville, 1887.

McClure, Alexander K., *Our Presidents and How We Make Them,* New York, 1900.

McCormac, Eugene Irving, *James K. Polk: A Political Biography,* Berkeley, 1922.

Phillips, Ulrich B., *Georgia and State Rights* (*American Historical Association, Annual Report, 1901,* vol. II), Washington, 1902.

Ramsdell, Charles W., "The Natural Limits of Slavery Expansion," *Mississippi Valley Historical Review,* XVI (September, 1929), 151-71.

Reeves, Jesse S., *American Diplomacy under Tyler and Polk,* Baltimore, 1907.

Schouler, James, *History of the United States under the Constitution,* 6 vols., New York, 1894-1899.

Schurz, Carl, *Life of Henry Clay* (*American Statesman Series*), 2 vols., Boston, 1897.

Sioussat, St. George L., "Tennessee and National Political Parties, 1850-1860," *American Historical Assocation, Annual Report, 1914,* I, 243-58.

. . . , Tennessee, the Compromise of 1850, and the Nashville Convention," *Mississippi Valley Historical Review,* II (December, 1915), 313-47.

Smith, Justin H., *The Annexation of Texas,* New York, 1919.

Steiner, Bernard C., "James Alfred Pearce," *Maryland Historical Magazine,* XVI-XIX (December, 1921-June, 1924).

Stoddard, W. O., *Life of Harrison,* New York, 1886.

White, Melvin J., "Louisiana and the Secession Movement of the Early Fifties," *Proceedings of the Mississippi Valley Historical Association,* VIII (1914-15), 278-88.

. . . , *Secession Movement in the United States, 1847-1852,* New Orleans, 1916.

Wise, Barton Haxall, *Life of Henry A. Wise of Virginia, 1806-1876,* New York, 1899.

Woodburn, James Albert, *Life of Thaddeus Stevens,* Indianapolis, 1913.

INDEX